Immigration and Citizenship in Japan

Japan is currently the only advanced industrial democracy with a fourth-generation immigrant problem. As other industrialized countries face the challenges of incorporating postwar immigrants, Japan continues to struggle with the incorporation of prewar immigrants and their descendants. Whereas others have focused on international norms, domestic institutions, and recent immigration, this book argues that contemporary immigration and citizenship politics in Japan reflect the strategic interaction between state efforts to control immigration and grassroots movements by multigenerational Korean-resident activists to gain rights and recognition specifically as permanently settled foreign residents of Japan. Based on in-depth interviews and fieldwork conducted in Tokyo, Kawasaki, and Osaka, this book aims to further our understanding of democratic inclusion in Japan by analyzing how those who are formally excluded from the political process voice their interests and what factors contribute to the effective representation of those interests in public debate and policy.

Erin Aeran Chung is the Charles D. Miller Assistant Professor of East Asian Politics and Co-Director of the Racism, Immigration, and Citizenship (RIC) Program in the Department of Political Science at the Johns Hopkins University. Previously, she was an Advanced Research Fellow at Harvard University's Program on U.S.-Japan Relations and a Japan Foundation Fellow at Saitama University in Urawa, Japan. Her articles on citizenship, noncitizen political engagement, and comparative racial politics have been published in the *Du Bois Review* and *Asian Perspective*. In 2009, she was awarded an Abe Fellowship by the Social Science Research Council to conduct research in Japan and Korea for her second book project on immigrant incorporation in ethnic democracies.

Immigration and Citizenship in Japan

ERIN AERAN CHUNG
Johns Hopkins University

CAMBRIDGE
UNIVERSITY PRESS

CAMBRIDGE UNIVERSITY PRESS
Cambridge, New York, Melbourne, Madrid, Cape Town, Singapore,
São Paulo, Delhi, Dubai, Tokyo

Cambridge University Press
32 Avenue of the Americas, New York, NY 10013-2473, USA

www.cambridge.org
Information on this title: www.cambridge.org/9780521514040

First published 2010

Printed in the United States of America

A catalog record for this publication is available from the British Library.

Library of Congress Cataloging in Publication data
Chung, Erin Aeran.
Immigration and citizenship in Japan / Erin Aeran Chung.
   p.   cm.
Includes bibliographical references and index.
ISBN 978-0-521-51404-0 (hardback)
1. Japan – Emigration and immigration.   2. Citizenship – Japan.   3. Assimilation
(Sociology) – Japan.   4. Japan – History – 1945–.   5. Japan – Social conditions.
6. Japan – Politics and government – 1945– .   I. Title.
JV8721.C58   2010
325.52–dc22   2009026332

ISBN   978-0-521-51404-0 Hardback

COVER ART: Antifingerprinting rally, 20 November 2007, Tokyo, Japan.
Photograph courtesy of Lim Young-Ki. © Mindan Seinenkai 2010.

To my parents, ChangBok Chung and ChoonHee Kim

Contents

Tables and Figures

Conventions and Abbreviations

Japanese and Korean names are written according to East Asian convention (family name followed by given name) except in cases where authors have identified themselves with given names first, for example, in English-language publications. Transliteration of Japanese words follows the standard Japanese romanization system, and transliteration of Korean words follows the McCune-Reischauer system. I have made exceptions where individuals or organizations prefer a particular romanization (e.g., Kim Il Sung rather than Kim Il-sŏng) and for commonly used place names (e.g., Tokyo instead of Tōkyō).

Unless otherwise indicated, all translations are my own.

DRPK   Democratic People's Republic of Korea
HRKJ   Human Rights Association for Koreans in Japan
ICCPR   International Covenant on Civil and Political Rights
ICESCR International Covenant on Economic, Social and
        Cultural Rights
JCP   Japan Communist Party
KCCJ   Korean Christian Church in Japan
KCIA   Korean Central Intelligence Agency
LDP   Liberal Democratic Party
MOE   Ministry of Education

NCCJ   National Christian Council in Japan
NTT   Nippon Telegraph and Telephone Public Corporation
ROK   Republic of Korea
SCAP   Supreme Commander of the Allied Powers
WCC   World Council of Churches

Acknowledgments

The support of numerous people made the completion of this book possible. I owe a special debt of gratitude to the many individuals in Japan who provided candid, thoughtful answers to my questions and who welcomed me into their communities, organizations, and homes. Although I cannot fit the names of all of the people who assisted me during my field research onto these pages, I want to mention those who went out of their way to make my research in Japan productive and enjoyable: Bae Jung Do, Kang Seong Sil, Kim Kyu Il, Kim Su Ryang, Reverend Kim Sungjae, Ko Yi Sam, Pak Yŏng Ho, Suh Jung Woo, and Yang Hae-ja. I hope this book conveys their wisdom, energy, and contagious passion for justice. I am also indebted to Professor Fukuoka Yasunori for taking me under his wing and helping me establish contacts with members of the Korean community, introducing me to a wide array of researchers, and providing valuable suggestions for improving my research design and interviewing techniques.

I am grateful to Leonard Schoppa and an anonymous reader for their careful reading of the entire manuscript and for their perceptive criticisms and insightful suggestions. This book is significantly improved as a result of their suggestions. Lew Bateman of Cambridge University Press has been a warm, brilliant editor who made the completion of this book especially rewarding.

The roots of this book go back to my dissertation, which I completed with the intellectual guidance of my committee members at

Northwestern University. I thank Michael Hanchard, who is now my colleague at the Johns Hopkins University, for his dynamic engagement with my ideas and enduring support. I am indebted to Meredith Jung-En Woo, who helped shape this project and offered invaluable mentorship and incisive criticisms throughout the process. I also wish to thank Bruce Cumings, Bonnie Honig, Peter Swenson, and Jeffrey Winters for sharing their theoretical insights. Chalmers Johnson provided valuable feedback on a chapter that was published as a working paper by the Japan Policy Research Institute.

Special thanks are due to Chikako Kashiwazaki, who not only offered extensive comments and suggestions at every stage of this project, but also provided countless introductions and alerted me to numerous events in Japan. Youngmi Lim, Noora Lori, Riva Kastoryano, and Susan Pharr generously shared their research with me and commented on various portions of the manuscript.

For their advice and support at various stages of this project, I thank Jane Bennett, Irene Bloemraad, Mark Blyth, Mari Calder, Mark Caprio, Bill Connolly, Jennifer Culbert, Margarita Estévez-Abe, Kentaro Fukumoto, Siba Grovogui, Kathryn Ibata-Arens, Richard Katz, Margaret Keck, Tobie Meyer-Fong, Reuel Rogers, Bill Rowe, Sonia Ryang, Mark Sawyer, Frank Schwartz, Katherine Tegetmeyer-Pak, and Ji Yeon Yuh. I am especially grateful to my friend, colleague, and mentor extraordinaire, Kellee Tsai, for her painstaking guidance and encouragement.

I presented chapters of this book at the annual meetings of the American Political Science Association and the Association for Asian Studies, as well as invited talks at the East-West Center–Washington, Georgetown University, Harvard University, MIT, the University of British Columbia, the University of Chicago, the University of Virginia, and Wesleyan University. I want to acknowledge, in particular, the suggestions and comments provided by Frank Baldwin, Thomas Berger, John Campbell, Julian Dierkes, Alexis Dudden, Carter Eckert, David Edgington, Shinju Fujihira, Mary Alice Haddad, Soo Im Lee, Hyung-Gu Lynn, Robert Weiner, Melissa Wender, and my dearly missed mentor, the late James B. Palais. I also benefited from the generous feedback of the participants in my graduate seminars on Comparative Racial Politics and Comparative Citizenship and Immigration at the Johns Hopkins University.

For their extraordinary research assistance, I thank Rameez Abbas, Adam Culver, Daisy Kim, Hitomi Koyama, Kyung Soo Rha, and Hanano Watanabe. Special mention must go to Taylor Percival for her speedy, superb work on the index. Any errors that remain are mine.

The Japan Foundation provided generous financial support for my field research in Japan from 1998 to 1999 and the Department of Liberal Arts at Saitama University provided me with administrative support. I also wish to thank the Program on U.S.-Japan Relations at Harvard University and the Department of Political Science at the Johns Hopkins University for providing me with the time and resources to finish my manuscript.

Earlier versions of Chapters 3 and 4 were previously published in *Asian Perspective* (24, no. 4: 159–78) and *Japan's Diversity Dilemma* (Soo Im Lee, Stephen Murphy-Shigematsu, and Harumi Befu, eds. [Bloomington, IN: iUniverse, 2006]). I thank the editors for their permission to reproduce portions of these publications in this book. I also wish to thank Lim Young-Ki of Mindan Seinenkai for providing me with the photograph that appears on the front cover of this book.

Finally, the completion of this book would not have been possible without the encouragement and love of my family. My mother, ChoonHee Kim, guided me through each hurdle of this project and continues to be my most ardent supporter and wisest teacher. I continue to strive to meet the benchmarks set by my father, ChangBok Chung, from whom I have learned the values of persistence, hard work, and writing at dawn. I dedicate this book to them with love and gratitude. My sisters, Loni and Sunglan, have sustained me with their unflinching encouragement and ingenious wit. My husband, Eric Clemons, has been my lifeline throughout this project with his patient support, candid advice, and tireless humor. My children, Daelia, Walter, and Nora, who were born at various stages of this project, are my sources of endless inspiration. I thank them for bringing laughter and joy into my life every day.

Immigration and Citizenship in Japan

Introduction

The Contradictions of Japan's Immigration and Citizenship Politics

> Achieving greater ethnic diversity within Japan has the potential of broadening the scope of the country's intellectual creativity and enhancing its social vitality and international competitiveness.
>
> – Prime Minister Obuchi Keizō's Commission on Japan's Goals in the 21st Century, 2000
>
> Foreigners are all sneaky thieves.
>
> – Kanagawa Governor Matsuzawa Shigefumi, 2 November 2003

On 20 November 2007, Japan reinstated its fingerprinting requirement for foreign residents as part of a counterterrorism measure. The bill had been passed in the Diet with little fanfare and received minimal coverage in the Japanese media. A small group of mostly North Americans, Europeans, and Australians worked with a handful of Japanese activists to organize a campaign against the bill in collaboration with Amnesty International Japan and the Solidarity Network with Migrants Japan (SMJ). Although this group contacted numerous proimmigrant and foreign-resident organizations and human rights activists, surprisingly few showed up for the rallies that the group organized in August and November 2007 to protest the measure. Most significant was the relative lack of participation by the largest foreign-resident groups in Japan: Chinese, Korean, *Nikkei* (ethnic Japanese) Brazilians, and Filipinos.

In many respects, the reinstatement of the fingerprinting requirement, with the stated aim of preventing the entry of potential terrorists and criminals into Japan, was consistent with developments in other industrial democracies to control their foreign populations following the 11 September 2001 attacks. The new immigration controls are modeled after the U.S.-Visit (United States Visitor and Immigration Status Indicator Technology) Program that was implemented in 2004 to collect and store biometric information on foreigners entering the United States. The anomaly in Japan's case, however, was that the bill exempted one particular group of foreigners: "special permanent residents," the vast majority of whom are prewar Korean immigrants and their descendants.

Lim Young-Ki (Im Yong-ki), a third-generation Korean resident born and raised in Japan and vice president of the Korean Youth Association in Japan, was making plans for a Korean festival when he received an urgent call at Mindan headquarters from an Amnesty International representative in November 2007.[1] The rally to protest the reinstatement of the fingerprinting requirement was scheduled to be held on Tuesday, but not a single Korean organization or activist had made the commitment to show up. In contrast to the decade-long antifingerprinting movement led by Korean activists in the 1980s, which ultimately led to its abolishment for special permanent residents in 1993 and for all foreign residents in 1999, the Korean response to its reinstatement was curiously weak. Although various Korean organizations issued public statements opposing the bill, Korean residents were noticeably absent among the foreign residents and activists who organized protests against the bill.

Lim, who was only a teenager when the fingerprinting requirement for Korean residents had been abolished in 1993 and, thus, had never been fingerprinted, understood the symbolic significance of Korean participation in the newly mobilized antifingerprinting movement. Most of his *senpai* (older colleagues) in Mindan felt that the Korean community did not have a stake in the current antifingerprinting movement because the bill explicitly exempted the Korean-resident community. Lim, however, saw the invitation to participate as an

[1] The Korean Youth Association in Japan (*Cheilbon daehan minkuk ch'ŏngnyŏn hoe* in Korean; also known as *Seinenkai* in Japanese) is a subsidiary organization of Mindan, the largest South Korean organization in Japan. I conducted an interview with Lim Young-Ki in Tokyo on 4 September 2008.

opportunity to shift the direction of his political activities in order to reach out to a broader community of foreign residents.

The representative from Amnesty International asked Lim if there was something from the 1980s movement that could be used in the rally. Lim recalled that Mindan headquarters housed the original giant thumbprint balloon used in various antifingerprinting movements during the 1980s, as displayed on the cover of this book. Although inflating the giant balloon would normally require work over an entire week, Lim, with the help of other members of his organization, managed to inflate the balloon in a single day and bring it to the rally. Despite his valiant efforts to demonstrate Korean solidarity with the protestors, Lim estimates that less than two hundred people were present with only a smattering of Korean activists. In contrast, a rally organized by Korean activists the following spring to demand local voting rights for foreign residents brought together nearly six hundred Korean and other foreign residents. When I asked another Korean activist why he and others did not join the renewed antifingerprinting movement, he replied, "It would have been better if more Korean residents supported the protests. But it is not as important as other issues like local voting rights. Anyway, the Japanese government was not stupid enough to include Korean residents [when it reinstated the fingerprinting requirement]. There would have been hell to pay if it did" (interview, 7 September 2008, Osaka).

Lim's story highlights a defining feature of contemporary immigration and citizenship politics in Japan. Japan is the only advanced industrial democracy with a fourth-generation immigrant problem. While other industrialized countries face the challenges of incorporating *postwar* immigrants, Japan struggles with the repercussions of its failure to incorporate *prewar* immigrants and their descendants. With the recent influx of new immigrants to Japan, the country's already fragmented, incoherent policies and practices regarding its foreign population developed into a world of extremes. The official stance toward immigrants suggests that non-Japanese do not have the capacity to become Japanese and, therefore, should be excluded. Meanwhile, some Japanese officials have publicly promoted the naturalization of Korean residents throughout the past two decades, arguing that they are de facto Japanese. Although immigration policies seek to uphold the commonly accepted idea that Japan is not a country of immigration, local officials and citizens have created immigrant integration programs based on the notion that foreign residents are local citizens. Public debate on immigration has hinged on either opening (*kaikoku*) or closing (*sakoku*) Japan's borders. Whereas permanent foreign residents have rights that are almost on par with Japanese citizens, permanent-residency status remains elusive for many recent immigrants to Japan.

Despite Japan's official closed-door policy, record numbers of immigrants have entered the country as laborers, students, and, to a lesser extent, refugees. Between 1985 and 2008, the total foreign population more than doubled from about 850,000 to more than 2.2 million (see Table I.1). Although recent immigrants to Japan come from more than 190 countries on every continent in the world, the majority are laborers from other Asian countries including China, the Philippines, South Korea, and Thailand. The Brazilian and Peruvian immigrant population also experienced phenomenal growth after the enactment of state-sponsored recruitment of *Nikkei* workers into the labor market. Finally, there were also an estimated 150,000 immigrants who overstayed their visas or entered Japan illegally in 2008.

The recent wave of immigrants arrived in Japan on the heels of a noncitizen civil rights movement led by prewar Korean immigrants and their descendants. As large numbers of new immigrants became established in their local communities, they found themselves in the middle of the movement's final stages, which have focused on securing local voting rights for foreign residents. In this context, in which the foreign population in Japan encompassed recently arrived immigrants as well as multigenerational permanent residents, foreign-resident claims in the 1990s ranged from proposals for alien suffrage to demands for multicultural education to appeals to gain special permission to stay in Japan among visa overstayers. Japan in the 1990s lacked national immigrant incorporation programs to provide recent immigrants with Japanese-language instruction, information about housing and schools, and other essential skills needed for settlement in Japan; at the same time, many foreign residents could, in principle, exercise many of the same rights as Japanese nationals. On the one hand, this gap has placed a significant burden on local governments that must meet the demands of an increasingly diverse community with insufficient support and guidance from the national government.

TABLE I.I. *Registered Foreign Residents in Japan by Nationality*

Year	North and South Korea	China	Philippines	United States	Brazil	Peru	Other[a]	Total[b]	%[c]
1985	683,313	74,924	12,261	29,044	1,955	N/A	49,115	850,612	0.70
1986	677,959	84,397	18,897	30,695	2,135	553	54,736	867,237	0.71
1987	673,687	95,477	25,017	30,836	2,250	615	58,393	884,025	0.72
1988	677,140	129,269	32,185	32,766	4,159	864	68,781	941,005	0.76
1989	681,838	137,499	38,925	34,900	14,528	4,121	72,644	984,455	0.80
1990	687,940	150,339	49,092	38,364	56,429	10,279	82,874	1,075,317	0.87
1991	693,050	171,071	61,837	42,498	119,333	26,281	104,821	1,218,891	0.98
1992	688,144	195,334	62,218	42,482	147,803	31,051	114,612	1,281,644	1.03
1993	682,276	210,138	73,057	42,639	154,650	33,169	124,819	1,320,748	1.06
1994	676,793	218,585	85,968	43,320	159,619	35,382	134,344	1,354,011	1.08
1995	666,376	222,991	74,297	43,198	176,440	36,269	142,800	1,362,371	1.08
1996	657,159	234,264	84,509	44,168	201,795	37,099	156,142	1,415,136	1.12
1997	645,373	252,164	93,265	43,690	233,254	40,394	174,567	1,482,707	1.17
1998	638,828	272,230	105,308	42,774	222,217	41,317	189,442	1,512,116	1.19
1999	636,548	294,201	115,685	42,802	224,299	42,773	199,805	1,556,113	1.23
2000	635,269	335,575	144,871	44,856	254,394	46,171	225,308	1,686,444	1.33
2001	632,405	381,225	156,667	46,244	265,962	50,052	245,907	1,778,462	1.40
2002	625,422	424,282	169,359	47,970	268,332	51,772	264,621	1,851,758	1.46
2003	613,791	462,396	185,237	47,836	274,700	53,649	277,421	1,915,030	1.50
2004	607,419	487,570	199,394	48,844	286,557	55,750	288,213	1,973,747	1.55
2005	598,687	519,561	187,261	49,390	302,080	57,728	296,848	2,011,555	1.57
2006	598,219	560,741	193,488	51,321	312,979	58,721	309,450	2,084,919	1.63
2007	593,489	606,889	202,592	51,851	316,967	59,696	321,489	2,152,973	1.69
2008	589,239	655,377	210,617	52,683	312,582	59,723	337,205	2,217,426	1.74

[a] The "other" category includes nationals of more than 190 countries in every continent. Among the largest numbers of foreign residents in this category include nationals of Thailand, Vietnam, Indonesia, the United Kingdom, India, Canada, Australia, and Bangladesh.
[b] As of 1 January 2008, there were also an estimated 150,000 illegal immigrants in Japan.
[c] This column refers to the percentage of the total Japanese population.

Source: Ministry of Justice 2003–2009; Japan Statistical Yearbook 2006.

On the other hand, the particular timing of recent immigration to Japan vis-à-vis developments in the Korean civil rights movement has had a profound effect on the ways in which proimmigrant organizations have mobilized foreign residents and how foreign residents, including new immigrants as well as multigenerational residents, are discussed in the public sphere. Rather than focus solely on the immediate needs of new immigrants, numerous advocacy groups, local government offices, and mainstream civil-society organizations put emphasis on the idea that foreign residents are citizens, linking their active engagement in the community with democratic revitalization.

This book seeks to explain the contradictions between policies that exclude foreigners and policies and practices aimed at incorporating foreign residents in contemporary Japan. Based on fieldwork conducted in Tokyo, Kawasaki, and Osaka and in-depth interviews with individual foreign residents, community activists, Japanese policy makers, journalists, and academics from 1998 to 2008, this book examines how traditionally underrepresented actors in Japan negotiate national policies and ideologies in their attempts to bring about social change. The inconsistencies of Japan's immigration and citizenship politics have created a delicate dilemma for Japanese authorities. Because permanent residents have social rights on par with Japanese citizens, officials have a strong incentive to keep permanent-residency status exclusive and maintain the official stance that discourages immigrant permanent settlement. At the same time, the unavoidable, continuing growth of the foreign population has pressured the government to politically assimilate the population of foreigners with the most privileged status in Japan: special permanent residents, the vast majority of whom are prewar Korean immigrants and their descendants. Korean-resident activists, in turn, have persistently contested the conditions of the community's political incorporation and have sought to diversify the meaning of Japanese citizenship from a discourse based on cultural homogeneity to one based on a multicultural, multiethnic society. In this way, Japan's stringent citizenship policies have unintentionally provided Korean residents with unprecedented bargaining power and specific opportunities for negotiating the terms of their political incorporation.

Recent scholarship by a new generation of Japan specialists analyzes how state and social actors have negotiated international norms, democratic ideals, and local pressures in an increasingly unstable social, political, and economic climate (Chan-Tiberghien 2004; Leheny 2006; Schoppa 2006). Unlike much of the earlier literature that questioned whether Japan is a democracy, these works ask why certain actors are able to influence public debate and successfully advance democratic reforms and why others fail at specific historical junctures. In particular, the events of the last two decades – including the economic recession, increasing voter discontent, large-scale immigration, and the looming demographic crisis – have led to significant shifts in Japan's political and social landscape for traditionally underrepresented social actors. Building on this scholarship, this book aims to further our understanding of democratic inclusion in Japan by analyzing how those who are formally excluded from the political process voice their interests and what factors contribute to the effective representation of those interests in public debate and policy. As Japan grapples with the issues of immigration, multiculturalism, and national identity, the political incorporation of the foreign community has important implications for understanding the quality of democracy in contemporary Japan.

This book is also about the dilemmas that Japan shares with other democracies in accommodating diversity. The recent wave of immigration to industrialized societies has placed the question of immigrant incorporation at the center of scholarship on immigration and citizenship. Although the problem of immigrant incorporation encompasses a variety of issues, such as cultural, linguistic, religious, and educational concerns, scholars as well as policy makers have given particular attention to the issue of political incorporation and political participation in recent years because of what many have identified as a troubling trend among the current wave of immigrants. That is, foreign communities are growing in size; at the same time, many immigrants and their descendants remain politically unincorporated. Scholarship on immigrant incorporation tends to focus on the role of structural, state-level variables or on individual-level variables to explain this paradox. In contrast, this book analyzes contextual factors and intermediate organizations in order to identify the unintended consequences of immigrant incorporation regimes and the political opportunities for noncitizens to engage in the polity.

The portrayal of immigrant incorporation as a two-way relationship between the state and immigrants does not reflect on-the-ground practices in which intermediary organizations and civil-society groups play central roles in shaping paths for immigrant political empowerment. Immigration and immigrant policy outcomes often do not reflect their objectives. States are then forced to revise their policies and, in cases in which international and domestic actors – including immigrant groups – exert pressure on the state, enact significant reforms. These revisions and reforms further institutionalize the limits and possibilities of immigrant politics by expanding (or constricting) alien rights, stabilizing (or destabilizing) foreign legal status, and shaping incentives for political engagement that can affirm or contest the official model of immigrant incorporation.

Intermediary organizations – in the forms of local state and nonstate institutions as well as mainstream and coethnic civil-society organizations – shape the political learning environment for immigrants and the paths for their political engagement in three central ways. First, prior activism by immigrant advocacy groups establishes the blueprint for subsequent movements by demonstrating the strengths and weaknesses of specific political strategies, such as lobbying, litigation, and protests, and by prioritizing the issues concerning immigrant communities. Established advocacy groups, furthermore, create networks of central actors who continue to play important roles in subsequent movements. These groups are also often the "training ground" for future generations of immigrant activists. Second, immigrant advocacy groups and local institutions provide resources that influence the direction of immigrant political engagement. Mainstream and coethnic civil-society organizations, for example, often provide immigrants with consultation services that shape the ways in which immigrants act on their grievances. Advocacy organizations can play a pivotal role in an immigrant's decision to either privatize social conflict – through prayer or mediation, for instance – or make public claims in the courts or on the streets. Likewise, state and nonstate institutions may influence an immigrant's decision to naturalize by providing information and assistance in the naturalization process, or they may encourage immigrants to voice their interests specifically as foreign residents through the establishment of foreign-resident assemblies and councils. Finally, the ideas that emerge out of early immigrant advocacy shape the ways that subsequent generations of immigrants, civil-society actors, and, at times, state officials approach immigrant political empowerment. These ideas form the basis for an immigrant group's collective identity, including the ways that they represent themselves in the public sphere, as immigrants, hyphenated minorities, or foreign-resident citizens, for example, and may set the agenda for immigrant claims making as well as state policies regarding immigrants. Accordingly, by examining the interactive relationship between state policies, intermediary organizations, and immigrant groups, this book aims to provide insights into the gaps among immigrant policy intent, interpretation, and outcomes.

THE PROBLEM OF IMMIGRANT INCORPORATION

Although the Japan case is unique in some ways, it is also emblematic of most immigrant incorporation regimes in contemporary democracies. None have actually resolved the so-called immigrant incorporation problem, which is evident in low naturalization rates, vast economic disparities, and racial and ethnic tensions. Given the history of Germany's restrictive citizenship policies until the implementation of major reforms in 2000, it should not come as a surprise that foreign residents in Germany have exhibited low rates of naturalization. Five years after the 2000 reform, the rate of naturalization in Germany was less than 2 percent of the total foreign population (SOPEMI 2007). Even in Britain, however, where immigrants are seemingly well integrated politically, immigrants and minorities engaged in violent forms of protest as often and sometimes even more than those in Germany between 1990 and 1995 (Koopmans and Statham 2000). Similarly, Jane Junn's (1999) study of racial minority political participation in the United States found that protesting was the only pattern of political activity in which racial minority groups outpaced whites. Although many have heralded the Swedish system of immigrant incorporation as an ideal model of multiculturalism, those with an immigrant background – regardless of nationality – are most at risk of unemployment and least likely to engage in active citizenship (Soininen 1999).

Scholars of immigration commonly describe immigrant incorporation as a necessary process for social and political stability. First, there is the real and imagined connection between the alien and the subversive. We generally assume that the more integrated the immigrant, the less likely that he or she will commit an act that threatens national security and public tranquillity (despite evidence that contradicts this assumption). Second, the rapid influx of immigrants from diverse ethnocultural backgrounds can be perceived as a potential threat to notions of a stable national identity and way of life (Rudolph 2003; Weiner 1993). Public resentment based on this perception is reflected in discriminatory policies and practices toward immigrants, community tensions, and violence. Likewise, the effects of political and social marginalization on the immigrant population – in areas such as education, employment, criminal justice, legal rights, health, living conditions, and civic participation – are potentially destabilizing for the receiving society. Finally, for putatively democratic states, the long-term exclusion of a significant fraction of the population from the rights and duties of full citizenship is untenable. The contradictions inherent in having a population of permanent residents who pay taxes, benefit from social services, and otherwise participate in the host civil society but remain disenfranchised threaten the political stability of liberal democracies.

The concept of immigrant incorporation has undergone significant changes in the scholarship on immigration and citizenship. Straight-line assimilation theory in early twentieth-century U.S. social scientific scholarship assumed that immigrant assimilation into the dominant society was inevitable. The current conception of incorporation implies a mutually constitutive relationship between the immigrant and the receiving society. Although immigrants adapt to the receiving societies, they also have a significant impact through a type of give-and-take process that ultimately results in the remaking of the immigrants and the receiving societies (DeWind and Kasinitz 1997: 1098). Rather than complete absorption, then, incorporation as it is used in the contemporary sense refers to a process of "becoming similar," "or treating as similar" (Brubaker 2001: 534). Hence, the emphasis is on mutual acceptance and inclusion.

The failure of immigrant incorporation in contemporary democracies, however, suggests that this interactive model of immigrant incorporation has yet to emerge in practice. The French republican model of immigrant incorporation is contingent on a type of ethnic privatization that requires immigrants and their descendants to contain, sanitize, and, at times, neutralize their differences in the public sphere in a type of "color-blind integration" (Bleich 2001, 2003). Although the model's stated aim is to assimilate immigrants into a nationally oriented political community, it has effectively denationalized those who appear unassimilated, such that second-generation French citizens of North African descent are regarded as "immigrants." In contrast, the Dutch "pillarization model" is based on state support of multi-culturalism, group rights, and group autonomy. But the process by which immigrants and ethnic minorities have been incorporated into this system involves a high degree of political assimilation. As a result, immigrants and ethnic minorities are less politically integrated and participate less in public debates than their counterparts in a number of other European countries (deWit and Koopmans 2005).

Moreover, immigrant incorporation – even political incorporation – is not equivalent to immigrant political empowerment. Whereas the former concept implies a passive process of being admitted, being included, and conforming to expectations or requirements, the latter entails participation and critical engagement. Thus, an immigrant can become incorporated politically by naturalizing but may not subsequently engage in political activities or feel that she is a member of her adopted society. The process of naturalization is highly contingent and almost always requires some form of assimilation, whether it is political or cultural. The individual applicant may be asked to demonstrate knowledge of the receiving society's history and language and have a history of "good behavior," which may be defined as no criminal violations, history of seditious activity, and/or engagement in religious or cultural activities that run counter to the receiving society's sensibilities. For example, recent additions to citizenship tests in the Baden-Württemberg region of Germany, where there is a relatively high concentration of Muslim immigrants, include questions such as: "What is your position on the statement that a wife should belong to her husband and that he can beat her if she isn't obedient? What do you think about parents forcibly marrying off their children? Do you think that such marriages are compatible with human dignity?" (Rothstein 2006). Although the current U.S. citizenship test focuses primarily on U.S. domestic history and state institutions, definitions of cultural, civic, and political assimilability have historically played prominent roles in determining who was eligible for naturalization. Asian immigrants remained ineligible for naturalization based on the "free white persons" clause of the 1790 Naturalization Law even after the law was amended to extend the right to blacks in 1870. Although the McCarran-Walter Act of 1952 removed racial restrictions to naturalization, it also introduced legislation that made immigrants who were suspected of having ties with the U.S. Communist Party or engaged in communist activities ineligible for naturalization (Chung 2009).

Citizenship acquisition almost always provides material benefits, residential security, and more opportunities for political participation. It does not, however, always lead to greater representation of the applicant group's interests or more political participation among naturalized citizens. Although the most prominent advantages of full citizenship are voting rights and the right to run for public office, the average naturalization applicant is most likely concerned about the immediate *material* gains: protection from deportation, unrestricted exit and entry rights, unrestricted access to social welfare benefits, freedom from employment restrictions, eligibility for fellowships and scholarships limited to nationals, the advantages of carrying a passport issued by the particular country, and, in the case of the United States, immigration sponsorship of relatives. For example, in a 2000 survey of 359 naturalized Japanese citizens, approximately 45 percent responded that the most important reason for naturalizing was to continue their lives in Japan (*kore karamo nihon de seikatsu shite iku tame*). Only 3 percent of the respondents chose "voting rights" as the primary reason, and none chose "in order to become a public official" (Asakawa 2003).

Furthermore, naturalization patterns are not indicative of a group's level of political participation. Noncitizens who are not eligible to vote can and do engage in a wide range of extraelectoral political activities in order to voice their concerns and shape public debate and policy. Likewise, studies of immigrant naturalization and voting behavior in North America have found significant gaps between immigrant naturalization and voting patterns (Ramakrishnan 2005). When the costs of naturalization are unreasonably high or when contextual factors pressure noncitizens to naturalize, naturalization may inhibit further political participation (Chung 2009; Jones-Correa 2002).

Rather than view immigrant political incorporation as a unidirectional process by which states integrate immigrants into the polity, I propose a relational approach that examines the interaction among state policies, intermediary organizations, and immigrant groups, specifically public policies and institutions that govern immigrant political incorporation – or immigrant incorporation regimes – and immigrant and civil society engagement with such policies and institutions. Immigrants do not simply adapt to the receiving society's policies and norms. They also negotiate them. Consequently, we cannot predict the social outcome of immigrant arrival and settlement in particular countries based on immigration and citizenship policies alone.

EXPLAINING JAPAN'S IMMIGRANT-HOSTILE, IMMIGRANT-FRIENDLY INCORPORATION REGIME

Large-scale immigration almost always provokes strong reactions from members of the receiving society. But Japanese responses to recent immigrants have been disproportionate to their numbers. Although the foreign community in Japan has grown at a rapid pace in recent years, foreigners still make up less than 2 percent of the total population. Japan has the smallest percentage of foreigners in its population among all advanced industrial democracies. Nevertheless, this relatively small population of little more than two million foreigners has provoked acute anxiety that is unusual even among countries that have only recently experienced large-scale immigration (Weiner 1998: 5). It is the only advanced industrial democracy that does not grant family reunification rights to migrant laborers (with the exception of ethnic Japanese immigrants).[2] It is also among a small handful of advanced industrial democracies that requires native-born generations of foreign residents to undergo the formal process of naturalization in order to become full citizens. Because Japanese nationality is closely associated with ethnocultural identity, naturalization applicants must not only renounce their allegiance to their country of origin but must also demonstrate evidence of cultural assimilation.

Based on what we know about Japan's immigration and citizenship policies, we would expect to find a highly deprived foreign community in Japan with little or no political voice. Foreign residents, however,

---

[2] All North American and West European countries with significant immigrant populations grant some form of family reunification rights to legal immigrants. In contrast, no country in East Asia grants family reunification rights to migrant laborers.

have access to a wide array of social welfare benefits – including housing assistance, unemployment insurance, and health insurance – that are comparable in scope to those offered in a number of Western European countries. Since the landmark Hitachi Employment Discrimination Trial in the early 1970s (see Chapter 3), permanent foreign residents have encountered fewer obstacles in gaining employment in Japanese firms and are eligible for employment in a number of public-sector jobs. Moreover, the Diet started to debate two bills introduced in 2000 and 2001 that would grant additional political citizenship rights to foreign residents. One bill would grant local voting rights to foreign residents, a measure that has been rejected by other countries with more liberal immigration and citizenship policies such as France and Germany. A survey of three thousand eligible voters in Japan conducted by the Asahi Shimbun in 2000 found that more than 60 percent of the respondents favored local voting rights for foreign residents. Only 28 percent of the respondents were opposed to granting foreign residents any electoral rights. Some municipalities have already passed ordinances to allow permanent foreign residents to vote in local referenda. In addition, foreigners in cities such as Kawasaki, Osaka, Kyoto, and Hamamatsu are able to represent their interests through consultative committees and foreign citizens' councils.

The level of hostility toward immigrants among some segments of Japanese society is on par with the degree of enthusiasm demonstrated by others. Proimmigrant groups, national and local government officials, business associations, and wide segments of the Japanese citizenry have encouraged foreign residents to participate in the public sphere, linking their active engagement with democratic revitalization. Many have identified foreign residents as "local citizens" who deserve equal access to social services and political representation. In addition, references to Japan's "multiethnic" and "multicultural" society routinely appear in the Japanese press as well as in local government documents despite the relatively small size of the foreign population.

How do we explain the paradox of a foreign community with substantial citizenship rights and social recognition in an immigrant-hostile society? Why are political rights for foreign residents an issue of national significance when immigration policies discourage immigrant permanent settlement?

International Norms

Some scholars argue that foreign residents have gained extensive rights without national state citizenship because national citizenship is becoming increasingly obsolete in the current era of globalization. For a number of observers, the expansion of rights granted to foreign residents signals the devaluation and decline of national citizenship in Western Europe and North America (Jacobson 1996; Schuck 1998). Others contend that economic globalization, international migration, and the development of supranational organizations have changed the territorial boundaries of citizenship and have led to the emergence of a type of postnational citizenship (Roche 1995; Soysal 1994). In applying this argument to Japan, Amy Gurowitz (1999) takes a more nuanced approach that focuses on how domestic actors, namely Korean and other proimmigrant activists and organizations, mobilized international norms to demand changes to discriminatory policies. Rather than assert that international norms forced changes, Gurowitz analyzes how they became powerful tools for domestic actors to pressure the government. Because these actors linked questions about integration and policies toward foreign residents to those of internationalization, government officials were especially sensitive to the perceptions of other states and the international organizations of which Japan was a member.

This focus on international pressure provides insight into the catalysts for democratic reforms and is especially useful for understanding changes to the political opportunity structure. It does not, however, explain the direction that these reforms took. Why were some specific gains made and not others? Why were democratic reforms applied unevenly to different groups within Japan? How do we explain cross-national variations among countries that face a common set of systematic factors (Earnest 2006)?

Foreign residents in Japan have gained rights that go above and beyond those prescribed in international human rights treaties. Although secure residential status and access to social welfare benefits are directly linked to international conventions, access to public-sector jobs and local voting rights are not. Furthermore, a number of landmark lawsuits pertaining to the rights of Korean residents filed in the 1970s, such as the Hitachi Employment Discrimination case, made their arguments based on domestic legal orders, not international human rights norms. Japan's ratification of international conventions, moreover, has been insufficient to their enforcement in relation to refugees and recent immigrants. Although Japan signed the International Convention on Refugees more than twenty years ago, it continues to hold the worst record of accepting refugees among the major industrialized countries. Japanese officials have granted permanent foreign residents expansive citizenship rights but have upheld restrictive immigration and citizenship policies. Consequently, the gains reflect not social change but a type of "preemptive-concessions strategy" that Susan Pharr (1990) argues Japanese officials use to introduce social change on their own terms. As the scholarship on Western Europe and North America demonstrates, the divergent ways that national states have applied a common set of international norms contradict the core postnational argument about declining state sovereignty (Earnest 2006; Joppke 1999, 2001; Lahav and Guiraudon 2006). Even European Union (EU) citizenship requires national membership in a European member state. International norms have little enforcement power because national states remain the principal institution for allocating individual and group rights (Brubaker 1992). Furthermore, the Japan case demonstrates that national states diverge in their application of international norms to specific groups *within* their boundaries.

Domestic Institutions

In order to explain why some states grant particular rights to foreign residents at different historical moments, scholars of European and North American immigration and citizenship politics have focused on domestic institutions. One approach weighs the roles that national courts and legislatures have played in granting and denying alien rights. For example, Christian Joppke's (1999) study of alien rights in the United States, Germany, and Britain demonstrates that activist courts were central to extending alien rights in accordance with domestic legal orders as opposed to international human rights. Similarly, Virginie Guiraudon's (1998) examination of Germany, France, and the Netherlands found that the bureaucracy and judiciary were more likely to extend alien rights when they worked behind closed doors, out of the public purview. Another approach links the extension of alien rights with partisan politics, arguing that leftist parties are more likely to propose measures to extend alien rights because they are more likely to capture their votes than are right-leaning parties (Hammar 1990; Rath 1990).

Although liberal democratic institutions are important pieces of the puzzle of Japanese immigration and citizenship politics, there is no evidence to suggest that any have played a proactive role in extending citizenship rights to foreign residents. In most cases, courts, legislatures, and political parties have only grudgingly responded to foreign-resident demands. And, as Thomas Berger (1998: 341) notes, there is no tradition of judicial activism in postwar Japan that is comparable to that in Western Europe and the United States. Although one could argue that the New Komeito Party introduced the local voting rights bill to the Diet because of its close relationship to the Soka Gakkai, a Buddhist organization with a substantial number of Korean members, it is highly unlikely that the bill's introduction was aimed at garnering potential votes among foreign residents. For example, a number of Japanese lawmakers have stated that they are reluctant to push for the passage of the local voting rights bill because the minuscule base of eligible foreign residents would provide little political payoff (*Nikkei Weekly*, 29 May 2006). The introduction of the voting rights bill in 2000 and subsequent attempts to pass the bill in the Diet were immediately preceded by diplomatic pressure from South Korea, especially during Kim Dae Jung's presidency (Calder 2002).

To be sure, the Diet debates about either granting permanent foreign residents local voting rights or easing naturalization procedures for them reflect the idea that liberal democratic states have two options in dealing with foreign residents' rights that are consistent with democratic principles. They can either grant extensive citizenship rights to permanent foreign residents to make them effective equals to citizens, or they can make citizenship acquisition easily accessible (Rubio-Marín 2000). However, one is hard-pressed to conclude that the Diet debates have been centered on Japan's liberal democratic principles. Here, again, Pharr's (1990) model of the official "preemptive-concessions strategy" seems more relevant since Liberal Democratic Party (LDP) officials introduced the naturalization bill in order to defeat the local voting rights bill and, ultimately, quell demands by foreign-resident activists.

Nonetheless, domestic institutions have served as significant constraints to extending noncitizen rights in Japan. As mentioned earlier, Japan's descent-based citizenship policies link nationality with ethnocultural identity, thereby making the material and symbolic barriers to naturalization high. As citizenship policies are, as Rogers Brubaker (1992) puts it, based on deeply rooted understandings of nationhood, they reflect shared understandings of what the "nation" should look like, who is worthy of membership, and who should be granted rights and privileges administered by the state. Accordingly, we would expect that societies with restrictive citizenship policies are likely to have equally restrictive naturalization procedures and highly restricted rights for foreign residents. This framework offers a probable explanation for one side of Japan's immigration and citizenship paradox: low naturalization rates, limited rights for recent immigrants, high barriers to permanent-residency status, and immigrant hostility. However, it does not make room for the other side of the paradox: why do foreign residents have extensive citizenship rights and social recognition in Japan?

Japan as a Recent Country of Immigration

The rapid growth of the immigrant community since the late 1980s has spurred a surge of English-language scholarship on the foreign community in Japan (Brody 2002; Sellek 2001; Shipper 2008; Tsuda 2003). Many of these studies build on the theories discussed in the preceding text but also examine their tensions. Based on the framework that Japan is a recent country of immigration comparable to countries such as Austria, Italy, and Spain, these works focus on the contradictions of Japanese immigration and citizenship politics, especially the conflicting imperatives to exclude particular categories of immigrants while meeting the demands of labor.

According to this approach, the relatively recent arrival of significant numbers of immigrants explains the contradictions of contemporary citizenship and immigration politics in Japan. The contradictions are built into the system: because national immigration and citizenship policies are so restrictive, national and local practices have had to be less rigid in order to adapt to constantly changing circumstances. Japanese authorities have created legal loopholes that open side doors to unskilled migrant workers in order to meet labor demands while upholding the façade that Japan is not a country of immigration (Tsuda and Cornelius 2004). Local governments and civil-society organizations have had to play central roles in helping immigrants to adapt to their new communities in the absence of national immigrant incorporation programs through ad hoc immigrant integration programs and services (Shipper 2008). In the process, foreign residents have gained access to social services and social recognition as local residents who contribute to their local communities.

The most significant limitation of this framework is the historical fact that Japan is *not* a recent country of immigration. Although recent immigrants have contributed to the growth of the foreign population, one of the largest segments of the foreign population continues to be former colonial subjects and their descendants. Despite assertions that immigration is a new phenomenon in Japan, Japanese politicians and pundits have been debating the problem of immigrant incorporation since at least the Meiji period (1868–1910) when Japan's first citizenship law was instituted.[3] Moreover, as was the case with former European colonial powers, Japanese state officials formulated citizenship criteria in the context of decolonization and reconstruction in the postwar period. Consequently, debates on nationality and citizenship policies were concerned not only with redefining Japanese national identity as a democratic nation-state but also with the legal position of Japan's former colonial subjects.

Similar to other countries that have recently experienced large flows of immigration, new immigrants to Japan often confront anti-immigrant sentiment and hostility, language and cultural barriers, exploitation, and social and legal discrimination. Immigrants with temporary visas face considerable hurdles to acquiring permanent residency, and those who overstay their visas are vulnerable to immediate deportation.[4] In contrast, nontemporary foreign residents enjoy social

---

[3] Japan's first comprehensive citizenship law was implemented in 1899. Meiji oligarchs institutionalized *jus sanguinis* (citizenship by descent) after concluding that it was the dominant principle of the time and as a means to prevent foreigners from politically and economically powerful Western countries from assuming positions of power. See ch. 2.

[4] Since 2000, however, the Ministry of Justice has given growing numbers of overstayers with established families in Japan "special permission" to remain in Japan.

welfare rights on par with Japanese nationals, which seemingly belies Japan's official closed-door immigration policies that discourage immigrant permanent settlement.

Japan's relatively generous provisions for foreign residents, however, were not implemented with new immigrants in mind. Almost a decade before large numbers of immigrants began to arrive in Japan in the late 1980s, the legal landscape for foreign residents in Japan had changed dramatically. Whereas foreign residents routinely faced discrimination in employment, housing, education, health care, and legal protection until the late 1970s, their legal status and rights were on par with those of immigrants in other advanced industrial democracies by the early 1980s. As I discuss in the following chapters, Korean residents had won a series of campaigns from the 1970s to combat employment and housing discrimination and remove the nationality requirement for employment in public-sector jobs and access to social welfare benefits. Japan's ratification of the International Covenants on Economic, Social, and Cultural Rights and on Civil and Political Rights in 1979 and the Convention Relating to the Status of Refugees in 1982 centralized many of these reforms to grant foreign residents social welfare benefits in such areas as national health insurance, public housing, and child care allowances. The 1985 amendment to the Nationality Act following Japan's ratification of the Convention on the Elimination of All Forms of Discrimination against Women allowed for individuals to acquire Japanese nationality through either their father or mother's nationality and, additionally, removed the requirement that naturalization applicants adopt a Japanese name.[5] Even as the Japanese government enacted measures to better control the rapidly growing numbers of immigrants in the 1990s, it nevertheless abolished the fingerprinting requirement for special permanent residents in 1993, in response to the decadelong antifingerprinting movement led by Korean activists. In Japan's case, therefore, major changes in policies regarding foreign residents *preceded* large-scale immigration.

---

[5] Although there was no explicit requirement in the Nationality Law, the Ministry of Justice "recommended" that naturalization applicants adopt Japanese names, and local officials typically enforced this unofficial policy.

Grassroots Pressure: Multigenerational Korean Activism and Strategic Citizenship

The contradictions of Japan's immigration and citizenship politics – especially those between official closed-door immigration policies and descent-based citizenship policies based on the principle of ethnic homogeneity, on the one hand, and citizenship practices and rights based on the principle that foreign residents are full members of Japanese society, on the other – do not necessarily reflect the primacy of international norms, domestic legal orders, or party politics. Although international or diplomatic pressure may act as immediate catalysts to reforms, they rarely offer tangible policies to be applied on the ground or templates for translating international norms into domestic policy (Earnest 2006: 269). Likewise, most reforms to Japan's immigration policies reflect the government's aim to better control immigration; in contrast, liberal reforms have been implemented only after considerable pressure has been applied from internal grassroots movements and external actors. In most cases, national-level reforms were preceded by local-level reforms enacted in response to Korean-led social movements.

Nor are these contradictions the inevitable outcome of recent immigration. Although other countries that have recently experienced heightened immigration have implemented liberal immigration and citizenship policy reforms, their content and context vary widely. For example, Spain implemented immigration and integration policies in the context of EU integration prior to the arrival of large numbers of immigrants (Agrela and Dietz 2006). In contrast, migrant workers in South Korea have made significant inroads in gaining rights in part because of the strong tradition of labor activism in South Korean history. In Japan's case, a dominant theme among advocacy groups has been foreign-resident citizenship, broadly conceived, and its significance for revitalizing Japanese democracy.

I argue that contemporary immigration and citizenship politics in Japan reflect the strategic interaction between state efforts to control immigration and Korean grassroots movements to gain rights and recognition specifically for foreign residents of Japan. Instead of a snapshot of immigration challenges that Japan currently faces, this book focuses on Japan's failure to either expel or incorporate former colonial subjects. The argument has two parts related to structure and agency.

First, postwar citizenship and immigration policies were formulated on the erroneous assumption that former colonial subjects, the vast majority of whom were Korean, would either repatriate or naturalize. Neither of these expectations was met. Rather than mass repatriation, more than six hundred thousand Koreans stayed in Japan following the end of World War II. The post–World War II division of the Korean peninsula into American and Soviet occupation zones and the outbreak of the Korean War in 1950 provided Koreans who remained in Japan with little incentive to repatriate in the near future. At the same time, newly established citizenship policies that equated nationality with ethnocultural identity and that contained strong colonial remnants deterred most from naturalizing. Japan's unilateral decision to strip former colonial subjects of their Japanese nationalities, moreover, contributed to the formation of a permanent foreign community with distinct identities and, eventually, limited rights. Although it is unlikely that most former colonial subjects would have kept their Japanese nationalities if presented with the option in the postwar period, Japan's failure to create immigrant incorporation policies for this population even after the establishment of a second generation posed significant obstacles for developing coherent immigrant policies in subsequent decades.

The second area related to Japan's failure to incorporate former colonial subjects concerns the agency of Korean residents. Unlike others who have attributed low naturalization rates among Korean residents to either stringent Japanese policies or Korean nationalism, I argue that low naturalization rates reflect political mobilization campaigns by Korean community leaders based on strategic purposes. In the wake of Japan's defeat in the Pacific War, most Koreans saw no advantages to holding Japanese nationality and viewed foreign citizenship as a source of empowerment. Korean leaders mobilized the community to demand specific rights as foreign nationals from the early postwar period. Foreign citizenship – specifically that of the victorious Allied forces – was not merely a tool for repatriation; on the contrary, it was a source of political power within Japan during the Occupation.

When a society fails to incorporate its immigrants, we normally expect to find signs of social instability such as antiimmigrant violence or riots. In Japan's case, the failure to incorporate immigrants, particularly former colonial subjects, in the postwar period resulted in a peculiar equilibrium for most of the Cold War era. The Korean community was left largely to fend for itself. A *modus vivendi* between Japanese authorities and Korean community leaders based on mutual noninterference allowed Koreans to develop a relatively autonomous community – a parallel society of sorts with Korean schools, governing bodies, and financial institutions – as long as they kept the community under strict control, obeyed Japanese laws, and did not involve themselves in Japan's domestic affairs. The combination of descent-based citizenship policies, restrictive naturalization procedures, discriminatory social practices, and Korean separatist politics led to the creation of a permanent foreign community in Japan.

Because this foreign community was relatively small, politically silent, and socially invisible, Japanese authorities could afford to ignore it for decades. On more than one occasion, Japanese officials denied the existence of minorities and foreign residents within Japan's borders, a claim facilitated by their physical indistinguishability from the Japanese majority. However, Japan's ascendance as a major economic power coincided with a significant turning point in the foreign community. As Japan's new international spotlight put pressure on officials to implement policies regarding immigrants and refugees that corresponded with international norms, native-born foreign residents began to demand changes based on the democratic values of postwar Japan that were, as Susan Pharr (1990: 11) describes, "incorporated into the Japanese constitution, spread by a mass educational system, and supported both by internal socioeconomic changes and by the process of Japan's internationalization" and that became "an ideological basis for status inferiors to improve their lot through protest."

Unlike first-generation leaders who focused their activities on repatriation and homeland politics, native-born generations of activists took aim at Japanese society and politics. As foreign citizens with roots in Japan, they had only two exit options: they could either naturalize or immigrate to another country. Because naturalization entailed giving up not only one's extant nationality but also one's ethnocultural identity, few chose this option. Likewise, those who "returned" to their homeland found that they were worse off as immigrants in South Korea and returned to their homes in Japan. "Voice," to borrow from Albert Hirschman's now classic work (1970), was the only viable option to improve their lot but, as foreign residents with no voting rights, their choices were limited. Rather than struggle against their status as permanent foreign residents with limited rights, native-born activists devised a strategy that would mobilize the community specifically as foreign residents permanently residing in Japan (*zainichi* or *teijū gaikokujin*), which gave birth to a noncitizen civil rights movement. At the heart of this movement is the struggle to gain equal rights and recognition for foreign residents, as opposed to racial and ethnic minorities with Japanese nationality. Using this strategy, foreign activists made a number of significant gains for the foreign-resident community, most notably the repeal of the fingerprinting requirement for permanent foreign residents in 1993.

By the mid-1990s, the permanent foreign-resident problem seemed to be coming to a close. Naturalization rates were rising and intermarriage rates between Korean and Japanese nationals had surpassed 80 percent of all marriages among Korean nationals. With the 1985 revision that permitted individuals to gain Japanese nationality through either their father or mother's nationality, it appeared that the vast majority of Japan's native-born Koreans would be Japanese nationals in the near future. Foreign-resident activists increasingly turned their attention inward, concentrating on how native-born generations with Japanese nationality could cultivate a distinct ethnic identity and overcome the persistent problem of social and political invisibility.

However, Japan's political and social landscape changed dramatically with the phenomenal growth of the immigrant community. Throughout a single decade, the total foreign population had grown by 65 percent. By 2005, the population had surpassed the two million mark. Their increasingly visible presence generated public debate on national identity and social diversity. At the same time, local governments were forced to address the discrepancy between national state policies aimed at excluding immigrants and local realities that called for the adoption of immigrant integration programs. Moreover, the growth of immigrant, and especially illegal immigrant, populations spurred the development of proimmigrant nongovernmental organizations (NGOs) led by Japanese activists.

Although the concerns of native-born generations of foreign residents may diverge significantly from those of recent immigrants, many of the former have chosen to align themselves with the latter. Part of the motivation for the alliances may lie in the idea of linked fate. For instance, Reverend Yi In-Ha, who many Korean activists refer to as the "Martin Luther King, Jr. of the Korean civil rights movement," stated that building multicultural coalitions with other marginalized groups was the logical next step in the Korean civil rights movement (interview with Yi In-Ha, 2 September 1999, Kawasaki). These alliances are also strategic: Korean activists realized the benefits of forming broad coalitions with new immigrants that would reach beyond the Korean community's specific issues.

In sum, Korean strategic responses to legal and social discrimination in Japan have institutionalized paths available to other foreigners for political empowerment at the levels of policies, local institutions, and ideas. First, a number of national and local policy reforms that have afforded foreign residents numerous social welfare benefits, a secure residential status, employment freedom, and protection from various forms of discrimination are direct and indirect products of Korean social movements, lobbying activities, and lawsuits. Second, grassroots movements by Korean and Japanese activists have led to the establishment of local organizations and networks of community activists that address the specific needs of Korean and other foreign communities through advocacy and service activities. Third, Korean activists and intellectuals have influenced mainstream ideas about citizenship, multiculturalism, and democratic inclusion in Japan. Ideas that were originally formulated in reference to Korean residents in Japan – such as *tomoni ikiru* (living together in harmony), *gaikokujin shimin* (foreign citizen), and *senshin shimin shakai* (advanced citizen society) – have entered mainstream discourse on immigrant incorporation and democratic revitalization in the Japanese press, publications by local governments, NGOs, and nonprofit organizations (NPOs), and, in some instances, public statements by high-ranking politicians. This three-pronged approach to political empowerment for the Korean community in Japan has shaped immigrant political incorporation in

Japan, affecting future generations of Korean residents as well as other immigrants in Japan.

Chapter 1 compares Japan's experience to those of other advanced industrial democracies, identifying the areas in which Japan's citizenship policies and politics parallel those of other industrial democracies grappling with immigration and diversity as well as the specific areas in which Japan stands out. Rather than approach immigrant incorporation as a unidirectional process by which states incorporate immigrants, this chapter examines immigrant incorporation as a relational process that involves interaction among state policies, local state and nonstate actors, and immigrant groups.

Chapter 2 focuses on the process by which citizens and noncitizens were constructed in postwar Japan. It explores the context in which citizenship policies were formulated to meet the often-conflicting goals of redefining Japan as a democratic nation-state and resolving the "Korean problem." I then discuss how the failure to either expel or incorporate former colonial subjects compromised Japan's postwar democratic project and set the foundations for the paradox of contemporary citizenship and immigration politics in Japan.

Chapters 3 and 4 investigate the impact that citizenship policies have had on noncitizen political engagement in Japan through the lens of prewar Korean immigrants and their descendants. Chapter 3 focuses on the Cold War period, tracing the evolution of the permanent foreign-resident community in Japan and the subsequent development of a citizenship-as-identity paradigm that Korean leaders used to gain political power. Although the first generation of Korean leadership was primarily interested in garnering support for competing homeland regimes, native-born generations applied this paradigm to create a civil rights movement specifically for foreign residents. Chapter 4 analyzes the changes in the post–Cold War era as native-born generations of activists reconceptualized possibilities for the distinct forms of citizenship that foreign residents can exercise in Japanese civil society. I concentrate on three central approaches that Korean-resident activists use in movements for social change: local citizenship movements, the group-rights approach, and the push for cosmopolitan citizenship in Japan.

Chapter 5 examines the transformation of Japan's political and social landscape following the influx of immigrants to Japan from the late 1980s. I discuss how previous movements by Korean activists institutionalized paths for new immigrants at the levels of national policy, local institutions, and ideas. Although different responses to the wave of recent immigrants by national state officials, local governments, and civil-society actors have aimed primarily to maintain social stability, the dichotomy between citizenship policy and practices has opened up opportunities for social change. The concluding chapter assesses the implications of Japanese immigration and citizenship politics for Japanese democracy and revisits the overarching questions of citizenship, political incorporation, and political empowerment for immigrants and their descendants.

I

Is Japan an Outlier?

Cross-National Patterns of Immigrant Incorporation and Noncitizen Political Engagement

Much contemporary literature on political participation in advanced industrial democracies has focused on the vexing problem of declining citizen participation (Fiorina 2002; Schlozman 2002). In particular, this scholarship is motivated by the disjuncture between citizenship policies and citizen political behavior: why don't citizens vote? Meanwhile, scholarship on immigration and racial politics in Western Europe and the United States has demonstrated increasing interest in a similar disjuncture between citizenship policies and noncitizen political behavior: why don't noncitizens naturalize?

Although foreign nationals make up a substantial proportion of the labor force in a number of industrialized societies, their rates of naturalization have been relatively low even among long-term and native-born residents. Tomas Hammar (1990: 22–3) estimated that, by 1987, more than half of the total foreign-resident population in Europe were permanent foreign residents who were eligible for naturalization but remained noncitizens by choice or circumstance. He labeled this category of foreigners "denizens."

Low naturalization rates especially among permanently settled populations of foreign residents – who are neither full citizens of the host country nor recent immigrants who lack a secure residence status – pose particular dilemmas for liberal democracies. On the one hand, the long-term exclusion of a significant fraction of the population from the rights and duties of full citizenship is untenable for putatively democratic states. Especially as debates about immigration and national identity become increasingly racialized, the line separating de facto and de jure second-class citizens is often blurred. On the other hand, low naturalization rates among permanently settled foreign populations reflect an unwillingness to assimilate into the receiving society and polity. Not only does this position pose a potential threat to what is commonly referred to as the "cultural integrity" of the receiving society, but it may also challenge the civic ideals upon which the society's citizenship policies are based. Additionally, the reluctance on the part of foreign residents to sever ties with their country of origin may be interpreted as a threat to the national security of the receiving society.

Scholarship that attempts to explain immigrant political incorporation – or the lack thereof – diverges significantly according to regions of study. North American studies often limit their analyses to naturalization rates with the assumption that naturalization is the primary indicator of political incorporation (Cho 1999; DeSipio 1996; Jones-Correa 1998; Lien 1994; Ramakrishnan and Espenshade 2001). Because the vast majority of this literature examines a single country – the United States – structure is assumed. If all eligible immigrants must meet the same requirements for naturalization and reap the same benefits from acquiring U.S. citizenship, then the source of variation in naturalization rates must lie within the individual immigrant or immigrant group.

In contrast, much European scholarship concentrates on formal citizenship and immigration policies with particular emphasis on structural constraints (Brubaker 1992; Hammar 1990; Soysal 1994). The central area of concern in this literature is explaining variations in citizenship policies and, especially in recent years, whether those variations are dissipating. These state-centered approaches tend to limit their discussions of immigrants to the symbolic roles that they play in policy debates and the entitlements that they receive from the state.

Recent comparative studies focusing on mediating institutions in North America and Western Europe provide an important intervention into the micro-macro gap. Although mediating institutions vary widely in their levels of formality and their relationship to the state – ranging from state-sponsored institutions to local governmental initiatives to mainstream or coethnic organizations – they generally intercede between individual interests and the formal institutions of the state (Wolbrecht 2005). Michael Jones-Correa's (1998; 2001) research on Latin American immigrants in the United States and Irene Bloemraad's (2005; 2006) comparative analysis of Portuguese immigrants and Vietnamese refugees in the United States and Canada are examples of works that examine how political institutions and contextual factors structure the incentives and disincentives for noncitizen political engagement in North America. In a similar vein, studies of immigrant politics in France and Germany have demonstrated that the groundwork for citizenship reforms involves a protracted, contentious process of negotiation between state and nonstate actors – from immigrant associations to the far Right – over public policies as well as ideas about national identity, community, citizenship, and democracy (Feldblum 1999; Kastoryano 2002; Wihtol de Wenden 1991).

Analyzing the mechanisms of political mobilization is enormously useful in understanding the process by which immigrants are encouraged – or discouraged – to participate in their country of residence. As an immigrant considers the process of naturalization, local institutions and organizations supply valuable information and resources, ranging from basic guidelines to translations of citizenship examinations to providing financial support. Local and coethnic organizations and communities may also provide incentives or compelling reasons why immigrants should naturalize. Coethnics may underscore the benefits of naturalization – such as immigration sponsorship of relatives or scholarships limited to U.S. citizens – or highlight the risks of not naturalizing, for example, after the U.S. Congress passed the welfare reform bill in 1996.[1] Or they may provide disincentives for naturalization, ranging from stories of difficult naturalization procedures to social ostracism. When new immigrants arrive, they may be greeted by community representatives who will attempt to guide them on the path to naturalization or, conversely, may encourage them to participate in the local community and inform them of their rights as foreign residents. Finally, in cases in which national immigration and citizenship policies are based on illiberal norms, mediating institutions can provide services in the absence of official programs and, at the same time, enable national policies by maintaining social stability.

---

[1] The 1996 welfare reform bill proposed to bar legal immigrants and permanent residents from a wide range of federal benefits and services.

Building on scholarship that highlights the role that mediating institutions play in shaping noncitizen political engagement and citizenship and immigration reforms, this book approaches immigrant political incorporation as a relational process that involves interaction and negotiation among state policies, local state and nonstate actors, and immigrant groups, rather than as a unilinear process by which states integrate immigrants into the polity. State policies set the structural boundaries of immigrant political incorporation and engagement by regulating movement within and between state borders, linking access to rights and goods to specific groups of people, and establishing the parameters of debate on national identity, community, and equality. By establishing the rules of the game, state policies further provide the political opportunities for noncitizen and minority exclusion and participation in political development. Mainstream and minority mediating institutions structure the political learning environment for noncitizens and provide the tools and resources for noncitizen political engagement. State policies and mediating institutions together shape noncitizen political identities, in terms of how noncitizens identify themselves with the receiving and sending societies as well as in terms of how noncitizens represent themselves in the public sphere and how they are inserted in public discourse. Finally, individual and group-level variables, combined with contextual factors (such as the political climate), push noncitizens toward or pull them away from political opportunities and social movements.

The concept of citizenship has multiple dimensions that are subject to interpretation, negotiation, and contestation by state and nonstate actors. When we examine only one dimension, such as state membership, we miss the constantly changing, interactive, and local process of citizenship in its everyday interpretation, communication, and exercise as well as the informal constraints and encouragements to its practice. An exclusive focus on structural or individual-level variables, moreover, overlooks the agency of noncitizens and is consequently not adequate for explaining the current dynamics of citizenship politics. In many cases, noncitizens are not merely the objects of reform movements but also active and central participants. Although the state may not recognize them as full members, noncitizens may directly influence debates about citizenship and help bring about citizenship reforms.

The remainder of this chapter compares Japan's citizenship and immigration politics to those of other industrial democracies by examining these multiple dimensions of immigrant political incorporation and their interrelationships. For the purpose of comparison, I have divided these dimensions roughly into two categories: citizenship and immigrant policies and noncitizen political engagement. The following section focuses on public policies and institutions that govern immigrant political incorporation – or immigrant incorporation regimes – and includes discussion of citizenship policies, formal and informal institutions for immigrant incorporation, and alien rights. The second section examines patterns of noncitizen political participation in Japan, looking at electoral and extraelectoral forms, with special attention given to the role played by mainstream and coethnic organizations. Finally, this chapter concludes with a discussion of the comparative insights that the Japan case offers.

JAPAN'S IMMIGRANT INCORPORATION REGIME

In this chapter, I use the term *incorporation regime* to refer to the policies and institutions that define and regulate the boundaries of membership in a political community, immigrant integration into the receiving society, and rights granted to noncitizens. These can be divided roughly into three categories. First, citizenship policies classify categories of people who are formally recognized as either belonging or not belonging to the political community.[2] By distinguishing between who is and is not worthy of membership as well as the terms of membership and nonmembership, these policies help structure relations between citizens and noncitizens as well as between state and nonstate actors. Second, states institutionalize boundaries between citizens and noncitizens by reserving certain rights and duties for citizens. Finally,

---

[2] This chapter focuses on citizenship policies rather than immigration policies as a comparative discussion of the latter is beyond its scope. Although numerous countries have made substantial reforms to their citizenship and immigration policies, the provisions of the latter tend to be less stable. A comparative discussion of immigration policies in various industrialized countries would require a snapshot of a particular segment of time, which would tell us more about the particular immigration challenges that a country faces at a particular time period than about how some sets of immigration policies compare to others. I analyze Japan's immigration policies in comparative perspective in ch. 5.

immigrant incorporation regimes include formal and informal institutions for incorporating foreign residents into the society and polity. These range from state policies to discretionary practices to intermediate organizations.

Citizenship Policies and Immigrant Incorporation Programs

Japan's citizenship policies are based on the principle of *jus sanguinis*, or citizenship by descent.[3] On this basis, critics argue that Japan's citizenship policies are anachronistic and out of step with other advanced industrial democracies. Patrick Weil's (2001) study of nationality laws in twenty-five industrial societies reveals, however, that Japan is one of a number of industrial societies with descent-based citizenship policies. In addition to Japan, Austria, Denmark, Finland, Greece, Israel, Italy, Luxembourg, Spain, and Switzerland are among the other industrialized societies in which citizenship attribution is based on *jus sanguinis*.

No country in the world has a pure system of *jus soli*, or birthright citizenship. For instance, the United States grants U.S. citizenship to all individuals born in U.S. territory regardless of their legal status and to children born overseas to U.S. citizens. Although a number of U.S. lawmakers have attempted to amend the former provision of *jus soli* to exclude descendants of undocumented immigrants, few have challenged the latter provision of *jus sanguinis*. Australia's and the United Kingdom's systems of limited *jus soli* are examples of cases in which birthright citizenship is contingent upon certain conditions being met by specific populations. For instance, a child born in Britain to foreign parents must have at least one parent who is an official resident of Britain and holds Indefinite Leave to Remain (ILR). In Australia, native-born immigrant children gain Australian citizenship only if one of the child's parents is a permanent resident or citizen. Thus, in these cases, *jus soli* applies only to a certain segment of the population; for groups outside of the designated population, *jus sanguinis* is the rule.

Moreover, citizenship policies based on a combination of *jus soli* and *jus sanguinis* are far more common than those based primarily

---

[3] The principle of *jus soli* applies to a few exceptional cases to avoid statelessness, such as when the parentage of a child born in Japanese territory is unknown.

Jus Soli   *Jus Sanguinis*
(Birthright citizenship)   (Citizenship by descent)

US, Canada, Mexico,   Belgium, Denmark,   Japan, Austria, Greece,
Ireland, New Zealand   France,   Luxembourg, Italy,
     Limited: Netherlands,   Switzerland, South Korea
     Australia, UK,   Sweden
     Germany

FIGURE 1.1. Citizenship attribution policies in various OECD countries.

on *jus soli* (see Figure 1.1). Those systems that combine elements of *jus soli* and *jus sanguinis* make second-generation citizenship attribution contingent on particular requirements but do not require second-generation immigrants to undergo the formal process of naturalization. For example, minors born in Sweden can acquire Swedish citizenship through a notification procedure after residing in the country for five years. These systems generally grant citizenship automatically to third-generation immigrants. In contrast, citizenship policies based on *jus sanguinis*, such as those of Japan, extend the descent requirement beyond the second generation and require all native-born generations of immigrants to undergo the formal process of naturalization in order to become full citizens.

Japan's official naturalization criteria are no more stringent than those of the United States, where naturalization is generally regarded to be relatively easy, as shown in Table 1.1. Naturalization applicants are not required to meet the five-year continuous residence requirement in Japan as permanent residents, which is the case in the United States. By comparison, applicants for permanent residency in Japan must meet the more stringent requirement of a ten-year continuous residence. Additionally, although the naturalization process can be costly because of the supporting documents that the applicant must prepare, there is no application fee for Japanese naturalization, which contrasts strikingly with the relatively expensive application fee for U.S. naturalization (more than $600 in 2009). Although official criteria are relatively straightforward, the substantial discretionary powers exercised by Ministry of Justice officials during the process make naturalization procedures opaque and arbitrary, as I discuss later in this chapter.

TABLE 1.1. *Naturalization Requirements in the United States and Japan*

United States	Japan
5-year continuous residence (as permanent resident)	5-year continuous residence
Good moral character	History of good behavior and conduct
Attachment to the constitution (Oath of Allegiance)	Must never have attempted overthrow of Japanese constitution or government, either individually or as a member of a group
English and civics knowledge	Applicant must be willing to give up existing nationality or be without nationality
	Applicant must be able to support him/herself financially
	Applicant must be at least 20 years of age

Finally, immigrant incorporation regimes include formal and informal mediating institutions for incorporating foreign residents into the society and polity. These range from state policies to discretionary practices to intermediate organizations. Examples of immigrant integration measures include host programs to help new immigrants with the process of integration and settlement in Canada and Switzerland, compulsory language and societal training programs for new immigrants and refugees in Denmark, the welcome and integration contract in France, and the Newly Arrived Youth Support Services in Australia (SOPEMI 2006). The state may also provide support for integration programs and advocacy organizations through funding and other material support or through political campaigns and initiatives. In countries that lack official integration programs at the national level, local governments may institute formal or informal programs of their own. In addition, political parties, labor unions, religious institutions, and immigrant organizations often play central roles in mobilizing noncitizens to naturalize and register to vote (Wong 2006).

Like many other industrial democracies, Japan has no official integration programs at the national level. Consequently, as I discuss further in Chapter 5, local governments and civil-society organizations have attempted to fill the gap by creating a number of immigrant integration programs that range from comprehensive to ad hoc.

Most programs and services offered by local governments, such as Japanese-language classes, multilingual information brochures, and cultural exchange programs, operate out of the local international-ization division as opposed to a distinct immigrant integration office. Nongovernmental organization (NGO) services also tend to be ad hoc and temporary.

Japan's descent-based citizenship policies, naturalization criteria, and embryonic immigrant incorporation programs, then, are not unique; although some of Japan's policies are on the far end of the spec-trum, they do not make Japan an outlier among industrialized democ-racies. At the same time, these policies have resulted in an anomalous outcome: Japan is the only advanced industrial democracy where a foreign community spans four generations. Although Austria, Greece, Luxembourg, and Switzerland have citizenship attribution policies that resemble those of Japan, they have not been countries of immigration long enough to have a fourth generation.[4]

Among former imperial powers, moreover, Japan is an outlier in some key interrelated areas. Japan experienced significant flows of voluntary and involuntary immigration before 1945 as a result of colonial expansion and wartime mobilization. Unlike its European counterparts, the bulk of Japan's postwar foreign population estab-lished itself before the conclusion of World War II. Whereas former European colonial powers sought to redefine the legal position of for-mer colonial subjects residing in newly liberated territories, Japan's policy debates centered on former colonial subjects who continued to reside within Japan proper and who were, for the most part, viewed as undesirable populations. Japanese lawmakers and American Occupa-tion officials, therefore, were primarily interested in repatriating these populations, not incorporating them.

With this goal in mind, Japan became the only former imperial power to unilaterally strip its former colonial subjects of their Japanese nationality after the war. Unlike former colonial subjects elsewhere, Korean and Taiwanese subjects did not have the option of choosing to either maintain or renounce their Japanese nationality. Thus, the only avenue through which former colonial subjects could regain Japanese

---

[4] Among these four countries, only Austria and Switzerland have third-generation for-eign residents.

nationality was – and continues to be – through the formal process of naturalization. As the second generation of largely Korean residents came of age, Japanese officials began to encourage them to naturalize from as early as the mid-1960s. There are, nevertheless, no specific provisions to ease naturalization requirements for former colonial subjects that exist elsewhere. For example, Belgium grants citizenship automatically to individuals born outside of Belgium to a parent who was born in the Belgian Congo before 30 June 1960 or Rwanda or Burundi before 1 July 1962.

The naturalization requirement for former colonial subjects and their descendants has posed a significant obstacle to their political incorporation in Japan. This problem, however, is not the consequence of formal naturalization requirements but is closely associated with the symbolic significance of Japanese citizenship. For the first generation of former colonial subjects, the process of naturalization was intricately tied to the colonial experience. Because Japanese nationality was imposed upon Korean colonial subjects, very few chose to go the route of renouncing their status as liberated Korean nationals in favor of acquiring Japanese nationality. As I discuss in Chapter 2, Japanese nationality, especially in the early postwar period, had few tangible benefits given Japan's status as a defeated power after the war. Moreover, the postwar reformulation of Japanese citizenship policies inserted a distinct ethnocultural understanding to citizenship status. Whereas imperial formulations of Japanese citizenship included racially and ethnically distinct colonial subjects who were united by the emperor, postwar discourse was based on consanguinity. To be a citizen of Japan implies that one is Japanese by blood.

In turn, postwar Korean organizations in Japan appropriated the dominant discourse on Japanese citizenship to equate Korean nationality with Korean ethnic identity, as I discuss in the following chapters. Especially among first- and second-generation Korean residents, the act of relinquishing one's Korean nationality is akin to giving up one's Korean identity. Up until the early 1980s, the Korean community often shunned Korean individuals who became naturalized Japanese citizens. The requirement to adopt a Japanese name and, therefore, give up one's Korean name, which was eventually abolished in 1985, further solidified the association between naturalization and ethnic dissociation. At the same time, the high rates of assimilation among native-born generations of Korean residents have made Korean nationality, for many, their last connection to the "homeland."

Legal Status and Noncitizen Rights

Although legal foreign residents in Japan made up only 1.69 percent of the total Japanese population in 2007, there are twenty-seven visa categories that are divided broadly into permanent and nonpermanent residents. Permanent foreign residents are further divided into two subcategories: general permanent foreign residents (*ippan eijyusha*) and special permanent foreign residents (*tokubetsu eijyusha*). The category of general permanent foreign residents made up 20.4 percent of the total foreign-resident population in 2007, thereby making this category the largest group among foreign residents in Japan (Ministry of Justice 2008b). The stated requirements for permanent residency are ten years of continuous residence (which is double the requirement for naturalization applicants), the ability to support oneself financially, and a history of "good behavior and conduct." As in the naturalization process, Ministry of Justice officials have a high degree of discretionary power in evaluating the last requirement and exceptions are made for particular categories of foreigners, such as *Nikkeijin* (ethnic Japanese) and spouses of Japanese nationals. In addition, Japan does not grant permanent-resident permits at the time of an immigrant's entry, a practice that diverges from the North American system but resembles numerous European systems (Kondo 2001: 14). Among general permanent foreign residents, Chinese nationals made up the largest group in 2007 (29%) followed by Brazilians (most of whom are *Nikkeijin*) and Filipinos (Ministry of Justice 2008a).

The category of special permanent residents was established in 1991 to cover former colonial subjects and their descendants, the vast majority of whom are South Korean and *Chōsen* (de facto North Korean) nationals.[5] Although South Korean nationals had previously

---

[5] Those who are registered as *Chōsen* nationals are legally stateless, because the country of *Chōsen* (which is the term used to refer to Korea prior to World War II) no longer exists, and Japan does not recognize North Korea as a legitimate state (some who are registered as *Chōsen* nationals consider themselves to be North Korean nationals). In order to engage in international travel, they must carry a special document to verify that they are permanent residents of Japan.

been granted "treaty" or "agreement" permanent residency (*kyotei eijyu*) as part of the 1965 Japan-Republic of Korea (ROK) Normalization Treaty, the 1991 reform stabilized the legal status of most other former colonial subjects residing in Japan regardless of nationality.[6] This category of foreign residents made up 20 percent of the total foreign-resident population in 2007. Among former colonial powers, Japan's system of categorizing foreign residents is relatively straightforward given that it is limited to those who reside in Japan. In contrast, the 1981 British Nationality Act created three major categories of British citizenship: British Citizenship, Citizenship of the British Dependent Territories, and British Overseas Citizenship. Although all three tiers of British citizens codified in the 1981 act can travel on a British passport and seek British consular protection, only the first category of citizens has the right of abode. National voting rights are reserved for special categories of foreign residents, namely resident Irish citizens and citizens of independent Commonwealth countries.

Nonpermanent residents, who made up almost 60 percent of the total foreign-resident population in 2007, can be divided broadly into visa categories that either allow or do not allow unrestricted economic activities. The former group, which made up 25.1 percent of the total foreign-resident population in 2007, refers to immigrants with one of three visa categories: spouse or child of a Japanese national, spouse or child of a permanent resident, and long-term resident. Because immigrants who hold one of these three visa categories can reside in Japan for up to three years and renew their visas an indefinite number of times, their status is not too far removed from that of permanent residents. They have a shorter residency requirement than other foreign residents in applying for permanent residency – five years for long-term residents and one year for spouse or child of a Japanese national or a permanent resident. Brazilian nationals, most of whom are *Nikkei*, made up the largest group among those with long-term resident (55.3%) and spouse or child of a Japanese national (26.3%) visas

---

[6] Reforms in 1982 changed the status of *Chōsen* nationals to "exceptional" permanent residents (*tokurei eijyuu*), which gave them greater residential security. The 1991 act unified the categories of "agreement" permanent residents and "exceptional" permanent residents to a single category of "special" permanent residents.

while Chinese nationals made up the largest group among those with spouse or child of a permanent-resident visa (34%) in 2007 (Ministry of Justice 2008a). As I discuss in Chapter 5, this population of immigrants has provided employers with the most effective way of legally importing unskilled foreign workers despite the official policy that prohibits immigration of unskilled workers. Among the remaining categories of nonpermanent residents, the largest groups in 2007 were (in descending order) college students, dependents, trainees, specialists in humanities/international services, engineers, and precollege students (Ministry of Justice 2008b).[7] Chinese nationals made up the largest group among foreign residents in all of these categories.

Although Japan maintains an official closed-door policy and has one of the smallest immigrant populations among Organization of Economic Cooperation and Development (OECD) countries in relative terms, their rights and privileges are comparable to those granted to permanent foreign residents in other advanced industrial democracies (see Table 1.2). As is the case in most other industrial democracies, permanent foreign residents enjoy a secure legal status that protects them from arbitrary imprisonment and persecution by the state. Unlike immigrants without a secure legal status – or permanent residents in the United States for that matter – permanent foreign residents in Japan cannot be deported for committing minor criminal offenses. On the contrary, permanent residents may be deported only if they are sentenced to more than seven years of imprisonment for crimes that the Ministry of Justice deems to be a major breach of Japanese national interests (Hanami 1998: 222). At the same time, permanent foreign residents in Japan are not necessarily guaranteed freedom of entry, even though they have freedom of departure, and must apply for reentry permits every few years (with longer permits granted to special permanent residents). In addition, there is no legislation that explicitly protects the civil rights of foreign residents, which makes foreign residents' rights contingent on the political climate, public debate, and

---

7 Although they made up more than 90% of new entrants to Japan in 2007, the number of registered foreign nationals with a "temporary visitor" visa made up only 2.3% of the total foreign-resident population in part because most foreign nationals in this group leave Japan without registering (Ministry of Justice 2008a). All foreign nationals residing in Japan are required to register with their local administrative office within 90 days of their entry into Japan.

TABLE 1.2. *Foreign Populations and Alien Rights in Selected OECD Countries (2006)*

Country	Foreign Population (thousands)	% of Total Population	Citizenship Rights
Austria	817.5	9.9	Civil, social, political[c]
Belgium	932.2	8.8	Civil, social, political
Canada	6,187[a]	19.8	Civil, social, political[d]
Denmark	278.1	5.1	Civil, social, political
France	3,506.5[b]	5.6	Civil, social
Germany	6,755.8	8.2	Civil, social
Japan	2,083.2	1.6	Civil, social
Netherlands	681.9	4.2	Civil, social, political
Sweden	492	5.4	Civil, social, political
Switzerland	1,523.6	20.3	Civil, social, political[e]
United Kingdom	3,392	5.8	Civil, social, political[f]

[a] Foreign-born population.
[b] 2005 figures.
[c] Voting rights in Vienna local elections only.
[d] Local voting rights extended only to immigrants of British nationality in certain provinces.
[e] No political rights at the national level. Foreigners may be able to vote or run for office at the local level, depending on the individual canton or commune.
[f] Voting rights in national elections for Commonwealth and Irish citizens only. Commonwealth citizens, however, do not automatically have immigration rights.
Sources: Earnest 2006; OECD in Figures, 2006–2007 ed.; SOPEMI 2008; Statistics Denmark 2005.

administrative interpretation rather than ensured in law. For instance, the fingerprinting requirement for foreign residents, which was abolished for all foreign residents in 1999, was reinstated in the fall of 2007 as part of an antiterrorist measure. Only special permanent residents are exempt from this requirement.

In the area of social welfare benefits, foreign residents have almost the same rights as Japanese nationals. Following Japan's ratification of the International Covenant on Economic, Social and Cultural Rights (ICESCR) and the International Covenant on Civil and Political Rights (ICCPR) in 1979 and the Convention Relating to the Status of Refugees in 1982, foreign residents became eligible for most state-administered benefits, such as health insurance, child care allowances, admission to public housing, and worker pensions. The only area in which foreign residents have not had equal access is in the national pension system.

When the nationality clause was removed from the National Pension
Law in 1982, approximately five thousand foreign residents (almost
all Korean residents) were unable to benefit from this measure because
those who were thirty-five years or older in 1982 lacked sufficient
contributory premiums (Kondo 2001: 17).[8] Additionally, foreign residents with temporary visas (less than 1 year) have only limited access to
the social welfare benefits provided to permanent residents. In regions
with relatively high concentrations of foreign residents, the cultural
rights of foreign residents have been addressed through the implementation, for example, of Korean "ethnic education" classes in several
wards in Osaka, bilingual education in Kanagawa Prefecture, and foreign citizens' councils in cities such as Kawasaki, Osaka, Kyoto, and
Hamamatsu.

Although permanent residency affords foreign residents residential
security and social welfare benefits, only full citizenship allows for
unrestricted opportunities to work in the public sector and to vote in
national elections. Although there is no explicit nationality clause in
Japan's constitution regarding civil servants, foreign residents are,
in principle, disqualified from positions that, according to the Cab-
inet Legislation Bureau's 1953 memorandum, pertain to the "exercise
of public power or participation in the formulation of national policy"
(Iwasawa 1998: 162). Nevertheless, foreign residents have been eligible
for a limited number of public-service jobs since the 1970s in the areas
of clerical and technical work, teaching, medicine, and transportation.
Some local governments, such as those of Osaka, Kobe, and Kawasaki,
have removed the nationality requirement for all civil-servant jobs –
including administrative positions – except fire fighters.

The political rights of foreign residents in Japan are consistent with
those instituted in many other industrial democracies. That is, local
governments have generally supported moves to grant voting rights

[8] Under the national pension plan, individuals are required to pay premiums over a
course of 25 years. Others who remained ineligible for the national pension were
disabled individuals who were 20 years or older in 1982 and those who were already
widows in 1982. Although the national pension system was revised again in 1986
to accommodate more foreign residents, it continued to exclude those who were
60 years or older in 1986 and disabled individuals who were 20 years or older in
1982.

and representation to foreign residents even against rigid opposition from the central government. From the early 1990s to 2004, more than twenty local governments in Japan instituted assemblies and advisory councils to represent the interests and opinions of foreign residents in the local community (Suh 2004). By 2005, more than 1,500 local assemblies (almost 76% of all local governments) submitted resolutions to grant local voting rights to foreign residents and more than 170 municipalities passed ordinances to allow foreign residents to vote in local referenda (*Asahi Shimbun*, 19 March 2005). Although the Diet did not pass the bill introduced by the New Komeito Party in July 2000 to grant foreign residents the right to vote in local elections, advocates continue to push for its resolution. Renewed support for the bill followed the January 2008 meeting between Ozawa Ichiro, the president of the Democratic Party of Japan, and Lee Sang-deuk, South Korea's National Assembly Deputy Speaker and special envoy of President Lee Myung Bak, in which Ozawa pledged to work toward the bill's passage. The issue remains under debate largely due to the 1995 Japanese Supreme Court ruling that the constitution neither prohibits nor demands local suffrage for permanent foreign residents and the legislature can amend the law to permit local voting by permanent foreign residents without a constitutional amendment (Kashiwazaki 2000: 457–8; Kondo 2001: 23). This ruling is noteworthy not only because it contradicts the primary argument used by opponents of local voting rights, but also because it diverges from those that struck down local voting rights bills as unconstitutional in France and Germany.

The extensive social and limited political rights enjoyed by foreign residents in Japan are in stark contrast with the highly restricted rights of immigrants with temporary visas. Like their Western European counterparts, Japanese government officials responded to the problems and responsibilities accompanying heightened immigration by implementing policies to tighten immigration controls while more fully incorporating foreign residents settled within Japan's borders. Although the Japanese central government has made efforts to improve conditions for permanent and long-term foreign residents throughout the past two decades, it has simultaneously renewed its efforts to curb illegal immigration. For example, a law that went into effect in February 2000, the same year that the local voting rights bill was proposed, made illegal immigration punishable by 300,000 yen, three years of imprisonment, or both. In addition, the law bars illegal immigrants from reentry into Japan for five years, up from the previous one-year ban (*Washington Post*, 18 February 2000). Additionally, the government has intensified police checks in areas where most undocumented foreigners are thought to work (SOPEMI 2004). These recent efforts to curb illegal immigration have resulted in a significant reduction of undocumented immigrants, from a high of 300,000 in 1993 to an estimated 150,000 in January 2008 (Ministry of Justice 2008a).

In sum, citizenship rights for foreign residents in Japan are on par with those of other democracies with relatively generous provisions including, but not limited to, access to most state-administered social welfare benefits, residential security, and limited political rights. Although Japan's foreign residents do not have local voting rights, they can represent their interests through representative assemblies and councils established specifically for foreign residents as well as through local referenda. However, these rights are generally limited to nontemporary foreign residents.

PATTERNS OF NONCITIZEN POLITICAL ENGAGEMENT

Naturalization Patterns

The impact of Japan's incorporation regime on one area of noncitizen political behavior is readily observed in the country's annual naturalization rates. The total number of naturalizations rose from a little more than four thousand in 1960 to more than ten thousand in 1993, and, since 1995, the annual rate has hovered between fourteen thousand and sixteen thousand (see Table 1.3). Despite the almost fourfold increase in annual naturalizations since the 1960s, the annual rate has not exceeded 1 percent of the total foreign population.

Table 1.4 lists naturalization rates in selected OECD countries with citizenship policies based purely on *jus sanguinis* or on a combination of *jus sanguinis* and *jus soli*. All of the countries listed in this table have relatively low rates of naturalization. Sweden is the only country listed where more than 5 percent of the total foreign population naturalized

TABLE 1.3. *Annual Naturalizations in Japan*

Year	(North and South) Korean Nationals	Total
1952	232	282
1955	2,434	2,661
1960	3,763	4,156
1965	3,438	4,188
1970	4,646	5,379
1975	6,323	8,568
1980	5,987	8,004
1985	5,040	6,824
1990	5,216	6,794
1991	5,665	7,788
1992	7,244	9,363
1993	7,697	10,452
1994	8,244	11,146
1995	10,327	14,104
1996	9,898	14,495
1997	9,678	15,061
1998	9,561	14,779
1999	10,059	16,120
2000	9,842	15,812
2001	10,295	15,291
2002	9,188	14,339
2003	11,778	17,633
2004	11,031	16,336
2005	9,689	15,251
2006	8,531	14,108
2007	8,546	14,680

Sources: Y. D. Kim 1990; Ministry of Justice 1986–2008; SOPEMI 2001–7.

in 2006.[9] Even among these countries, Japan's naturalization rate (less than 1%) is among the lowest. Only Luxembourg has lower rates.

There are no discernable patterns in Table 1.4 that would suggest a relationship between naturalization patterns and citizenship policies. Although the countries with the lowest rates of naturalization have citizenship policies based purely on *jus sanguinis*, one of the four

[9] Naturalization rates among the countries listed in Table 1.4 were somewhat higher during the years between 2000 and 2005, when naturalization rates exceeded 5% of the total foreign population more than once in Austria, Belgium, Denmark, the Netherlands, and Sweden.

TABLE 1.4. *Naturalizations in Selected OECD Countries* (2006)

Country	Total	% of Foreign Population	Span of Foreign-Resident Generations	Citizenship Attribution for Second Generation	Jus Soli for Third Generation?
Austria	25,746	3.2	3	Naturalization required	No
Belgium	31,860	3.5		Conditional entitlement[a]	Yes
Denmark	7,961	2.9	2	Conditional entitlement[b]	No
Germany	124,832	1.8	2	Conditional entitlement[c]	Yes
Italy	35,766	1.3		Conditional entitlement[b]	No
Japan	14,108	0.7	4	Naturalization required	No
Luxembourg	1,128	0.6	2	Naturalization required	No
Netherlands	29,089	4.2	2	Conditional entitlement[b]	Yes
Spain	62,339	2.3		Conditional entitlement[b]	No
Sweden	51,239	10.7	2	Conditional entitlement[b]	Yes
Switzerland	46,711	3.1	3	Naturalization required	No

[a] Dependent on parents' years of residence in receiving society.
[b] Dependent on individual's years of residence in receiving society.
[c] Dependent on parents' residency status.

Source: SOPEMI 2008; Weil 2001.

countries with the highest rates of naturalization in this table also has descent-based citizenship policies. In addition, the naturalization requirement for second- (and, in some cases, third-) generation foreign residents does not necessarily have a negative effect on naturalization rates given Austria's case. Finally, the size of the foreign population in relation to the total population has no obvious impact on naturalization rates. Foreign residents make up 20 percent of the total Swiss population but naturalized at a rate of only 3.1 percent in 2006. This rate is only slightly higher than that of Denmark, where foreign residents make up only 5 percent of the total population. Likewise, Japan and Luxembourg had similar rates of naturalization despite the fact that foreign residents make up less than 2 percent of the total Japanese population and approximately 40 percent of the population in Luxembourg.

Nonetheless, Japan stands out again in one central area: Japan is the only country with low rates of naturalization *across* four generations of foreign residents. Only about 30 percent of the total Korean population in Japan are naturalized Japanese citizens even though more than 90 percent were born in Japan and span four generations. The prevalent scholarship on immigrant political behavior that focuses on either individual or group-level characteristics to explain naturalization patterns, especially in the United States, is insufficient for understanding this phenomenon. For example, various studies of immigrant naturalization and voting behavior in the United States point to the significance of immigrant-related variables such as length of residence in the United States, English-language ability, generational status, and homeland ties (Ramakrishnan and Espenshade 2001). If we applied these theories to the Korean population in Japan, most of whom are native-born, Japanese-language speakers who attend Japanese schools and intermarry with Japanese nationals at a rate exceeding 80 percent, we would expect to find high rates of naturalization especially among the later generations. Instead, naturalization rates among Koreans in Japan are far outpaced by those among Korean immigrants to the United States, despite the fact that the former exhibit much higher rates of cultural assimilation.[10]

---

[10] Naturalization rates in the Korean American community are slightly higher than the national average. Slightly more than half of all foreign-born Koreans were naturalized U.S. citizens according to the 2000 Census, compared to 43% of the total foreign-born population in the United States.

Another area in which Japan stands out is in the unofficial practices surrounding the naturalization process. Although Japan's official naturalization criteria are similar to those of other industrialized democracies, the unusually stringent informal prerequisites pose significant constraints for individuals to naturalize. In addition to meeting the official naturalization criteria, applicants must submit tax records as well as extensive documentation related to their family histories, including a copy of their family registry from their country of origin. If an applicant is granted an interview, she may be required to provide painstaking details about her individual and family history that range from the applicant's employment history to the nationalities of the applicant's friends (e.g., Korean or Japanese) to facts about the applicant's parents' marriage (Asakawa 2003: 53–4). In most cases, naturalization applicants must also demonstrate evidence of cultural assimilation. Japan's naturalization procedures confer a great deal of discretionary power to the Ministry of Justice in determining if an applicant meets the requirement of "good behavior and conduct." Ministry of Justice officials have been known to conduct meticulous verifications of cultural assimilation, involving home inspections and interviews of neighbors, and often pressure individual applicants to adopt Japanese names despite the abolishment of the official requirement to do so (Kim 1990).[11] Naturalization applications may be rejected if the presiding official deems the applicant "inappropriate" or "incongruous" with the general understanding of a Japanese national. To my knowledge, the only other industrialized democracy with naturalization procedures that involve a close inspection of individual applicants' cultural assimilation is Switzerland, where applicants are required to demonstrate familiarity with Swiss habits, customs, and traditions and integration into the Swiss way of life in addition to language fluency (in German, French, Italian, or Romansch); show compliance with Swiss laws; and pose no danger to Swiss internal and external security. Until 2003, Swiss citizens voted in plebiscites on each naturalization application in some areas of Switzerland (Oezcan 2003b).

[11] David Aldwinckle, a naturalized Japanese citizen from the United States, describes the "good behavior survey" (*sokō chōsa*) as follows: "The Justice Ministry will visit your house, look at your décor, open your refrigerator, even check your children's toys. They will talk to your neighbors to find out how 'Japanese' you are…" (Aldwinckle 1999).

Taken as a whole, Japan's naturalization rates are consistent with those of other countries that have citizenship policies based solely on *jus sanguinis* or in combination with *jus soli*, albeit at the low end of the spectrum. However, the unofficial practices surrounding the naturalization procedure – particularly in the assessment of whether an applicant fits the definition of a "good Japanese national" – make the process arbitrary and opaque. The significant constraints posed by Japan's naturalization procedures, however, do not fully explain low rates of naturalization among native-born generations of Korean residents. Given their high rates of cultural assimilation, native-born Korean residents generally do not have to pass significant hurdles to become Japanese citizens. Particularly in recent years, Ministry of Justice officials have used their discretionary powers to ease naturalization procedures especially for native-born Korean applicants. The 1985 revisions to the Nationality Act, following Japan's ratification of Convention on the Elimination of All Forms of Discrimination against Women, changed citizenship attribution criteria so that individuals could acquire Japanese nationality through either their mother or father and, as mentioned earlier, officially abolished the requirement to adopt a Japanese name. Since 2000, some members of the Liberal Democratic Party (LDP) have pushed for a bill to ease naturalization requirements for permanent foreign residents, creating a simple process of registration and declaration on par with the procedures of other industrial democracies.

Nevertheless, no other country exhibits such low naturalization rates across four generations. Naturalization rates in Austria, which has three generations of foreign residents, have increased significantly from a little more than 2 percent in 1996 to 5.5 percent in 2004. Switzerland, which also has three generations of foreign residents, has experienced only an incremental rise in naturalizations and could well join in Japan's distinction. Still, Japan may be the only industrial democracy where foreign residents have resisted official efforts at incorporation. The strongest opposition to the LDP bill to ease naturalization requirements, for example, has come from the Korean community. Therefore, in order to understand why the majority of foreign residents remain politically unincorporated in Japan, we must also examine the political interests and strategies of foreign residents.

Noncitizen Extraelectoral Political Participation

Aside from a handful of high-profile non-Korean foreigners and nat-uralized citizens – such as Marutei Tsurunen, a naturalized Japanese citizen from Finland who was the first person of European descent to be elected to the Diet in 2002, and Ana Bortz, a Brazilian journal-ist and resident of Hamamatsu City who won a racial discrimination lawsuit in 1999 – the vast majority of non-Korean foreigners do not participate directly in the public sphere, even when they are the objects of public debate and policy. Rather, their political engagement tends to be indirect: their rights are defended by Japanese NGOs, Japanese human rights lawyers, Korean umbrella organizations, and, in some cases, local governments. Although most proimmigrant NGOs, orga-nizations, and lawyers work primarily to provide medical, legal, finan-cial, and practical assistance to recent immigrants, legal and illegal, they also act as spokespeople for immigrants in the public sphere and mediators between immigrants and local governments. In partic-ular, NGOs and Japanese human rights lawyers have played pivotal roles in publicizing the harsh conditions faced by foreign workers and pressuring the central and local governments to respect the commu-nity's human rights and basic needs through petitions, protests, and lawsuits.

This lack of direct political engagement by non-Korean foreign res-idents is due in part to the recent arrival of many immigrants to Japan. Most recent immigrants to Japan do not have the requisite linguistic and cultural fluency, much less political capital, to influence public debate and policy in Japan. Even among those who do, especially the Chinese-resident community, political engagement has tended to focus on the homeland. To be sure, many Korean community organiza-tions have long focused their political activities on homeland politics, and groups such as Chongryun continue to adhere to the principle of noninterference in Japanese domestic politics. Additionally, several Korean organizations are part of the transnational networks of Korean diasporic communities that have worked to attract international atten-tion, raise funds, and/or change policies about issues such as Korean reunification, the North Korean famine, and justice for former "com-fort women." But, by and far, the modes of Korean-resident political engagement among native-born generations in contemporary Japan are aimed explicitly at advancing the democratic process in Japan. Social movements for local voting rights for foreign residents, protests against recent state efforts to revise Japanese textbooks, participation in local foreign-resident assemblies, and petitions to remove the nationality requirement for local civil service jobs are direct action methods through which Korean residents have engaged in Japanese – not homeland – politics.

Korean-resident political activism – especially their focus on issues concerning their incorporation in Japan, rather than the homeland, and their relative success in gaining public support and political attention in a few key areas – can in part be explained by the length of the community's residence in Japan. First, their legal status as permanent foreign residents since 1981 explains the timing and capacity of their social movements. Until the early 1970s, Korean political activism in Japan resembled that of recent immigrants. The limited rights-based movements were almost entirely spearheaded by Japanese human rights lawyers and activists. Direct political engagement by Korean residents focused primarily on homeland politics led by Mindan and Chongryun. Mindan and Chongryun explicitly discouraged their members from assimilating into Japanese society, whether in the form of naturalization, cultural assimilation, or political engagement in Japan's "domestic" affairs. Individual attempts to gain employment in Japanese corporations or challenge social discrimination or otherwise demand civil, social, or political rights were condemned as acts of assimilation into Japanese society. Thus, rather than challenge their precarious status as foreigners with limited rights, Mindan and Chongryun cautioned their members against any form of political activity that would challenge the status quo.

With the establishment of permanent residency for the community, prewar Korean immigrants and their descendants no longer had to rely on either South or North Korea – or their representative organizations in Japan – to represent their interests or to protect them from either persecution by the Japanese state or deportation. Although they do not possess the full gamut of rights and privileges accorded to Japanese citizens, permanent foreign residents nevertheless enjoy a secure legal status. They are, furthermore, typically accorded a special status among foreign residents in official policy. Because this category of foreigners already enjoys a secure legal status, there is no imperative to demand changes to immigration policies, labor laws, and other areas that do not directly impact them.

Second, native-born Korean residents in Japan have to their advantage a wealth of social capital that recent immigrants lack. For example, those who were born and raised in Japan have the linguistic and cultural fluency to navigate Japan's social and political landscape to the point of passing as Japanese. Moreover, most have established social, economic, and psychological roots in Japan and, thus, have no realistic plans to "return" to their homeland. Although a substantial portion of the Korean-resident community sustain an interest in homeland politics, their everyday civic activities indicate that they are first and foremost members of their local communities. To be sure, Korean residents are more likely to identify themselves as Kawasaki city residents or Kobe citizens than as Korean citizens. Even those who are not politically active are likely to engage in civic activities related to their local communities. In this respect, they have more at stake in Japanese politics than do recent immigrants.

Finally, foreign residents permanently residing in Japan have the political capital to influence public debate and policy in Japan. As long-term residents of their local communities – or local citizens – they are as likely to have some bearing on local officials or policies as their fellow community members with Japanese citizenship. Some may be actively involved in their local community politics and may even have leadership roles. For example, one of my interviewees was a leading figure in the Kobe community movement to block the construction of the Kobe Airport in the late 1990s. Furthermore, the decades of political activism within the Korean community – even when directed primarily toward homeland politics – has afforded the community with individuals who possess the requisite leadership and mobilizational skills to engage in any form of political activity. As research on Latin American immigrants in the United States has shown, immigrants who are politically active in transnational organizations are likely to be active in their country of residence as well because of political socialization (DeSipio 2006). Their previous political activism has also supplied them with a network of allies among the dominant Japanese population. These include activists on the Left from earlier movements in the 1960s and 1970s, *burakumin* and other minority activists, as well as contemporary proimmigrant activists.[12]

Nonetheless, their legal status as foreign residents – as opposed to ethnic minorities with full citizenship of their country of residence – has had a significant influence on the direction and scope of their political engagement within Japan. Aside from a handful of attempts in the 1960s and 1970s, Korean community activists have generally not engaged in joint movements with Japan's other ethnic minorities, such as the *burakumin*, Ainu, or Okinawans.[13] Rather than a civil rights movement to recognize the equality and humanity of ethnic and racial minorities within Japan, Korean activists have engaged in a civil rights movement specifically for foreign residents and have thus pushed to the forefront a number of issues that we do not necessarily see in minority communities elsewhere, such as local voting rights for foreign residents. In sum, the generational status of the Korean community has shaped foreign residents' concerns and demands, the types of political action in which they can engage within their structural boundaries, and the social and political capital available to foreign residents to influence public policy and debate.

THE RACIAL POLITICS OF PASSING

Mr. Pak, a first-generation Korean resident who immigrated to Japan in 1969, visited Europe for the first time in 1996. Although he had made several trips to South Korea in the past, this was his first visit outside of Asia. As he walked the streets of Paris, Venice, and London, he recalls that he felt a freedom that he had never experienced before: "This was the first time I had ever been completely free of my identity. I didn't have to hide who I was. In these countries, I was simply yellow, an Asian. I didn't have to negotiate any issues of identity. I didn't have to worry whether or not someone might suspect that I am Korean. My identity [as an Asian] was already marked on my skin. But as soon as I returned to Japan, I felt suffocated again. It was

---

[12] The *burakumin* are descendants of historical outcasts who have been discriminated against since the Tokugawa Period (1600–1868).

[13] The Ainu refer to the indigenous population of northern Japan who currently reside mainly in Hokkaido.

back to the pass-or-not-pass dilemma" (interview, 6 September 2008, Kawasaki).

Although a growing number of Korean residents have begun to publicly use their Korean names, most Korean residents continue to negotiate the politics of "passing" as Japanese in their daily lives. Even among those who are not especially ashamed of their Korean identities, passing as Japanese is often more convenient, as a second-generation Korean resident in her fifties puts it: "When I go to the store or to the post office or meet someone for the first time, it's just easier to use my Japanese alias. I don't want to have to explain that I am a South Korean national who was born and raised in Japan. I don't want to deal with the stupid remarks about how well I speak Japanese. I don't want to answer the inevitable question of why I am a foreigner even though I was born in Japan" (interview, 5 September 2008, Tokyo). Others, however, note that the choice to "pass" or "not pass" is not necessarily voluntary. A second-generation businessman described the "passing" dilemma accordingly:

I have to carry two sets of business cards: one with my Korean name and one with my Japanese name. When I think that my Korean identity will pose a problem for me, I always use my Japanese name. Sure, the elite can use their Korean names freely. But when you work for someone else, you don't have that freedom. . . . What has troubled me most during my entire life in Japan has been the name problem. I have a real name and a Japanese alias. . . . Where else in the world can you find a whole community of people who all have two completely different names?" (interview, 10 April 1999, Kawasaki)

Racial minority groups in many advanced industrial democracies are typically marked by their hypervisibility, whether they are recently arrived immigrants, native-born residents, or legal citizens. As Stephen Castles and Mark Miller (2003: 238) argue in their comparative analysis of North American and European societies, phenotypical difference is the central marker for minority status in that it may "coincide with recent arrival, with cultural distance, with socioeconomic position, or, finally, it may serve as a target of racism." Since the 1960s, the majority of noncitizens in advanced industrial democracies have originated from postcolonial societies. Thus, they are not only foreigners but also racial and ethnic minorities. Consequently, not only is immigration a central area of public concern in most industrial democracies, but also immigrants and their descendants are targets of public discontent.

Among advanced industrial democracies, the foreign population in Japan is one of the only groups for which phenotypical difference is *not* the basis for the formation of new ethnic minorities. Most Korean residents in contemporary Japan rarely experience direct forms of discrimination in part because they are indistinguishable from the Japanese majority in terms of physical appearance, speech, mannerisms, and, for many, customs and rituals. There are no particular religious or cultural customs that have been passed down from generation to generation that would set Koreans apart from the Japanese majority. For instance, *kimchee*, the ubiquitous Korean side dish, has made a regular appearance in meals among Japanese households since the late 1990s.[14] The Korean ritual of *chesa* (ancestor worship) is the only major cultural tradition that is practiced among many Korean residents in Japan; nevertheless, *chesa* is not incongruous with a number of Japanese cultural rituals. Aside from their nationalities, most Korean residents have more in common with the Japanese than they do with South or North Koreans in the peninsula. To be sure, contemporary Korean social movements in Japan are not aimed at gaining the "right to difference," because Korean residents are not terribly different from the Japanese majority.

Given their physical indistinguishability from the dominant Japanese population and their high rates of assimilation, native-born generations of Korean residents routinely "pass" as Japanese in their everyday lives. On the one hand, passing as Japanese is the most expedient, and thus common, method that individual Korean residents use to avoid discrimination. Unlike minority groups elsewhere that face racial profiling, harassment, and discrimination based on their physical appearance alone, native-born Korean residents are often able to choose when and to whom they reveal their Korean identities. On the other hand, passing goes beyond the act of nondisclosure – of simply not revealing one's Korean identity – because it involves the conscious act of concealing one's ancestry and legal status, complete with the

---

[14] According to a number of scholars and Korean activists that I interviewed, more than a handful of Japanese citizens have been surprised to learn that *kimchee* originates from Korea, not Japan.

use of a Japanese alias. Not only are Koreans at risk of being "outed" like others who hide their identities, but also their daily practice of passing contributes to the foundation of their social and legal discrimination: Korean identity is hidden because it is a source of shame and the basis for their legal status as foreigners. Although phenotype does not play a role in distinguishing Korean and other Asian foreign residents from the Japanese majority, their exclusion from full membership in the polity is nevertheless based on biological heredity. That is, the majority of Korean residents in Japan hold Korean nationality because Japanese (and, for that matter, South Korean) citizenship policies are based on the principle of *jus sanguinis*, which states that citizens are tied together by blood.

The case of Turks in Germany is a particularly illustrative comparison to that of Koreans in Japan. In comparative studies of citizenship in Western Europe, Germany is frequently cited as the case study *par excellence* of the "ethnic" citizenship model, in which common descent, language, and culture is the basis for membership in a community of citizens (Baldwin-Edwards and Schain 1994: 11). As in Japan, German nationality is closely related with ethnic, racial, and national identity. For almost an entire century, German citizenship policies were based on a pure system of *jus sanguinis* that not only limited citizenship attribution to those of German descent but also made the naturalization procedure an exceptional measure rather than "a regular procedure terminating a process of immigration" (Hailbronner 2001: 102).

Although Germany and Japan have enacted policies to simultaneously incorporate foreign residents who are permanently settled within their borders and restrict new immigration, citizenship policy reforms in Germany have been more liberal and implemented at a much swifter pace than those in Japan, despite the fact that Korean settlement in Japan began well before the arrival of "guest workers" to Germany in the 1960s. This difference may be attributable to the timing and intensity of public debate about immigrants and citizenship in both countries. In Japan, public debate regarding immigrant incorporation and multiculturalism did not develop until the large-scale influx of new immigrants from the 1980s, most of whom originated from other Asian countries or are of Japanese descent. The high rates of cultural assimilation within the long-term Korean-resident community – coupled with the phenotypical similarity between Koreans and the dominant Japanese population – resulted in public ignorance and apathy about the Korean minority in Japan until the 1980s.

In contrast, the mere presence of the non-European foreign population, most of whom are phenotypically different from the majority German population, has generated public debate over immigrant integration, German citizenship, and German multiculturalism. Moreover, antiforeign violence reached its peak between 1992 and 1993 when there were reportedly an average of fifty to one hundred antiforeigner incidents daily (Berger 1998: 333; Martin 1994: 189). Consequently, incorporating the noncitizen in Germany is not simply a problem that is localized to the noncitizen community; on the contrary, the intense public debates and extremist violence have made immigrant incorporation impossible for policy makers to ignore.

Thus, visibility is not likely to be the basis for social movements within foreign communities in Germany – or for most of Western Europe for that matter – as it is for foreign residents in Japan. For example, because most Turks cannot "pass" as ethnic Germans, the large-scale naturalization of the Turkish community would not lead to their de facto eradication. Whereas the political assimilation of the Korean community can facilitate the state's attempt to "re-create" Japan as a homogenous society and, thus, maintain exclusionary policies toward foreigners, the incorporation of the long-term Turkish community in Germany poses a formidable challenge to ethnocultural definitions of German nationhood. In the German case, the question at hand is not about the existence of ethnic minorities but what the state should do about them. Specifically, the major political parties have engaged in heated debates over the terms and conditions of citizenship acquisition for foreign residents since the 1990s.

The findings of this chapter place Japan squarely among other advanced industrial democracies that face the challenges of immigration control, immigrant incorporation, and social diversity in a globalizing world. Overall, Japan's immigrant incorporation regime is largely similar to those of other industrial democracies, especially in Europe, based on citizenship policies, naturalization criteria, and alien rights. However, Japan's immigration history as a former colonial power coupled with its policies toward former colonial subjects has resulted in anomalous outcomes. That is, most former colonial subjects and their descendants living within Japan's borders remain politically unincorporated and continue to make up one of the largest groups of foreign residents despite the phenomenal growth of the immigrant community since the late 1980s, such that Japan has the distinction of being the only advanced industrial democracy with a fourth-generation immigrant problem.

Citizenship and immigrant policies alone did not determine these outcomes. On the contrary, as I argue in the remainder of this book, these anomalous outcomes reflect the strategic interaction between state officials who have sought to control immigration and hide the so-called minority problem and multigenerational Korean activists who have aimed to gain political visibility and power specifically as foreign-resident citizens of Japan. At the crux of this struggle is the question of visibility. For Korean activists, the community's social and political invisibility is the greatest obstacle to transforming Japanese society. Not only does it pressure individual Koreans to pass as Japanese, but also it has enabled policy makers and the general population to ignore the community and the issues that it faces for decades. One Korean activist went so far as to state that, "Some ethnic Koreans wish that they could look different from Japanese like Blacks do from Whites" (Bae Jung Do, lecture, Yokohama Asia Festival, 27 October 1998).

By denying the existence of native-born, permanent foreign residents within Japan's borders (despite official statistics to the contrary), public officials are able to perpetuate the myth of Japanese homogeneity in their attempts to restrict immigration as well as to dismiss the need to institute immigrant incorporation policies or grant further rights to permanent foreign residents. This ideological veil of cultural homogeneity in Japan has encouraged a complacent attitude toward racism in general and has perpetuated the marginalization and denial of Japan's minorities. Mainstream and progressive forces in Japan pressure foreign residents and ethnic minorities to pass as Japanese not only to shield them from discrimination but also to maintain social harmony. As a vocal Korean activist put it,

Some people say that Japan has changed considerably in this era of "internationalization." . . . But despite the changes on the outside – such as discussions of a "borderless society" – the inside hasn't changed very much. Although

Korean residents have been granted "special permanent residence" status, they are accepted as part of Japanese society only when they use their Japanese names. Perhaps the internationalization of Japanese society assumes the assimilation of Koreans [in order to present a picture of a discrimination-free Japanese society]. (Kim Kyu Il, panel discussion on the "Borderless Society," Yokohama Asia Festival, 3 November 1998)

2

Constructing Citizenship and Noncitizenship in Postwar Japan

According to Rogers Brubaker (1992), citizenship policies in the modern world have demonstrated remarkable continuity because they are based on the deeply rooted national traditions of each nation-state. His comparative historical study traces modern German citizenship policies, which were based predominantly on the principle of *jus sanguinis* until recently, to the ethnocultural understandings of nationhood that preceded the development of the German nation-state. Likewise, he argues that liberal citizenship policies in France have their origins in the assimilationist understandings of nationhood that date back to the rationalist, cosmopolitan tradition of the eighteenth century.

If we were to apply Brubaker's "national traditions" model to the Japanese case, we might surmise that deeply rooted understandings of racial purity in Japanese history inevitably gave rise to descent-based citizenship policies. To be sure, the idea of a "unique" Japanese identity has been a powerful mobilizational tool since the Meiji Restoration of 1868. As John Dower's (1986: 222) powerful study of racial images used during the Pacific War demonstrates, the emperor symbol and the idea of "one blood and one mind" under the emperor became the basis for an ideology that dramatized the "unique character of the nation" and the "racial homogeneity of the people" in order to bring about national unity. In a similar vein, Peter Duus (1995: 415) notes that, although a number of Meiji intellectuals acknowledged the heterogeneous character of the population in ancient times, they argued that these various ethnic groups were "blended" (*dōka*) and "fused" (*yūgō*) into the superior Yamato race.

Nevertheless, Japan's modern citizenship policies that were formulated during the Meiji era did not necessarily link citizenship with ethnocultural identity. Carol Gluck's (1985) study of Meiji Japan describes the ways that the imperial system determined the boundaries of a unique Japanese political order, or *kokutai* (national polity), rooted in immutable principles. Gluck notes that the term *kokumin* (national, or citizen) came into widespread use from the late Meiji period, shortly before the promulgation of Japan's modern constitution in 1889. Meiji oligarchs characterized *kokumin* as a privileged category to which the Japanese people should aspire. Whereas the "people" were defined as (imperial) subjects (*shinmin*), Meiji oligarchs declared that all those born and raised in Japan were not automatically *kokumin*. Rather, *kokumin* were those that had a "sound sense of nation (*kokkateki kannen*)" (Gluck 1985: 23–5). Political assimilation – rather than ethnocultural identity – was a prerequisite for acquiring the status of *kokumin*.

The debate preceding the passage of the 1899 Meiji citizenship law had little to do with any deep-rooted ethnocultural understandings of nationhood. Despite the existence of a community of Chinese and Korean settlers in Japan, Meiji oligarchs were more concerned about the imperialistic aims of a small number of Westerners living in Japan at the time. In addition, many of the foreign advisors to the Meiji government came from continental European countries where citizenship policies were based on the principle of *jus sanguinis*. Following a careful study of nationality laws in about thirty different countries, Meiji jurists concluded that *jus sanguinis* was the dominant principle of the time (Kashiwazaki 2000). Consequently, Japan's institutionalization of *jus sanguinis* into the country's first nationality law was motivated by the pragmatic aims of implementing a modern legal code and preventing foreigners from politically and economically powerful Western countries from assuming positions of power (Takenaka 1997: 193).

Although postwar Japanese citizenship policies perpetuated *jus sanguinis* from the 1899 Meiji law, they nevertheless marked a distinct shift from prewar policies. Whereas the imperial state granted colonial subjects Japanese nationality on the basis that they constituted part of

Japan's multiethnic empire, postwar officials stripped former colonial subjects of their Japanese nationalities on the premise that they were not part of the Japanese nation (Onuma 1986). Japan's postwar reconstruction effectively reinvented Japan – from an authoritarian imperial state to a developing democracy, from the "champion of the colored races" to the "Yankees of the East," and from a multiethnic empire to a homogenous nation. These ideas were neither new to the postwar era nor deeply embedded in Japanese national traditions. Rather, they can be characterized as the institutionalization of select prewar ideas and ideologies that variously complemented, competed with, and contradicted one another at different points leading to the postwar era. Moreover, the particular context of postwar Japan's state formation – including the configurations of state power during the American Occupation of Japan, the historical context of the Cold War, racial politics in U.S.-Japan relations, and the organization of Japanese and Korean interest groups – created political opportunities to implement citizenship policies that simultaneously enfranchised all Japanese nationals, including women, and disenfranchised former colonial subjects.[1]

This chapter examines how postwar citizenship policies formulated in the context of decolonization and democratic reconstruction created the opportunity for Japanese officials to effectively remove former colonial subjects from the body politic. Although the transition from an imperial, multiethnic system to a democratic, homogenous one marked a profound shift in ideology, Japanese authorities and American Occupation officials set off to implement the necessary changes virtually overnight. Former colonial powers in Europe faced similar tasks of decolonization and democratic reconstruction. However, unlike Japan, they did not have a substantial population of former colonial subjects living within their national boundaries. Whereas large numbers of imperial subjects from neighboring territories migrated to the Japanese metropole up until the end of World War II, former colonial powers in Europe did not experience large-scale immigration from the colonies until after the war. In addition, whereas European colonial powers opened their doors to former colonial subjects and affirmed their rights to citizenship during the process of decolonization, Japan

---

[1] Here, I am borrowing elements of Theda Skocpol's (1992) "polity centered" approach.

closed its borders and unilaterally stripped former colonial subjects of their Japanese citizenship.

For U.S. and Japanese authorities, former colonial subjects had no place in Japan's postwar democratic project. On the contrary, they were viewed as obstacles that needed to be expelled. As a democratic nation-state, however, Japan could not forcibly repatriate this unwelcome population and, instead, created policies based on the assumption of mass repatriation. Thus, Japanese and American officials formulated immigration policies that closed Japan's borders in order to keep former colonial subjects from returning to Japan and devised citizenship policies that would ensure the complete assimilation of those who stayed. The division of the Korean peninsula after the war and the outbreak of the Korean War in 1950 halted the repatriation process and left more than six hundred thousand Koreans in Japan. Additionally, those who remained had no intention of naturalizing after thirty-five years of colonial domination. Thus, postwar Japan was left with a body of politically unincorporated foreigners permanently residing in Japan who would shape the dynamics of immigration and citizenship politics in the years to come.

CITIZENSHIP AND SUBJECTHOOD IN A MULTIETHNIC EMPIRE

A few years before the outbreak of the Russo-Japanese War in 1904, an article appeared in the Sunday *New York Times Magazine* entitled, "Who Are the Japanese? Their Ethnic Mixture and Future as a World Power." The author, Charles De Kay, a writer and poet, attempted to explain Japan's rapid development as the leader "among nations of the Orient" by analyzing the Japanese "ethnic mixture," which was said to consist of "a strain of that race we consider the highest, the Aryan, and also strains of two conquering races of Asia, the Mongols and the Manchus" (DeKay 1901). He concluded that although the Chinese, who have clung to their "old view and antique methods," have been brought to their knees by European powers, the Japanese, through their "suppleness and imitation," have modernized themselves and have every right to make their claim on other Asian territories.

Less than ten years before, observers in England and the United States had applauded Japan's victory over China in the Sino-Japanese War (1894–5) as a struggle "against the evil ways of the Government of Corea" as well as "against the encroachments of China" (*New York Times*, 18 April 1895, 7). Editors of the *Nation* explained that China and Japan went to war because "China has never forgiven Japan for discarding Oriental in favor of Western civilization" (January–June 1895, 377). A *New York Times* editorial stated in 1895 that, "The sympathies of the American people have been with the Japanese throughout the war. They are with the Japanese now" (27 April 1895, 4). However, Russia's defeat by Japan in 1905 ushered in the period of the "yellow peril," which "bid the world shudder at what may be the reflux of the great Mongol invasions" (*Nation*, 15 September 1904, 212–13). As an article in the *Nation* explained, "when we slapped them on the back two years ago and told them they were the greatest people on earth, they believed us" (16 January 1908, 51–2). But few actually believed that the Japanese "race" was capable of beating the white powers at their own game:

Here matters hung until those upstart Japanese had the presumption to take a hand in a game which only white nations could play.... [B]ut the idea that they could be a serious factor when Powers of the first class should begin to partition Asia, was preposterous. It was to be America for Americans, Asia for the Anglo-Saxon Alliance, and Nirvana for the Japanese. But what a situation now confronts us! Here is a yellow nation that is actually "doing things" to one of the great world-powers which, by a fixed law of "sociology," was to have an important part in the cosmic process of wiping inferior races off the map.... The people of Asia can never be allowed to possess their own soil, worship such gods as they choose, and attend to their own concerns.... Asia must be opened, at all costs, to the white man's armies, missionaries, and capitalists. Why not, then admit the Japanese to the Anglo-Saxon alliance? (*Nation*, 29 September 1904, 254–5)

Whether the Japanese were described as a "civilized island race" (*Nation*, 5 January 1905, 14–15) or as possessing "Superhuman malice, superhuman ability, and superhuman guile" (*Nation*, 16 January 1908, 51–2), it was clear that Japan was no longer an insignificant Asian country. As Bruce Cumings (1993: 98) notes, Japan's defeat of Russia heralded its "first clear moment of 'emergence' in the modern world-system."

By 1922, Japan had assembled a formal empire consisting of territory in Formosa, Korea, the southern half of Sakhalin Island (Karafuto), Kantōshū (leased territory on the Kwantung peninsula and railway rights in Manchuria), and the Nan'yō (the mandated Micronesia islands) (Chen 1984: 241). As in Europe, race played a prominent role in Japanese imperial discourse. Japan preached and practiced the "scientific" racist discourse of the times, which asserted that, "There are superior and inferior races in the world and it is the sacred duty of the leading race to lead and enlighten the inferior ones" (Nakajima Chikuhei, 1940, quoted in Dower 1986: 217).

At the same time, as an object of Western imperialism in the non-European world, Japanese leaders were acutely sensitive to racial issues in the United States and in the international environment. By the late 1920s, approximately 618,000 Japanese were living abroad on a more or less permanent basis, including approximately 125,000 Japanese in Hawaii and 8,000 in the U.S. mainland (Iriye 1974: 252). Japanese immigration to the West Coast was met with hostility and alarm. In 1905, the California legislature unanimously passed a resolution calling on the federal government to limit immigration from Japan, characterizing Japanese immigrants as "immoral, intemperate, quarrelsome men bound to labor for a pittance" (quoted in Pyle 1978: 135). In the following year, the San Francisco School Board established an "Oriental Public School" in Chinatown for Japanese, Korean, and Chinese children. This act of segregation sparked international controversy and vocal protests from the Japanese government. U.S. policy makers were confronted with the fact that they could not restrict Japanese immigration in the same way that they had done so with Chinese immigration in 1882 (Hing 1993: 29).

Consequently, the United States and Japan signed the so-called Gentleman's Agreement in 1907 and 1908 whereby the Japanese government would refrain from issuing visas to laborers bound for the mainland United States and the San Francisco School Board would rescind its segregation order. Nevertheless, the reactionary, isolationist political climate that followed World War I, culminating in the Red Scare of 1919 to 1920, led to greater exclusionist demands. Finally, in 1924, the U.S. Congress passed the Japanese Exclusion Act as part of the Immigration Act of 1924.

Ironically, the legal status of Koreans in Japan became the bedrock for vocal protests from the Japanese government regarding the comparably unjust treatment of Japanese immigrants in the United States. For example, Kiyo Sue Inui's (1925) *The Unsolved Problem of the*

Pacific analyzed the discriminatory character of the 1924 National Origins Quota Act, which excluded Japanese immigrants, according to its inconsistencies in relation to American democratic theory and international law. Moreover, Inui specifically compared the immigration and naturalization laws of the United States with those of Japan in order to suggest the anachronism of the former and the modernity of the latter. Having recently made an unsuccessful attempt to insert a racial equality clause in the Preamble to the Covenant of the League of Nations at the Paris Peace Conference in 1919, Japan was said to have entered a new era as the "champion of the 'principle of the equality of nations and just treatment of their nationals'" (250). Inui argued that "no law of Japan discriminates against persons within the jurisdiction of the Japanese Empire on account of racial affiliation or nativity" and that Japanese immigration and naturalization laws were free from any reference to "race, creed or nationality" (253–8).

As the world situation became more hostile – with the world depression, closed markets, and exclusionary measures adopted by the West against Japan – Japan's economic vulnerability became an issue of national security. In particular, Germany's collapse in 1918 had profound implications for Japan. Japan's leaders concluded that future wars would be protracted, "fought not only with guns but with the entire resources of nations, from engineers to doctors, from cotton to iron ore" (Barnhart 1987: 18). In its preparation for a "total war," Japan embarked upon a quest for economic security that eventually culminated in its formidable Asian empire and the creation of the Greater East Asian Co-Prosperity Sphere. The Korean colony served as a much-needed industrial base that provided cheap labor and an abundant supply of cheap hydroelectric power in the north (Woo 1991: 38–9). For Koreans in the Japanese empire, mass mobilization for industrialization developed into forced assimilation (*kōminka*, or imperialization) in the 1930s that involved the eradication of Korean language and cultural expression, compulsory emperor and Shinto worship, and the forced adoption of Japanese names (*sōshi kaimei*). At the same time, this assimilation policy was premised on the existence of immutable biological differences to ensure that the Japanese empire's assimilated subjects, albeit *kokumin*, would assume their "proper place" (Weiner 1994a: 31).

The romantic vision of Pan-Asianism combined the idea of a linked fate that Japan shared with other Asian countries and the notion that Japan had become the "champion of the colored races." Among African Americans, Japan came to be seen as a model for political and economic development as well as a potential military ally against American racism (Allen 1994: 28–9). In 1925, Marcus Garvey was contacted by the Indian revolutionary, Rash Behari Bose, then residing in Japan, who forwarded Garvey a copy of the Japanese book, *The Negro Problem*, in which Garvey's Universal Negro Improvement Association was prominently featured (Allen 1994: 29; Hill 1989: 297). The author, Mitsukawa Kametaro, was one of the founders of *Gyochisha* (Society to Carry Out Heaven's Way on Earth), which was modeled after the more prominent *Kokuryūkai* (Amur River Association or the so-called Black Dragon Society). Both of these organizations declared their mission to "check the expansion of the western powers" and emancipate the "colored races" from white domination (Beasley 1987: 78; Maruyama 1963: 27–38, 291, 326). By 1938, Japan's attempts to lead a coalition of non-Western, nonwhite peoples had gained widespread attention as embodied in the pamphlet published by the Communist Party of the United States (1938) entitled, "Is Japan the Champion of the Colored Races?"

Japan's Pan-Asiatic slogans of the 1920s and 1930s manipulated these sentiments with images of Japan as the "leader of Asia," "the protector of Asia," and the "light of Asia" (Dower 1986: 6). The discourse on Pan-Asianism also contrasted ideals of Asian prosperity and union with the divisive and self-serving designs of Western colonialism in Asia (Peattie 1984b: 103). Maruyama Masao (1963: 31) noted, "Because of Japan's historical position as the first Asian country to construct a modern State and to check 'the thrust of Europe towards the East', the ideology of Japan's continental development always contained this side-issue of the emancipation of East Asia."

Meanwhile, as the war between China and Japan expanded after 1937, the army began to draft skilled Japanese workers from factories and mines. To alleviate labor shortages, more than half a million Koreans were mobilized to Japan between 1941 and 1945 as labor or military conscripts – including an estimated one hundred to two hundred thousand "comfort women" – such that, by January 1945, Koreans made up 32 percent of the industrial labor force in Japan (Cumings 1981: 28–9; 1997: 177–9). Although Korean residents accounted for only a fraction of the total foreign community in Japan in 1910, by the end of World War II, the Korean community had a population of more than 2.3 million. No other colonial power had comparable populations of colonial subjects residing in the metropole at any time during their rule.

As anti-Japanese sentiment crystallized in the United States, international condemnation of Japan's brutal colonial rule in Korea grew louder. Following the abortive March 1 Korean Independence Movement in 1919 and Japan's violent response, the Japanese colonialists inaugurated its "enlightened" administration that, in word, reformed the local administration in Korea and allowed for greater Korean political participation, demilitarized police operations, and an expanded education system for Koreans.[2] The reforms also relaxed controls on the press and permitted the publication of Korean-owned newspapers. But in its actual implementation, the military police merely became part of the civilian police and the network of town and village police stations virtually monopolized local communications until after the Korean War (Henderson 1968: 79). Nevertheless, increased international scrutiny of Japan's colonial administration pressured Japanese leaders to substantiate their claims of "enlightenment" and "equality" in Japan's laws. In 1922, legal restrictions on the entry of Koreans into Japan were abolished, and, in 1925, a universal manhood suffrage act that allowed Korean males in Japan to vote in Japanese elections was passed. In 1932 and 1937, 187 Koreans ran for political office and 53 were elected, including a Korean elected to the Diet in 1932 (Okamoto 1994). By the end of World War II, there were 410 Koreans holding civil service posts in the Japanese government (Chee 1983: 83).

In Imperial Japan, the hierarchy of power was characterized by a family state, or *kokutai*, with heterogeneous subjects who were

---

[2] The March 1 Movement in Seoul sparked nationwide protests in more than 600 different places and involved at least half a million Koreans. Caught by surprise, Japanese authorities reacted with mass arrests, beatings, and, in a few cases, massacres. Japanese authorities estimated more than 12,000 arrests, 1,409 injuries, and 553 deaths compared to some 45,000 arrests, 15,000 injuries, and more than 7,500 deaths according to Korean nationalist sources (Cumings 1997: 155; Eckert et al. 1990: 278–9).

united under the emperor. Consequently, state discourse focused on the common past and common destiny between colonizers and colonized. Prewar officials justified Japanese imperialism on the basis that their fellow Asians welcomed Japanese leadership and that all of Asia constituted one big family. As Mark Peattie (1984a: 40) describes, the colonial doctrine of assimilation (*dōka*) was based on a cluster of assumptions concerning the relationship among Japan, the colonies, and the emperor: "the supposedly indissoluble bond between Japan and the other countries of the Chinese culture area, the Confucian faith in the benevolence of the emperor toward all his subjects, and the mystical linkage which Japanese had for the centuries drawn between the emperor and his people." Although colonial subjects were granted citizenship status and, thus, referred to as "children of the emperor" (*tennō no sekishi*), they were never granted *equal* status in Japan's hierarchical imperial system. On the contrary, like peasants, the urban poor, the *burakumin*, the Okinawans, and the Ainu, colonial subjects were part of the imperial family's outer circle who – according to numerous officials, intellectuals, and popular writers – were a "race" apart from the rest of the population (Weiner 1994b: 259–60). Colonial peoples were principally subjects – and second-class citizens at best – and, thus, ultimately controllable, exploitable, and disposable. Consequently, the problems posed by Koreans and other "inferior" subjects could be controlled with an array of repressive measures and political concessions.

CREATING CITIZENS AND NONCITIZENS IN POSTWAR JAPAN

Although Japanese imperialism was in many ways modeled after its counterparts in Europe, population movements between the colonies and the metropole differed significantly in terms of density and timing. Unlike European imperial powers, Japan colonized neighboring territories, which allowed for large numbers of colonial migrants to enter the metropole in the early stages of colonization in response to social dislocation in the colonies and facilitated the forced recruitment of colonial subjects in the later stages as laborers and soldiers. Although France and Britain enlisted colonial subjects during World War I, their numbers were much lower – somewhere between five hundred thousand to eight hundred thousand in France and between ten thousand to thirty thousand in Britain – and most were forcibly repatriated during the interwar years (Hargreaves 2007; MacMaster 2001). In contrast, more than two million colonial subjects were residing in Japan proper at the end of World War II.

The process of decolonization in Japan also contrasted starkly with that among former imperial powers in Europe. Whereas Britain and France engaged in a gradual process that opened the doors to hundreds of thousands of immigrants from their former colonies, Japan's decolonization endeavors were hasty and incomplete.[3] Although restrictive immigration policies implemented at the end of the Occupation and tight border controls prevented the mass influx of former colonial subjects to Japan proper, Japan faced a unique challenge among former imperial powers: how to manage, and ultimately repatriate, two million former colonial subjects who were residing in Japan.

The decolonization process reflected the fast pace at which reforms were implemented during the American Occupation (1945–52). With Japan's surrender to the Allied Powers in 1945, the authoritarian imperial state became a developing democracy under the leadership of the Supreme Commander of the Allied Powers (SCAP). Although the emperor system remained intact, the idea of an imperial hierarchy or "family state" was no longer sustainable in a developing democracy that renounced imperialistic aggression. However, in keeping the emperor system, the Japanese state – with the cooperation of Occupation authorities – maintained a symbol of unity among its citizens. Instead of claiming that Japanese subjects, regardless of race or ethnicity, were united by the emperor, the postwar state could claim that they were united by blood under the emperor. Hence, the imperial family became more literal, based on consanguinity rather than on a common past and common destiny. Whereas prewar Japanese state ideology explicitly included Koreans as part of the imperial "family" nation, the postwar discourse on Japanese national identity explicitly excluded them based on consanguinity.

---

[3] E.g., in the early postwar period, Britain admitted all former British subjects and granted them virtually all of the rights and privileges of full citizenship upon entry. The Immigration Acts of 1962, 1968, and 1971 eventually imposed controls on the entry of Commonwealth citizens, and the Nationality Act of 1981 drew the boundaries of national citizenship that included the creation of a special secondary-citizenship status without the right of immigration (Brubaker 1989: 11, 107).

Japanese authorities further adopted the term *kokumin* to represent "the people" in their translation of the new constitution in 1946. Japanese representatives at the constitutional drafting sessions argued that *kokumin* implied a harmonious relationship between the people and the nation-state, compared to the term commonly used to refer to "the people" in translations of the U.S. Constitution, *jinmin*, which had socialist and communist connotations at the time. However, *kokumin* also had conservative undertones as it had been used in wartime propaganda to connote "the Japanese" and even "the Yamato race." According to John Dower's (1999: 381–2, 393–4) compelling study of postwar Japan, Japanese authorities deliberately chose the term *kokumin* to weaken the significance of popular sovereignty and exclude former colonial subjects from rights guaranteed by the state through "linguistic subterfuge." Consequently, citizenship status, rather than race or ethnicity, became the primary means by which the Japanese state differentiated former colonial subjects from the remainder of its population.

Under General Douglas MacArthur's leadership, the Occupation administration implemented sweeping reforms with a high sense of idealism and faith in the universality of American values and institutions. Occupation officials believed that the United States was, despite its faults, the most advanced of all societies and, therefore, the model for a new democratic Japan (Chapman 1991). Many civilian reformers sent out from the United States to Japan were "New Dealers," and Japan's new labor laws mirrored reforms adopted in the United States in the 1930s (Cohen 1987). Moreover, Occupation officials assumed that they could unleash the democratic tendencies in Japan by giving the Japanese people control over their own destinies. SCAP operated on the philosophy that if the causes of militarism and nationalism were removed, then democracy would sprout spontaneously. Whereas the occupying powers in Germany abolished the existing government and governed the country directly, SCAP acted as a supervisory organ over the existing Japanese government. Accordingly, Japan became a laboratory for the transference of American ideals and institutions to an Asian setting. Thus, historians often refer to the period especially from 1945 to 1947 as "Japan's American Revolution" (Pyle 1978: 151–66).

Koreans in Japan did not figure prominently in the Occupation's plans for Japan's postwar "democratic revolution." Although

Occupation authorities implemented a constitutional provision prohibiting "discrimination in political, economic, or social relations because of race, creed, sex, social status or family origin" (Article 14) in Japanese society, neither Occupation nor Japanese authorities applied such democratic idealism to the Korean population. On the contrary, Occupation policies regarding Koreans in Japan reflected the view that Koreans belonged outside of Japanese society and were obstacles to Japan's democratic revolution. They were also seen as a destabilizing force because of their involvement in black-market activities.

Hence, SCAP's primary aim for the Korean population was repatriation. Shortly after the end of the war, almost two-thirds of the more than two million Koreans residing in Japan returned to the Korean peninsula. American Occupation forces slowed the pace of repatriation by placing severe limitations on the amounts of money and property that could be taken back, but they nevertheless actively encouraged repatriation and provided free transportation to repatriates. Korean repatriates, particularly demobilized soldiers and former forced laborers, were often given priority over repatriates to the former colonies in Formosa, the Ryukyu Islands, and China in order to prevent congestion in evacuation areas (Cheong 1992: 44). Although SCAP terminated the official repatriation program in December 1946, this program continued unofficially until the end of 1949 using Japanese shipping facilities that were controlled by Occupation authorities. However, by the end of 1946, the rate of Korean repatriation slowed considerably while that of illegal immigration to Japan from Korea, mostly by former repatriates, increased rapidly. In July and August of 1946 alone, Japanese authorities arrested more than thirteen thousand Korean repatriates attempting to return to Japan illegally (Lee and DeVos 1981: 60; Wagner 1951: 49). From 1947, the Japanese government used the same shipping facilities to return voluntary repatriates and illegal immigrants to Korea (Wagner 1951: 47). Fukuoka Yasunori (2000: 9–10) estimates that most of those who were forcibly recruited to Japan in the prewar period returned to Korea early in the repatriation movement. Accordingly, the majority of the remaining Koreans were likely to have migrated to Japan before the war as a result of the social and economic dislocation caused by Japanese colonial expansion. Social, political, and economic conditions remained unstable following Korea's liberation from Japan, which was the basis for many Koreans to return – illegally – to Japan and provided the approximately six hundred thousand Koreans who remained in Japan with little incentive to repatriate immediately. In contrast, only about thirty thousand of the one hundred to two hundred thousand former colonial subjects from China and Formosa remained in Japan in mid-1946 (Takenaka 1997: 295). As David Conde (1947: 44), a former SCAP official, explained, "Many families had returned to Korea highly enthusiastic at the prospect of rebuilding their homeland, only to find that Japanese or Japanese collaborators remained in key positions and that they had less freedom south of the thirty-eighth parallel than they had in postwar Japan."

Despite their dubious positions as liberated nationals and potential enemies, Koreans in Japan were above all a source of irritation for the Occupation authorities as Edward Wagner observed in 1951:

In the eyes of the Occupation authorities the Koreans have constituted an unwelcome additional administrative burden. The contrast between Korean defiance and apparent placid Japanese acceptance of American rule has been strikingly evident. Not only has this helped to heighten the esteem in which the Japanese have come to be held, but it also has fostered violent dislike as the typical attitude of Occupation personnel toward Koreans. (Wagner 1951: 2)

Japanese authorities were quick to point to the Korean community's involvement in "illegal activities" such as the black market and their subversive potential as hostile former colonial subjects and allies of the Japan Communist Party (JCP). Public anger over Korean and Formosan involvement in black-market activities became especially pronounced following the so-called Shibuya incident in July 1946. Tensions between Japanese and Korean and Formosan gangs over the division of black-market territories culminated in a violent confrontation between Formosan vendors and Japanese gangsters that left seven Formosans dead and thirty-four injured as well as one Japanese policeman dead and another critically injured. This incident reinforced the belief that former colonial subjects were responsible for black-market abuses and the rising crime rate (Dower 1999: 143–4).

As the following statement by Shikuma Saburo, a Progressive Party member from Hokkaido, demonstrates, liberation of former colonial subjects implied chaos for many Japanese:

We refuse to stand by in silence watching Formosans and Koreans who have resided in Japan as Japanese up to the time of surrender, swaggering about as if they were nationals of victorious nations. We admit that we are a defeated nation but it is most deplorable that those who lived under our law and order until the last moment of the surrender should suddenly alter their attitude to act like conquerors, posting on railway carriages "Reserved" without any authorization, insulting and oppressing Japanese passengers and otherwise committing unspeakable violence elsewhere. The actions of these Koreans and Formosans make the blood in our veins, in our misery of defeat, boil. (quoted in Conde 1947: 42)

Shirasu Jirō, a close personal advisor to Premier Yoshida Shigeru, proposed mass deportation as the optimum solution to the "Korean problem": "In his opinion the Koreans in Japan were almost to a man engaged in illegal or non-gainful pursuits and that it was grossly unfair that the Japanese Government... assume obligations on behalf of this parasitic group" (Butterworth to Acheson, 3 May 1950, quoted in Cumings 1990: 856n68).

Assuming that all Koreans in Japan would eventually repatriate, SCAP made no clarification regarding their legal status. Wagner (1951: 56) notes that no single agency in SCAP was charged with primary responsibility for Korean-resident affairs and, as a result, disparate agencies prepared ad hoc directives in response to daily matters concerning the Korean population. Without a uniform policy toward Koreans in Japan, SCAP's often-contradictory responses to the "Korean problem" set the tone for the strained, ambiguous relationship between Korean community organizations and the Japanese state throughout the Occupation to the present day. On the one hand, Koreans were given special guarantees and privileges as "liberated nationals." Several early directives from SCAP to the Japanese government prohibited discrimination against Koreans and other minorities in employment, social welfare distribution, and public assistance.[4] Other

---

[4] There is little evidence to suggest that Japanese authorities heeded these directives. Given the fact that Jim Crow laws in the U.S. Army did not officially come to an end until 1951, the Occupation did not provide much of a blueprint for racial toleration.

directives placed Koreans beyond Japanese criminal jurisdiction. On the other hand, SCAP did not include Koreans among Allied nationals because of their service – compulsory or not – in the Japanese military during the war against the Allies. Further, because Koreans in Japan remained Japanese nationals in law until 1952, they were not eligible for the special supplementary rations that Occupation authorities gave to most foreign nationals in Japan. A Joint Chiefs of Staff directive to SCAP in November 1945 added to the confusion by stating that Koreans and Formosans could be treated as "liberated peoples" and as enemy aliens: "You will treat Formosan-Chinese and Koreans as liberated peoples in so far as military security permits. They are not included in the term 'Japanese' as used in this directive but they have been Japanese subjects and may be treated by you, in case of necessity, as enemy nationals" (JCS1380/15 1945). The Occupation's policy toward Koreans and other former colonial subjects as belonging neither to the Allied Powers nor to the enemy country provided the basis for the derogatory Japanese term *daisangokujin* (third country people).

When it became clear that many remaining Koreans would not repatriate, SCAP conferred authority over their treatment to Japanese officials on the basis that Koreans technically remained Japanese nationals. In May 1946, SCAP reformulated the previous directive issued by the Joint Chiefs of Staff so that the status of "liberated nationals" would apply to Koreans only in the case of repatriation. In November 1946, an official news release announced, "Koreans who refuse to return to their homeland under the SCAP repatriation program will be considered as retaining their Japanese nationality until such time as a duly established Korean Government accords them recognition as Korean nationals..." (Conde 1947: 45). Hence, SCAP's answer to the "Korean problem" was to repatriate as many Koreans as possible and assimilate those who chose to stay in Japan. While relaxing regulations on repatriation such as restrictions on currency and personal effects that repatriates could take back to Korea, SCAP placed strict controls on Korean activity and movement within Japan.

The Japanese government exploited the Korean community's ambiguous position by heightening police intimidation and surveillance to control the population while denying them full citizenship rights. Defying SCAP's orders, local Japanese officials refused to release some Koreans convicted of political offenses unless they repatriated.

In December 1945, the Diet passed an amendment to the Election Law that denied voting rights to those whose family registers (*koseki*) were not located in Japan. As was the case during the colonial period when the family registry system was first institutionalized, this legal loophole provided the government with a tool to demarcate colonial subjects among Japanese nationals. In September 1946, Osaka officials instituted a local registration system specifically for Koreans that resembled the prewar police surveillance system (Wagner 1951: 60). In 1947, the Diet passed the Alien Registration Law that identified Koreans as belonging to *Chōsen* based on their family registers and required Koreans to carry alien registration cards at all times.[5] However, because the Republic of Korea (ROK) and the Democratic People's Republic of Korea (DPRK) were not established until 1948, Koreans in Japan during this time were held to be stateless. Consequently, *Chōsen* referred not to a nationality but to an ethnic group.

Declaring Japan a homogeneous nation, the Diet passed the 1950 Nationality Act perpetuating without controversy the principle of *jus sanguinis* from the Meiji law of 1899 (Takenaka 1997: 291). Moreover, the Immigration Control Order of 1951 – designed to supplement the 1947 Alien Registration Law to monitor aliens within Japan as well as movement in and out of Japan – was based on the American model that set specific immigration quotas based on country of origin. Thus, postwar Japanese policies regarding foreigners were based on a German-style citizenship model and an American-style immigration model, which, in combination, protected Japan's external and internal borders. In terms of internal security, this combination was a powerful tool: Koreans remaining in Japan were subject to Japanese laws as residents but were excluded from the privileges of Japanese citizenship as foreigners. The arduous naturalization process virtually guaranteed the cultural, social, and political assimilation of Koreans who elected to become Japanese nationals and the constant threat of deportation ensured the docility of those who remained in Japan as foreigners. In effect, postwar immigration and citizenship policies provided the second-best solution to the "Korean problem" during the Occupation. Although SCAP could not forcibly repatriate all Koreans in Japan because of its early commitment to voluntary repatriation,

5 Korea was called *Chōsen* by the Japanese until Korea's liberation from Japan.

the Japanese government could deport any "troublemakers" among those who remained in Japan. Finally, when Japan concluded the San Francisco Peace Treaty with the Allied Powers in 1952, Japan's former colonial subjects were formally declared aliens.

From the onset of the Occupation, Korean community members regarded themselves as part of the victorious Allied armies. Many Koreans demanded the rights and privileges of Allied nationals. Some believed that they were no longer subject to Japanese law and openly engaged in the flourishing black market of the postwar economy. However, the greatest threat posed by the community was in the realm of politics.

The first postwar Korean organization of national significance, Choryŏn (Chōren in Japanese, or League of Koreans in Japan), was established in October 1945 with the primary purposes of repatriating Koreans and protecting their rights. In addition, Choryŏn offered educational programs such as Korean-language classes to prepare Korean children for their future lives in Korea. At the same time, a number of Choryŏn's leaders played central roles in the reorganization of the JCP following SCAP's release of approximately 2,500 political prisoners. For example, Kim Chŏn-ae (Kim Ten-kai in Japanese), who had been imprisoned for seventeen years for his alleged involvement in communist activities, was a member of the JCP Reconstruction Committee and was named "supreme advisor" of Choryŏn (Pak 1989: 52).[6]

Consequently, as repatriation slowed and the organization began to focus its attention on the issue of Korean liberation in Japan, Choryŏn members frequently joined forces with the JCP. They maintained that the welfare of Koreans in Japan could not be secured within the present Japanese political establishment that perpetuated the emperor system, which was a claim that paralleled the JCP's call for the overthrow of the emperor system and the creation of a "people's republic" (Pak 1989: 50–5). As Sonia Ryang (1997: 80–1) notes, Choryŏn's Japanese edition of its official publication, *Haebang Sinmun*, closely resembled the JCP's official publication, *Akahata*, which highlighted the two organizations' overlapping interests and close ties. Changsoo Lee

---

[6] Choryŏn's leftist orientation was consistent with prewar Korean political movements in Japan opposed to Japanese rule that supported Korean revolutionaries in China or worked with Japanese communists.

(Lee and DeVos 1981: 65–7) observes that direct appeals made by the JCP to the Korean community resonated powerfully among the majority of Koreans in Japan at a time when anti-Korean sentiment was widespread in Japanese society and government. Choryŏn and Korean members of the JCP exhorted Koreans to take the matter of Japan's democratic revolution into their own hands. This "call to action" involved not only working from the margins of society but also demanding political enfranchisement.

Hence, the leaders of Choryŏn did not believe that their status as foreigners would preclude their participation in Japanese politics. After all, foreign nationals – specifically Occupation officials – were leading the project of rebuilding Japan. Most of Choryŏn's protests were in response to their treatment as Japanese nationals rather than as foreigners. Choryŏn's fiercest protests – including the violent Kobe incident in 1948 that led SCAP to declare a state of emergency – concerned their rights as foreigners to operate Korean schools in Japan autonomously.

After the establishment of the two separate Korean regimes (ROK, or *Kankoku* in Japanese, and DPRK, or *Kita Chōsen*), Choryŏn declared its solidarity with the DPRK and referred to the Rhee government established in the ROK as an American puppet regime. Choryŏn's position was most likely consistent with that of the majority of the Korean community. From the onset, the Japanese government encouraged Koreans in Japan to change their existing *Chōsen* nationalities to *Kankoku* because *Chōsen* now referred only to North Korea. Nevertheless, as many as two-thirds of the Korean population maintained their *Chōsen* nationalities, which, by default, made them North Korean nationals despite the fact that most first-generation Koreans in Japan had come from southern Korea.[7] Although some kept their *Chōsen* nationalities because they did not support either the North or South Korean governments, for others, allegiance to North Korea was the nationalistic choice.

With the approach of the Cold War and the growing power of the Chinese Communists in the region, SCAP no longer deemed Koreans in Japan merely a source of irritation; on the contrary, the "Korean

---

[7] In 1952, e.g., 94% of Korean residents in Japan were reported to have originated from southern Korea (Kang and Kim 1989: 118).

problem" became a security issue that required immediate attention. The mass protests organized by Choryŏn, which often led to violent clashes with the police, as well as Choryŏn's ongoing alliance with the JCP threatened political stability and, thus, national security. In reaction to Choryŏn's support of North Korea, SCAP issued a ban in 1948 against the public display of the North Korean flag, which Choryŏn defiantly disregarded. At last, Choryŏn's joint declaration with the JCP to "overthrow the Japanese government" and violent clashes with the Japanese police provided fodder for the enactment of the Organization Control Law in April 1949, which outlawed organizations construed to be subversive to the Japanese state. With SCAP's consent, the Japanese government declared Choryŏn a terrorist organization and dissolved it in September 1949, part of the "red purge" that began earlier that year.

THE FAILURE OF IMMIGRANT INCORPORATION IN POSTWAR JAPAN

In 1951, Edward Wagner warned that American Occupation directives regarding citizenship policies would have significant consequences for the future of the "Korean problem" in Japan:

> ... the forthcoming peace treaty with Japan would do well to contain provisions designed to ease the entry of individual Koreans into Japanese citizenship status. If practical considerations of the moment permit, Koreans should be given a clear option of electing Japanese or Korean citizenship, and all possible guarantees should be established to militate against the continuation of discriminatory practices on the part of the Japanese, and also against exploitation by Koreans of dual nationality status. Although the Korean problem in Japan is relatively minor, it is one which merits the continuing attention of the United States. It is a problem for the solution of which the United States cannot avoid accepting major responsibility. The issue is one which the rest of Asia may well watch to determine how closely American professed aims and actual performance coincide. (Wagner 1951: 3)

Even before the peace treaty brought the U.S. Occupation of Japan to a formal end, the vexing problem of Korean citizenship status had been resolved to the satisfaction of SCAP, the Japanese government, the South Korean government, and the dominant Korean organizations in Japan. All sides agreed that Koreans in Japan were not Japanese nationals. For security reasons, neither Japan nor South Korea was willing to grant dual-citizenship status to the Korean population. Moreover, all sides assumed that most of the Korean population in Japan would eventually repatriate to South or North Korea. Until that time, citizenship and immigration laws created during the Occupation would ensure that those Koreans who posed a security threat would be deported and those who remained would submit to Japanese laws. However, none of the parties involved in the negotiations addressed the problem of persistent discrimination against Koreans in Japan or Korean integration into Japanese society.

SCAP implemented many radical reforms in Japanese society, including a new constitution (1946) and a number of revolutionary changes in the Japanese political and social order, to reflect democratic principles. Although the Japanese empire was destroyed and the emperor declared to be human and not divine, the imperial institution remained intact as a symbol of the state and national unity. Not only did postwar Japanese citizenship policies expand the system of rights for state members, they also blurred the distinction between legal and primordial membership. The transformation of Japanese citizenship policies during the Occupation institutionalized the conflation of nation and ethnie as well as of nation and nation-state.[8]

Japan faced a problem common to former imperial powers: postwar reconstruction included the imperative to define the legal status of former colonial subjects. However, unlike former imperial powers such as France, Great Britain, and the Netherlands, the Japanese government automatically forfeited Japanese nationality for Koreans. Rather than having the option to preserve their Japanese nationality, former colonial subjects were required to undergo the same naturalization process as other foreigners if they wanted to become Japanese nationals. As colonial subjects, Koreans were incorporated into a hierarchical imperial system through forced assimilation. Postwar citizenship policies became the principal institutional device employed to sever Koreans from the Japanese body politic and quarantine them from potentially

---

[8] Anthony Smith (1986: ch. 2) defines *ethnie* as a named human population with myths of common ancestry, shared historical memories, one or more elements of common culture, a link with a homeland, and a sense of solidarity among at least some of its members.

contaminating Japanese society and culture. Moreover, in the context of the Cold War, the existence of Koreans in Japan – two-thirds of whom initially registered by claiming North Korean nationality – became a security threat to an otherwise politically stable and economically dynamic postwar era.

In contrast, former colonial powers in Europe structured their citizenship and immigration policies generously toward former colonial subjects. Later revisions were responses to the large flows of immigration that resulted from such generous policies. Japan's immigration and citizenship policies were based on the erroneous assumption that most, if not all, former colonial subjects would repatriate to their home countries and that those who chose to stay would eagerly seek naturalization. Accordingly, naturalization was the only remnant of an immigrant incorporation regime in postwar Japan. Japanese officials simply did not anticipate that there would be any foreign community to incorporate. As the following chapter demonstrates, the failure to incorporate former colonial subjects led to the formation of a permanent foreign community in Japan that would make citizenship – specifically foreign citizenship – the center of its collective identity and political activities. Hence, Japan's postwar citizenship policies effectively removed former colonial subjects from the body politic and created political opportunities for foreign residents to contest the conditions of their exclusion and incorporation.

3

Negotiating Korean Identity in Japan

WHAT'S IN A NAME?

Discussion of Koreans in Japan – in English as well as in Japanese – often begins with the thorny issue of names. In English, this community is most often referred to as "Korean residents in Japan" (in reference to their legal status) or "ethnic Koreans in Japan" (which would include Japanese nationals of Korean ancestry), or the "Korean minority in Japan" (to signify their discursive position in Japanese society), or simply, "Koreans in Japan."[1] Although some use the term *Korean-Japanese* (or *Japanese-Korean*) to refer to this group, the concept of hyphenated identities has yet to be widely accepted in Japanese society. The official Japanese term for Korean residents is *Zainichi Kankoku Chōsenjin* (South and North Korean Residents in Japan); however, the actual term used by individuals and groups is inextricably linked to the identity politics of this community. The official term in itself

---

[1] Incidentally, reference to Koreans in Japan in Korean is least controversial. Koreans are simply referred to as "Overseas Koreans in Japan" (*Chaeil Kyopo*, literally brethren, or compatriots in Japan). Some members of the Korean community in Japan have adopted this term (although the term *dōhō*, rather than the direct translation, *kyōhō*, is more often used in the Japanese version). Although all overseas Korean populations are named in Korean in this way, the politics of this term is controversial among some Korean Americans who identify themselves primarily as Americans of Korean ancestry (literally *Hankuk kye mikukin*, but more often referred to as *Hanin dongpo*, or ethnic Korean brethren, and *Komerikan*, the Korean slang for Korean American) rather than as "overseas Koreans" who reside in the United States (*Chaemi Kyopo*).

divides the community according to nationality – with the implication that *Chōsen* refers only to North Korea – and privileges South Korean nationals by placing *Kankoku* before *Chōsen*. Although some prefer the term *Zainichi Korian* because of its neutrality and its apparent reference to Koreans as an ethnic group, others identify themselves according to their specific nationalities (e.g., *Zainichi Kankokujin* if they are South Korean nationals).[2] Still, some prefer *Chōsenjin*, which was the term used to refer to Koreans prior to the war, while others simply use the abbreviation *Zainichi* as a reference to their permanent residence in Japan.[3] There are those who would like to be rid of the term *Zainichi* altogether because they see themselves as part of an autonomous nation separate from the Japanese state and not as a Japanese minority group. As one third-generation Korean activist stated, "I don't like to be referred to as a *Zainichi*. I am Korean and therefore should be recognized as being a whole Korean person, not as someone whose identity is compromised by the country in which I reside" (interview, 27 March 1999, Tokyo).

The problem of "naming" the Korean community extends to the actual names of individual Koreans. Most Korean residents have two names: a Korean name (*honmyō*: real name, or official name) and a Japanese name (*tsūmei*: assumed name, or alias). Not only is the Japanese name often used in daily life, but it is routinely printed on the individual's alien registration form in brackets next to the Korean legal name (Fukuoka 2000: 28). In comparison, although it is not uncommon for Korean Americans to have Korean and English given names, rarely do they adopt a non-Korean family name, except in the cases of marriage or adoption. Moreover, the symbolic difference

---

[2] Harajiri Hideki (1997) has devised the term *Nihon teijū Korian* (permanent-resident Koreans in Japan) to emphasize the Korean community's permanent-resident status.

[3] The term *Chōsenjin* is no longer used regularly by the general public to refer to present-day Koreans in Japan because of the negative connotations associated with its usage from colonial times. The term is often used by children as a slur to taunt other children who are suspected of or are identified as being Korean. However, members of the Korean community continue to use the term to refer to their history in Japan as colonized subjects and their present situation of statelessness (because *Chōsen* as a unified state no longer exists). In recent years, the term has been reappropriated by some members of the community as a symbol of ethnic Korean pride in a manner similar to the Black Power movement and the gay rights movement in the United States.

84 Immigration and Citizenship in Japan

between the names Hyun-Ju Kim and Helen Kim pale in comparison to that between Kim Hyun-Ju and Kanemoto Kashiko.[4] The practice of adopting Japanese names among Koreans derives from the policy of *sōshi kaimei* (the forced adoption of Japanese names) under the cultural assimilation program of the Japanese colonial period. Although this policy was abolished with Japan's defeat in World War II, the practice continued with second-generation Koreans who, like Jews in nineteenth-century North America who "Anglo-sized" their names, used their Japanese names to pass as Japanese. Hence, although names can serve as an important source for distinguishing an ethnic minority group from the dominant population, the Korean community's invisibility has been further exacerbated by the prevalent use of Japanese aliases among individual Korean residents and naturalized Japanese citizens of Korean descent.

In the past two decades, public figures, such as the award-winning novelist Yi Yang-ji and the filmmaker Sai Yoichi, and younger generations of Korean residents have increasingly begun to use their Korean names or hybrid versions of their Korean and Japanese names.[5] Nevertheless, these cases are exceptional. Surveys of Korean residents conducted in 1984 and 1993 showed that approximately 80 percent of ethnic Koreans use their Japanese names regularly (Fukuoka and Kim 1997; Kimpara et al. 1986). In contrast, the 1984 survey of Kanagawa prefecture residents revealed that more than 80 percent of the Chinese residents in the same prefecture did not even have a Japanese alias.

The methods that Korean residents have adopted to grapple with the predicaments of being Korean in Japan highlight the community's

[4] During my fieldwork in Japan, I personally experienced the politics of "names" and "naming" in the Korean community. When I first arrived in Japan, my business cards displayed the romanized version of my English-language name in *katakana* (Erin Chung). Although few Japanese questioned this usage, many Korean residents that I met were disappointed that I had chosen not to use my "real [Korean] name." As a result, I promptly changed the name on my business cards to my Korean name (Chung Ae-Ran) using the original Chinese characters (with the *katakana* reading on top). Incidentally, some Korean residents instructed me to include my English name as well to indicate that I am Korean American and not a South Korean national or resident (Chung 1999).

[5] Hybrid names combine either the Korean family name with a Japanese given name such as "Son Masayoshi," the name of Yahoo Japan's president, or a Japanese or Korean family name with a Japanese reading of the Korean forename such as "Takayasu Keisai" or "Kim Chika." Others use the Japanese pronunciation of their Korean names (e.g., "Ri Tai-Ei" instead of "Yi Tae-Yŏn").

complexity and diversity. National identities, regional ties, class, and generations divide them.[6] In addition, there are different political agendas for achieving social parity, which are mixed and often antagonistic. Although some Korean groups lobby for voting rights and political inclusion, others vehemently oppose these efforts because they are said to promote assimilation and collaboration with the Japanese government.

The identity politics of this highly assimilated, legally foreign community is directly related to their ambiguous position between recent immigrants and Japanese nationals. Because Japanese citizenship policies are based on the principle of *jus sanguinis*, native-born generations of foreign residents do not automatically qualify for Japanese nationality. Thus, despite the fact that they now span four generations in Japan, the Korean-resident population constitutes one of the largest foreign-resident communities in Japan. Although naturalization procedures have become less restrictive for permanent residents throughout the past few decades, there were only about 300,000 naturalized Koreans in Japan by 2008.[7] By comparison, almost 890,000 persons in the United States naturalized in the year 2000 alone, including approximately 24,000 persons who were born in South Korea.[8] By the year 2000, more than half of all foreign-born Korean Americans had naturalized in the United States whereas only about 30 percent of the total Korean-resident population (including native-born generations) had naturalized in Japan.

At the same time, according to the conventional indicators of language, education, and marriage, the Korean community in Japan does

---

[6] Regional divisions include those within Japan, such as the Kansai and Kantō regions, as well as South Korea, such as the Kyŏngsang, Chŏlla, and Cheju regions.

[7] According to Kim Yŏng Dal (1990: 110), there were 145,572 naturalized Koreans in 1988. The annual naturalization rate in the 1980s fluctuated between an average of 4,500 to 6,800. Although the rate for 1991 remained consistent with the previous decade (at 5,665), the annual average increased to 7,244 in 1992 and 7,697 in 1993 (Tanaka 1996: 52–3). Since 1995, the annual average has remained consistent at about 10,000.

[8] These figures are based on the *2000 INS Statistical Yearbook*, Table 49. The total Korean population in the United States in the year 2000 numbered about 1.2 million, including a little more than 700,000 (57%) who were foreign born. Since 1991, the total number of naturalizations by Korean immigrants in the United States has been almost twice that of Korean residents in Japan (before that time, the number was much higher in the United States) despite the fact that the vast majority of Korean residents in Japan are native born.

not show signs of maintaining a strong Korean sociocultural identity. An estimated 90 percent of this population was born in Japan, and the majority are not fluent in Korean. The overwhelming majority of school-age Korean residents attend Japanese elementary and secondary schools using their Japanese names. Since 1990, the intermarriage rate between Koreans and Japanese has made up more than 80 percent of all marriages among Korean nationals.

Given that most Koreans in Japan have already assimilated into Japanese society for the most part, why does Korean citizenship remain the last vestige of Korean identity in Japan? A top-down analysis of citizenship policies at the level of the state alone would lead us to the same variables found in earlier English-language studies of Koreans in Japan: the difficult procedures and requirements of state immigration and naturalization policies and the maintenance of sociocultural identity by Korean residents (Lee and DeVos 1981). We would be left with a static, dichotomous portrait of an "oppressive" Japanese state and "oppressed" Koreans that masks extraelectoral forms of political participation in Korean communities as well as in Japanese civil society.[9]

Contrary to the conventional wisdom on this subject, Korean residents were not merely passive victims of repressive Japanese state policies and social discrimination, even in the early postwar period. Instead, as the previous chapter illustrates, Korean organizations played a significant role in the reclassification of the community as foreign nationals and actively discouraged their members from naturalizing despite the obvious disadvantages of foreign citizenship status. To be sure, postwar Japanese citizenship policies shaped Korean collective identity formation by conflating nationality and ethnicity, thereby equating Korean nationality with Korean identity. At the same time, the dominant postwar Korean organizations interpreted and responded to these institutional changes by making citizenship a political strategy in their dealings with the Japanese (and, at times, North and South Korean) state.

During the Occupation, Koreans objected to their treatment as Japanese nationals by Occupation authorities, arguing that they were "liberated nationals" with rights and privileges that surpassed the

---

[9] See Sonia Ryang's (1997: 7–16) critique of English-language studies of Koreans in Japan.

defeated Japanese. Even after the passage of restrictive citizenship and immigration laws that made foreign citizenship a primary source of social closure from the dominant Japanese society, Korean citizenship continued to be the basis for political organization within the community. By equating orthodox definitions of Korean identity with Korean citizenship, Korean community groups, particularly state-based organizations, were able to maintain a steady base of supporters for their political agendas throughout most of the Cold War. However, in their departures from these organizations and their corresponding ideologies, new generations of Korean activists have reinterpreted the meaning of Korean citizenship as identity and practice in movements to democratize Japanese society.

CONFLATING NATIONALITY AND ETHNOCULTURAL IDENTITY DURING THE COLD WAR

Although Choryŏn involved itself heavily in Japanese politics, its successor organizations, the pro–South Korea Mindan (Korean Residents Association in Japan; *Chae Ilbon Taehan Minkuk Mindan* in Korean, *Zainippon Daikanminkoku Kyoryū Mindan* in Japanese), established in 1946, and pro–North Korea Chongryun (General Association of Korean Residents in Japan; *Chae Ilbon Chosŏnin Ch'ongryŏn Haphoe* in Korean, *Zainippon Chōsenjin Sōrengōkai*, or *Sōren* in Japanese), established in 1955, made clear from their inceptions that they would submit to Japanese laws but would not involve themselves in Japan's domestic affairs. Rather than mobilize to gain rights for Koreans as residents of Japan, they centered their activities on homeland politics and repatriation for the Korean community and discouraged their members from acquiring Japanese nationality. Unlike prewar Korean groups and the short-lived Choryŏn, Mindan and Chongryun focused their political activities on opposing each other, not on contesting Japanese state policies and social discrimination. Thus, under the leadership of two insular organizations that encouraged them to maintain their precarious status as foreigners with limited rights, Koreans in Japan remained a severely deprived minority for at least the first half of the Cold War era.

Mindan was the successor to Kŏndong (the League for the Establishment of a New Korea), an anticommunist organization formed in

January 1946 in opposition to Choryŏn. With the enactment of the South Korean nationality law in 1948, Mindan became the official organ of South Korea, with the primary purpose of registering Koreans in Japan as overseas nationals of South Korea. Chongryun emerged as the official overseas organization of North Korea and the successor to Choryŏn; nevertheless, the organization cut all ties with the Japan Communist Party (JCP). Rather than declare a "people's revolution" in Japan, Chongryun adhered to North Korea's *juche* philosophy of self-reliance and divorced itself from Japanese domestic politics. In her study of the organization, Sonia Ryang (1997: 117–18) argues that Chongryun's policy of "mutual noninterference" in Japanese domestic affairs has allowed it to exist within Japanese society as "a lawful, self-governing body that not only rarely causes problems in society at large but also vigilantly checks its own members' behavior with regard to the Japanese legal system."

As I discuss in the previous chapter, postwar Japan's citizenship and immigration policies were formulated under the assumption that most, if not all, former colonial subjects would either repatriate to their home countries or naturalize. Even before former colonial subjects were officially stripped of their Japanese nationalities in 1952, the Diet passed a series of legislation that would institutionalize the association of nationality with ethnocultural identity, on the one hand, and legalize nationality-based exclusion, on the other. For example, the 1945 amendment to the Election Law and the 1947 Alien Registration Law demarcated former colonial subjects among Japanese residents as aliens based on the location of their family registries (*koseki*). Although American Occupation officials introduced legislation that prohibited discrimination against women and racial and ethnic minorities, noncitizen residents are notably absent in antidiscrimination legislation. As one Korean activist puts it, "Korean residents do not exist in Japanese law. They have only been recognized as people who do not count, people outside of society" (interview with Suh Jung Woo, 8 September 1999, Osaka).

Although postwar legislation declared that former colonial subjects were not Japanese nationals, their legal status remained undetermined for more than a decade thereafter. Shortly after passing the 1951 Immigration Control Order, the government froze its plans to enact special legislation regarding the legal status of Korean residents upon reaching a stalemate over the matter with South Korea. Instead, Koreans who had resided continuously in Japan from before September 1945 were provisionally declared "126-2-6 aliens" who could "continue to stay in Japan without having a qualification to stay, until their qualifications to stay and periods of stay" were determined in later legislation, which was finally enacted as a result of the 1965 Japan-Republic of Korea (ROK) Normalization Treaty (Iwasawa 1986: 150). Instead of naturalizing, which remained closely associated with the colonial policy of forced assimilation and submission to the emperor, most individual Korean residents in postwar Japan remained in a type of legal limbo and attempted to avoid discrimination by using the most expedient, and historically tested, tool that was available to them: "passing" as Japanese.

The 1965 Japan-ROK Normalization Treaty stabilized the legal status of a section of the Korean-resident population for the first time during the postwar period. In addition to providing a total of $800 million to South Korea in grants, loans, and commercial credits, the treaty granted permanent residency to Koreans who resided continuously in Japan from before the end of the war and who applied for South Korean nationality by January 1971. This so-called treaty-based permanent residency (*kyotei eijyū*) applied up to only the third generation of South Korean residents in Japan – or, the children and grandchildren of South Korean nationals eligible for permanent residency under the treaty – with the stipulation that the matter would be revisited in 1991 to determine the status of future generations of Korean residents. Treaty-based permanent residency afforded those who qualified with expanded freedom of foreign travel and fewer grounds for deportation than other foreign residents. Soon after the treaty was signed, the South Korean government sent annual funds to Mindan and extended university scholarships to second-generation Korean-residents to study in South Korea. According to Mindan, more than eighty-five thousand Koreans changed their registered nationalities from North to South Korea between 1965 and 1970 (Mindan 1998). By 1970, South Korean nationals outnumbered North Korean nationals by almost fifty thousand people, thus forming a majority in the community (Toitsu Nippo 1982; Yi 1980).

Although Mindan and Chongryun dominated the Korean community through the 1970s, a few small splinter groups provided a critical voice in the community. Chominryŏn (the League of Koreans in Japan for the Promotion of Democracy) was one of the few splinter groups to emerge from Chongryun, formed by a group of former high-ranking Chongryun officials in January 1975. Mindan encountered a more severe division following Park Chung Hee's 1961 military coup in South Korea, with its membership split into progovernment and antigovernment camps. In August 1973, Korean Central Intelligence Agency (KCIA) agents kidnapped Kim Dae Jung from his hotel room in Tokyo while he was organizing a mass rally protesting Park Chung Hee's dictatorship in South Korea. Not only was this a flagrant violation of Japanese law, one that stirred international interest, but it also widened the ideological divisions within Mindan. Shortly thereafter, the majority of those in the antigovernment camp abandoned Mindan to join the South Korean democratization movement in Japan and Korea that included the creation of splinter groups such as Hanmindong (National Congress for the Restoration of Democracy in South Korea and Promotion of Unification) and its subsidiary, Hanch'ŏngdong (*Seinendō* in Japanese, or Korean Youth Alliance).

Because Mindan and Chongryun were founded with the purposes of repatriation and nationality registration, they discouraged their members from acquiring Japanese nationality. The legal status of Koreans in Japan as resident aliens was essential to Mindan and Chongryun's survival throughout the Cold War. Not only did both groups compete to gain more members through nationality registration, but they also proclaimed themselves to be the vanguards of South and North Korean nationals against Japanese discrimination.

Practical considerations were also a factor in discouraging naturalization. Koreans who naturalize are highly unlikely to either maintain their memberships in Mindan or Chongryun or contribute funds. Even for Koreans who have not naturalized, membership in these organizations can be peripheral, functional, and/or interchangeable. Among the Korean residents I interviewed, there are a number who are or have been members of both organizations for the purpose of expanding their networking opportunities. Others have changed their nationalities from North to South Korean (and thus their membership from Chongryun to Mindan) as a result of marriage, not for political reasons. Non-Chongryun Koreans often send their children to Chongryun schools not so much for the purpose of ideological education but so that their children can learn the Korean language and be among other ethnic Koreans. Some have simply stopped paying dues. Mindan suffered a drop in active (due-paying) membership in 1988 when the South Korean government opened its embassy in Japan. Up until this time, Mindan was the only organization through which a South Korean national could obtain a passport in Japan. Hence, active membership in Mindan was required in order to travel overseas. Today, most South Korean nationals in Japan make arrangements for international travel at the South Korean embassy, which issues passports free of charge.

Much of the dissatisfaction with Mindan and Chongryun lies in the organizations' dogmatism. Second-, third-, and fourth-generation Koreans are warned against assimilating into the society in which they were born and discouraged from naturalizing despite the difficulties associated with noncitizen status. Rather than challenge the exclusionary ideology of Japanese homogeneity, both groups have, until very recently, constructed their own ideologies of "authentic identities" for the Korean community based on blood ties and nationality. Their declarations of noninvolvement in Japanese domestic politics and their rigid antiassimilationist stance – at the expense of gaining rights for Korean residents – relieved the Japanese state from the burden of administrative change in regard to citizenship policies. Consequently, for much of the Cold War, Koreans in Japan were a model minority of sorts – they were law-abiding, culturally assimilated (despite Mindan and Chongryun's antiassimilationist rhetoric), and politically silent regarding Japanese domestic politics.

FROM KIKOKUSHUGI (REPATRIATION) TO ZAINICHI (PERMANENT RESIDENCY)

Three major events in the late 1960s and early 1970s fueled the transition from state-based identity politics to the birth of independent movements in the Korean community. First, in February 1969, Kim Hŭi-ro, a second-generation Korean resident in his forties, made national news when he killed two loan sharks in the Japanese mafia (*yakuza*) to whom he owed money and, rather than surrender to authorities, subsequently held thirteen people hostage for eighty-eight hours at a nearby hotspring inn in Shizuoka prefecture in order to publicize his demands. Upon contacting the media, he demanded a public apology from a local detective who had harassed him with anti-Korean slurs. He also announced that he killed the two gang members because they had been harassing him relentlessly, which he linked to what he characterized as the unbearable discrimination he suffered as a Korean in Japan. He was eventually sentenced to life imprisonment by the Shizuoka district court following eight years of a series of dramatic trials (Lee and DeVos 1981: 252–4). After years of remaining an "invisible" minority in post-war Japan, this incident suddenly threw the Korean community into the public spotlight. During the early years of his thirty-one-and-a-half years in prison, Kim continued to speak out about the discrimination he encountered as a Korean in Japan. When he was released on parole in September 1999, he moved to Pusan, his deceased parents' hometown in South Korea, where he received a hero's welcome. Shortly before his release, Kim stated, "I was not fighting all Japanese people, only the ones that discriminated against us because we are Koreans. If I ever meet those kind of people, I will fight again" (*Yomiuri Shimbun*, 8 September 1999: 2).

Second, in April 1971, came the arrest of the Suh brothers while they were students at Seoul National University in South Korea. Suh Sung and Suh Jun-sik were second-generation Korean residents in Japan but had been active in student demonstrations during the bitterly fought 1971 presidential elections between Park Chung Hee and Kim Dae Jung (Suh 1994). Following an unauthorized visit to North Korea, the brothers were arrested for violating South Korea's National Security Law, which bans unauthorized contact with North Koreans, any activity that "praises" or "benefits" North Korea, and any involvement in organizations alleged to be pro–North Korean. South Korean authorities also charged Suh Sung with masterminding an espionage ring of students, which included his younger brother Suh Jun-sik, under orders from North Korea. They sentenced Suh Sung to death and Suh Jun-sik to fifteen years in prison. At their second trial in 1972, their sentences were commuted to life imprisonment (reduced to 20 years in 1988) and seven years, respectively. Following his release in 1978, Suh Jun-sik was detained for another ten years for refusing to submit a statement of ideological conversion. Partially through the efforts of their younger brother, Suh Kyung Sik, a professor at Hōsei University in Tokyo, their cases attracted international attention to the treatment of political prisoners in South Korea, and Amnesty International considered the brothers to be Prisoners of Conscience.[10] However, they were merely the best known case: between April 1971 to February 1976, some thirty-six second-generation Koreans from Japan were arrested in South Korea for their alleged links with the "pro-North Korean" community in Japan and for violating South Korea's National Security Law (Chen 1988: 391).

Third, the highly publicized Hitachi Employment Discrimination Trial of the early 1970s that I discuss in the following section, which involved a second-generation Korean resident, brought to light the widespread discrimination against Koreans in employment, housing, and social welfare, among other areas. Not only did the Korean plaintiff eventually win the case in 1974, setting a legal precedent against nationality-based discrimination in employment, but also the trial generated a grassroots movement led by a coalition of young Korean and Japanese activists. As I explain further in the following section, this movement, which was the first of its kind, created the blueprint for independent Korean social movements in the decades to come.

These events coincided with the coming of age of second-generation Koreans and the subsequent development of the concept *zainichi* (residence in Japan), which emerged in opposition to the prevalent *kikokushugi* (repatriation) ideology of first-generation Korean residents. Whereas the first-generation leadership of Mindan and Chongryun absorbed themselves in homeland politics, second-generation members began to question their connections to the homeland. Many of those who visited South Korea to "rediscover" their roots returned disillusioned. Their experiences resembled those of U.S. African Americans in the 1960s and 1970s who "returned" to the homeland to discover, as John A. Williams described in 1963, "There is nothing like a trip to Africa to make an American Negro realize just how American he is" (quoted in Walters 1993: 56). Rather than welcoming them as one of their own, South Koreans in the "homeland" treated

---

[10] Suh Jun-sik, who remained in South Korea as a human rights activist following his release, was arrested again in 1997 during a human rights film festival that he helped organize. Suh was charged with violating the National Security Law for screening the film "Red Hunt," a South Korean documentary about the 1948 Cheju Island uprising and subsequent massacre of suspected communist sympathizers. For more information, see the Amnesty International Report, "Republic of Korea (South Korea): On Trial for Defending His Rights: The Case of Human Rights Activist Suh Jun-Sik" (AI Index: ASA 25/18/98), May 1998.

Immigration and Citizenship in Japan

many Koreans from Japan as foreigners or criticized their lack of pro-ficiency in Korean language and culture. Consequently, many of those who expected to become more "Korean" during their visit to South Korea returned to Japan with the realization that they were neither Korean nor Japanese, but they were *zainichi*.

Zainichi signifies the permanent nature of Korean residence in Japan and became the basis for seeking civil and social rights in Japan as the following section illustrates.[11] At the same time, this concept did not challenge the equation of nationality with identity. On the con-trary, *zainichi* proponents endeavored to define and maintain a dis-tinct Korean identity in Japan that embraced neither repatriation to the homeland nor assimilation into Japanese society. Ironically, the struggle to define a specific Korean identity in Japan reinforced the equation of nationality with identity.

Because second-generation Koreans were born and raised in Japan, few distinguishing characteristics tied them together as Koreans. Not many were fluent in Korean because the majority of second-generation Koreans were educated in Japanese schools. In addition, many first-generation Koreans were unable or unwilling to teach the Korean language to their children. Those who came to Japan as uneducated laborers were likely to be illiterate and/or unable to maintain their fluency in Korean under harsh conditions in Japan. Others chose not to teach Korean to their children to protect them from discrimination. The overwhelming commonality that the community shared was Korean nationality. In this sense, (North or South) Korean nationality came to signify not only one's legal status but also one's politics and, ultimately, one's ethnic identity. As Kang Chae-ŏn (1996: 178), a first-generation Korean-resident writer, puts it, Korean nationality became the final "fortress" (*toride*) for native-born Korean residents to demonstrate their Korean ethnic identity.

In the late 1970s and early 1980s, writings on *Zainichiron* (dis-courses on *Zainichi*) by second-generation Korean residents sprouted in various journals and newspapers. In 1987, Ko Yi Sam, a second-generation Korean resident, founded the publishing company Shinkan-sha with the purpose of giving a voice to second-generation Koreans

[11] For a wide-ranging discussion of the *zainichi* concept in historical, social scientific, literary, and pop-cultural forms, see Lie 2008.

in Japan.[12] Ko notes that the concept of *zainichi* became more concrete as second-generation Korean residents published and refined their arguments (interview with Ko Yi Sam, 9 March 1999, Tokyo). His company began publication of *Horumon bunka* [Hormone Culture], a widely read journal about Koreans in Japan, in 1990.[13] Although the well-known Korean-resident writers of the time were of the first generation, *Horumon bunka* featured the writings of second-generation Koreans exclusively. *Horumon bunka* and another similar journal, *Kikan seikyū* (which began publication in 1989), were successors to the journal *Kikan sanzenri* (published from 1975 to 1987), which was among the first journals in Japan that explored issues specifically related to Korean residents in Japan (Lie 2000). Ko predicted that the second-generation contributors to the journal would be the opinion leaders of the Korean community in ten years. His prediction was correct: almost all of the seven original members of the editorial board, such as Pak Il and Kang Sang-jung, are now among the best-known Korean-resident nonfiction writers in Japan.

Until the 1970s, there was little discussion of the specific forms of discrimination facing Koreans in Japan within the community. Rather, the existing state-based organizations tended to rely on political slogans that supported their particular agendas. Ko Yi Sam explains the difference between first- and second-generation Korean organizations according to education:

The first-generation were not *zainichi* Koreans as the word is used today; they were "foreigners" whose identities were based on repatriation [*kikokushugi*].... The second-generation, on the other hand, have been concerned more about their rights in Japan as permanent residents. A big difference between the two generations is that the first were educated during the Japanese colonial period while the second were educated during the postwar period.

[12] Shinkansha publishes a wide range of books, particularly those related to Koreans in Japan, North and South Korea, human rights issues, foreigners in Japan, the Korean diaspora, and Japanese politics and history.

[13] *Horumon*, or hormone, in this case refers to animal intestines (chitterlings) that are as ubiquitous to Korean food in Japan as *bulgogi*, known in Japanese as *yakiniku* (grilled beef, or Korean barbeque). Like chitterlings in African American "soul food," the origins of this cuisine date back to the colonial period during which time Koreans were more likely to have had access to animal by-products than animal flesh. The consumption of chitterlings is not as common in South Korea as it is in Japan's Korean community.

In other words, this is a difference between imperial versus "democratic" education. . . . Members of the second-generation use the premise that Japan is a democracy as the basis for many of their arguments. This reasoning does not occur as naturally for the first-generation. (interview with Ko Yi Sam, 9 March 1999, Tokyo)

TOWARD A NONCITIZEN CIVIL RIGHTS MOVEMENT

With the coming of age of second-generation Korean residents, the 1970s witnessed the birth of a full-fledged noncitizen civil rights movement led by Korean activists. Although Korean identity and foreign legal status remained integral components of this movement, the emphasis was on their position as permanent residents of Japan. Korean demands for rights and democratic inclusion were based not on their status as nationals of another sovereign country but as rightful members of Japanese civil society. A second-generation Korean activist describes the change in oppositional strategies as one from powerlessness to empowerment:

Up until now, different segments of the Korean community have attempted to use "normal" channels of political participation to influence Japanese and Korean state policies from the position of powerlessness [*mukenri*, literally, without rights] and semi-statelessness. Korean residents in Japan are not full members of any state. I may be a national of South Korea but I am not even permitted to enter the country, much less participate in its political process. . . . But we have entrusted our fates to governments that neither represent our interests nor include us as full members of their societies. That is why most of our demands have been based on general appeals to human rights. . . . What we need to do is either influence government policy as full citizens of the society or engage in revolutionary politics to change both the state and the society. (interview, 10 May 1999, Tokyo)[14]

As noncitizens without voting rights, Korean activists – often in coalition with Japanese activists – employ the political tools available to all members of a civil society regardless of citizenship status. The strategies that they have used to gain institutionalized rights and recognition

---

[14] Korean activists in Japan who have been active in movements to reunify North and South Korea or have made unauthorized visits to North Korea are not permitted to enter South Korea. South Korea's National Security Law prohibits actions construed to be antistate or procommunist.

for the Korean-resident community can be divided broadly into three categories: litigation, lobbying, and protest. Disenfranchised minorities elsewhere have historically used these political tools primarily to gain *access* to citizenship, as was the case among Asian immigrants in the United States in the early twentieth century who attempted unsuccessfully to gain the right to naturalize through the courts. Korean efforts to secure institutionalized rights in Japan, however, have aimed to empower the status of foreign residents rather than ease the path to full citizenship.

The Hitachi Employment Discrimination Trial of the 1970s marked the beginning of a series of campaigns and lawsuits intended to challenge legal and social discrimination against Korean residents based on their alien legal status. These campaigns are notable not only for their triumphs but also by their leadership. The Korean civil rights movement of the 1970s and 1980s, which converged around high-profile lawsuits and local and national campaigns, was spearheaded by Korean and Japanese activists who were not affiliated with either of the dominant Korean organizations in Japan. Both Mindan and Chongryun initially opposed many of the campaigns, claiming that they would encourage Korean assimilation into Japanese society. These campaigns are equally significant for creating a blueprint for Korean-resident and proimmigrant activism in subsequent decades: 1) centralized movements focusing on the Japanese legal system that aim to expand institutionalized rights and protections for Korean, and other foreign, residents at the national level and 2) local, grassroots campaigns and organizations aimed at changing Japanese society.

Hitachi Employment Discrimination Trial

Shortly after Arai Shōji, a nineteen-year-old South Korean national born and raised in Japan, learned that he had qualified for one of seven vacancies at the Hitachi Software Plant in Totsuka, he was asked to submit a copy of his family registration certificate (*koseki*), a document that often serves as a form of identification for Japanese nationals. He notified the company by phone that he did not have a family registration certificate in Japan and would submit a copy of his alien registration card instead. The company later informed him that they did not employ foreigners and that his employment was cancelled.

When he filed his lawsuit against Hitachi for employment discrimination in 1970, Arai Shōji – who began to use his Korean name, Pak Chŏng-sŏk, during the course of his trial – had the support of a broad spectrum of Japanese activists, including students, teachers, intellectuals, and lawyers. The 1960s had radicalized a generation of activists worldwide in what Martin Luther King Jr. described as a "revolutionary" time: "All over the globe men are revolting against old systems of exploitation and oppression, and out of the wombs of a frail world, new systems of justice and equality are being born" (King 1967). Organized struggles against racism, sexism, poverty, war, and exploitation throughout the world gave rise to new social movements in Japan that, by the late 1960s, had become confrontational, and often violent, in their protest tactics. Students, labor unions, and members of the Communist and Socialist parties had previously organized mass protests against the renegotiation of the U.S.-Japan Mutual Security Treaty (*Anpo*) in 1960 and the Japan-ROK Normalization Treaty in 1965, and the Buraku Liberation Movement had succeeded in pressuring the Diet to pass the Law on Special Measures for Dōwa Projects in 1969, which provided funds for improving housing conditions and education for *burakumin* (Pharr 1990: 85). Student protests had reached their peak in the late 1960s, beginning with the campuswide University of Tokyo strikes in 1968 that eventually shut the university down for two days in January 1969 (Steinhoff 1989, 1999). The beginning of the Hitachi trial coincided with three mass-protest movements: the anti–Vietnam War movement, protests against proposed changes to the Immigration Control Law and Alien School Act in the late 1960s and early 1970s, and mass demonstrations against the *Anpo* renewal in 1970. The Committee to Support Pak (*Paku-kun o kakomu kai*), which assembled a legal team and held monthly study meetings to publicize the trial as well as discuss the broader social and political problems of the day, was initially formed by members of Beiheiren (Citizens' Alliance for Peace in Vietnam), a Keio University student organization with roots in the anti–Vietnam War movement.

Korean supporters were harder to come by. Most Korean activists at that time backed Mindan and Chongryun's position that employment in a major Japanese corporation encouraged Korean assimilation into Japanese society. The minority of Korean residents that were not associated with Mindan or Chongryun focused their efforts on the South

Korean democratization movement or other issues related to homeland politics. Arai Shōji (hereinafter referred to as Pak) approached members of Beiheiren only after he had already been rebuffed by members of the Korean community – even his own siblings – who criticized his attempts as misguided, hopeless, and "assimilationist" (Wender 2005: 74). Pak's alliance with Japanese activists intensified claims that Pak and his supporters were assimilationists.

Although Pak's case faced strong opposition from the dominant factions of the Korean community, two sources of support proved to be pivotal in garnering international attention for the case as well as in establishing the foundations for a full-fledged civil rights movement for Korean residents in Japan. First, Reverend Yi In-ha (Lee In Ha), who immigrated to Japan in 1941 at the age of fifteen and had been serving as the general secretary of the Korean Christian Church in Japan (KCCJ) since 1960 and was senior pastor of the Kawasaki Korean Christian Church (*Zainichi Daikan Kirisuto Kyōkai*), was a founding member and spokesperson for the Committee to Support Pak. Often referred to as the "Martin Luther King, Jr. of the Korean civil rights movement" in Korean activist circles, Yi's active involvement in the aforementioned Kim Hŭi-ro trial in 1969 and his connections to national and international Christian organizations, including the National Christian Council in Japan (NCCJ) and the World Council of Churches (WCC), were instrumental in recruiting seasoned activists and lawyers to Pak's campaign and publicizing the case worldwide. In the same year that Pak filed his lawsuit against Hitachi, Yi joined the WCC's commission on the Programme to Combat Racism, which, in 1974, contributed 4.5 million yen to the Committee to Support Pak and passed a resolution for an international boycott of Hitachi products (interview with Yi In-ha, 2 September 1999, Kawasaki).

Second, Pak's case attracted a handful of young second- and third-generation Korean residents who had cut ties with Mindan and Chongryun and struggled to establish an identity that transcended the prevalent assimilation versus repatriation dichotomy described in the previous section. One of Pak's earliest supporters was Ch'ŏe Sung-gu, a member of the KCCJ, who was subject to ostracism from his Korean youth church group when he championed Pak's case. As the Korean-resident writer Pak Il (1992) notes, Ch'ŏe's support of Pak's case was significant not only because he helped form the Committee to Support Pak but also because his stated position on the Korean identity issue, which he formulated in response to Pak's struggle, stimulated debate on the *zainichi* concept.

By the time that the Yokohama district court made its landmark ruling in favor of Pak in 1974, the Committee to Support Pak had mobilized a total of 7,800 activists as well as eight regional committees in Japan and had garnered international attention, including boycotts of Hitachi products led by the WCC and three Christian church bodies in South Korea (Hicks 1997: 41). The coalition of Japanese and Korean activists outlived the trial to form one of the most influential groups to come out of the *zainichi* movement of the 1970s, Mintōren (*Minzoku sabetsu to tatakau renraku kyōgikai*, or the National Council for Combating Discrimination against Ethnic Peoples in Japan, which is the official English name used by the organization), formally established in 1975. In the spirit of the Hitachi trial, Mintōren activists defined Koreans as permanent members of Japanese society and directed their efforts at securing equal rights for Koreans and other marginalized groups in Japan.

At its inception, Mintōren was made up of Korean and Japanese members that supported neither North nor South Korea. Rather, the group defined *zainichi* Korean identity according to their colonial and postcolonial history in Japan. "Living together in harmony" (*tomoni ikiru*) became the central platform of the group. Although the Hitachi trial had gained national, and even international, attention and the Committee to Support Pak had become a national organization, Mintōren was organized as a decentralized grassroots organization made up of several local chapters that focused on local issues in communities with relatively large Korean populations. Consequently, the issues that Mintōren tackled were specific to each local community. Because most Korean residents at the time struggled with fundamental barriers in their daily lives specifically as foreigners with limited institutionalized rights, however, Mintōren activists often made their claims based on the idea that Korean residents were local citizens who deserved rights equal to Japanese nationals based on their membership in Japanese civil society, often with appeals to their human rights.

Local Movements

Many accounts of citizenship and immigration politics in Japan point to Japan's ratification of international conventions in the late 1970s and early 1980s as the catalyst for sweeping reforms that dramatically changed the social and legal status of foreign residents in Japan. This assessment places primary emphasis on external pressure, suggesting that social change was top-down. To be sure, the reforms that followed the ratification of these treaties granted foreign residents in Japan substantial citizenship rights that would correspond with international human rights norms regarding minorities, foreigners, and refugees. Moreover, it is unlikely that the Japanese government would have implemented such dramatic reforms without pressure from the UN Committee on Human Rights and other members of the international community. Not only was the Japanese government acutely sensitive to international criticism as Japan joined the ranks of the world's major economic powers, but also Japan's ratification of the treaties had a binding effect on policies regarding foreigners residing in Japan. As Yuji Iwasawa (1998: 2–5) points out, treaties have the force of law in Japan and, consequently, the Japanese government makes "scrupulous efforts to bring Japanese law into conformity with the treaty" before entering into a treaty.

Korean residents, however, were not passive beneficiaries of top-down reforms during this period. On the one hand, Korean activists and their allies were instrumental in drawing international attention to what they characterized as human rights violations against Koreans in Japan. In the same year that Japan ratified the International Covenant on Economic, Social and Cultural Rights (ICESCR) and the International Covenant on Civil and Political Rights (ICCPR), a group of Korean and Japanese activists and lawyers filed a report detailing human rights violations against Korean residents in Japan to the United Nations, which was refiled by the Washington, D.C.–based International Human Rights Law Group the following year in 1980. The UN Commission on Human Rights officially took up the case in 1980 and terminated its investigation only after the Japanese government outlined plans to implement legal reforms to rectify the situation (Iwasawa 1986: 132; 1998: 124). As Amy Gurowitz (1999) argues, domestic actors – in this case, Korean and Japanese activists and lawyers – appealed to the international community by using the language and logic of international human rights norms that ultimately put powerful pressure on the Japanese government to implement reforms. Drawing on Margaret Keck and Kathryn Sikkink's (1998) concept of "boomerang" patterns of influence by transnational advocacy networks, Jennifer Chan (2008: 7–10) notes that, since as early as 1975, a wide range of domestic actors in Japan have bypassed the Japanese state and directly lobbied international organizations to exert pressure on Japan from outside.

On the other hand, grassroots movements by Korean and Japanese activists had been putting pressure on local governments, national policy makers, and individual companies since the early 1970s. The Hitachi case fueled an explosion of local campaigns and lawsuits that challenged the basic connection between institutionalized rights and nationality. As more Korean residents came to terms with the idea that they would live out their lives in Japan, rather than "return" to the homeland, they sought to remove structural barriers to their prosperity and well-being as permanently settled, noncitizen members of Japanese society. In many cases, Mintōren activists and human rights lawyers who supported Pak during the Hitachi trial spearheaded these efforts at the local level by organizing protests, lobbying officials, and organizing legal teams. In addition, Japanese activists who were not affiliated with Mintōren frequently supported these local Korean movements, which they characterized as one of many local citizens' movements of the day.

A number of local governments had already granted Korean residents rights to social welfare benefits *prior to* national reforms that followed the ratification of international conventions during the late 1970s and early 1980s. Nagoya city granted Korean residents rights to National Health Insurance in 1972 and a number of other municipalities with relatively large Korean populations – including Osaka, Kobe, Kawasaki, Yokohama, and all the wards in Tokyo – followed suit in the 1970s (Iwasawa 1998: 170). Kawasaki city was among the first to enact a wide range of progressive legislation in response to Korean movements against discrimination in the 1970s. In 1975, foreign residents were given access to public housing and child support from the city, and, in 1986, the city announced plans to expand education for

Korean residents, leading to the publication of local educational policies for Korean residents in municipalities throughout the Kanto and Kansai regions in the 1980s (Yamawaki 2003). Also in 1975, the city of Osaka granted Korean residents access to public housing in response to a petition written by fifteen organizations (UNESCO Japan 2008). Finally, after Japan's ratification of the ICESCR and ICCPR in 1979, the Ministry of Construction announced that foreign residents were eligible for public housing in 1980. Following Japan's ratification of the Convention Relating to the Status of Refugees in 1982, the nationality requirement was formally removed from the Child Allowance Law, the Child Dependency Allowance Law, and the Special Child Dependency Allowance Law in 1982, and foreign residents have been eligible for National Health Insurance since 1986.

Korean residents also made significant progress in expanding their rights to employment in the public sector even without national-level reforms. Although there is no formal nationality requirement for public-sector jobs, local governments limit certain positions involving decision making or the exercise of public authority to Japanese nationals only. Until the early 1970s, most local governments interpreted this stipulation strictly, barring foreign residents from taking their qualifying examinations. As young, native-born generations of Korean residents came of age in the 1960s and 1970s, however, they increasingly pressured their local governments to abolish the nationality requirement for public-sector jobs through petitions and protests. In Yao city, for example, Mintōren activists worked with local labor unions in a series of protests in the 1970s that led to the removal of the nationality requirement for postal delivery workers and made Korean residents eligible for employment in the local city government. As early as 1973, six cities and one town in Hyōgo prefecture had removed the nationality requirement for clerical and technical positions in the public sector (Ishikida 2005). These local developments were followed by the high-profile case of Nippon Telegraph and Telephone Public Corporation (NTT), one of the largest semipublic organizations in Japan. After two Korean residents attempted unsuccessfully to sit for the company's licensing examination in 1975 and 1976, teachers from one of the student's schools, the Nishinomiya Nishi High School, asked their local labor union for help, which eventually led to a national movement that pushed the issue on the floor of the National Diet in 1977. Finally, in September 1977, NTT removed the nationality requirement and, in April 1978, hired a Korean resident who had passed the company's licensing exam. In the same year that NTT removed the nationality requirement from its licensing examination, Kim Kyŏng-deuk, a second-generation Korean resident, became the first foreign-national lawyer in Japan. After passing the bar examination, Kim refused to naturalize despite the nationality requirement for entry into the Legal Training and Research Institute, which provides mandatory training for more than two years after a candidate has passed the bar examination. Subsequently, the Supreme Court removed the nationality requirement for entry into the institute, thereby making foreign residents eligible to practice law in Japan (Kim 1995).

In the late 1970s and early 1980s, movements by Korean residents and their allies pressured the Ministry of Education (MOE) to allow public universities to hire foreign nationals as formal members of their faculty and remove the nationality requirement for public school teachers. Suh Yong-dal, a first-generation Korean resident and professor at Momoyama Gakuin University, led a group of Korean-resident professors in 1975 who submitted a petition to the MOE encouraging public universities to hire Asian nationals and another petition to the Japanese Association of National Universities and the Japan Association of Public Universities urging them to eradicate employment discrimination. Japanese supporters who formed the Association to Promote Foreign Residents as College Professors in 1977 joined their efforts. In 1979, the Japan Association of Public Universities issued a statement declaring that the exclusion of foreign professors from employment in public universities based on their nationality was unreasonable, and, in 1982, the Diet passed a law that permits national and municipal universities to hire foreign nationals as faculty with full voting rights in faculty meetings (UNESCO Japan 2008).[15]

The movement to eradicate the nationality requirement for public school teachers began in the Kansai area in the 1970s. In 1974, a total of nineteen foreign-resident teachers had been hired by Osaka

[15] Although foreign nationals can be hired as full-time faculty in public schools who can vote in faculty meetings, attend teachers' conferences, and join the school administration, they cannot participate in board meetings and are ineligible for promotion to managerial or top administrative posts.

prefectural and municipal schools, and, in 1979, a Korean resident was hired to teach at a public school in Mie prefecture. The Hyogo and Saga prefectures followed suit in 1981 by abolishing the nationality requirement for public school teachers, and the Aichi prefecture did the same in 1982. These developments came to a halt when the MOE declared in 1982 that foreign nationals could be hired by public schools as lecturers only and would not be permitted to attend faculty meetings. Following a storm of protests and demonstrations, the Nagano Prefecture Education Committee reversed an earlier decision to revoke a Korean resident's teaching license based on the MOE guidelines and hired her to teach as a full-time faculty member in 1985. This decision set a precedent for hiring foreign nationals as public school teachers, and, finally, in 1991, the MOE declared that the nationality requirement no longer applied to public school teachers.

As the Diet began deliberations about ratifying the international covenants on human rights in 1979, Korean residents gained tools through which they could strengthen their claims. For example, Kim Hyŏn-jyo, a first-generation Korean resident, filed a lawsuit with the Tokyo District Court claiming that the Social Insurance Agency owed him his old-age pension for which he had paid premiums throughout the course of twelve years. Because the National Pension Law contained a nationality requirement until 1982, Kim was denied pension payments based on his nationality. Although Kim made his case based on Japanese and international human rights laws, the Tokyo District Court dismissed his case in 1979. After the nationality requirement was removed from the National Pension Law following Japan's ratification of the Convention Relating to the Status of Refugees in 1982, the Tokyo High Court overturned the 1979 decision in favor of the plaintiff. Another high-profile lawsuit by a naturalized Japanese citizen of Korean descent related to the national pension, commonly referred to as the "Shiomi case," made similar claims based on international human rights law on appeal – after the case had been rejected by the Osaka District Court in 1980 – but was ultimately dismissed by the Supreme Court in 1989 (Iwasawa 1998: 171–4).

Accordingly, although the reforms that followed the ratification of international conventions in the late 1970s and early 1980s were the first of their kind at the national level, they did not necessarily bring about top-down change. In some cases, the reforms nationalized policies that had already been implemented at the local level in a number of communities with relatively large Korean populations. In others, they provided the basis for resolving claims that had already been made in the courts and in direct appeals to local officials. Japan's ratification of international human rights treaties, moreover, provided Korean activists with a powerful tool through which they could make their claims. It was not, however, the *catalyst* for claims making within the Korean community. As one Korean activist puts it, "While external pressure has changed the structure of Japanese society, only grassroots movements can change the content of Japanese society" (interview with Suh Jung Woo, 8 September 1999, Osaka).

National Movements

As I discuss in Chapter 2, Korean activists were involved in various facets of political life in early postwar Japan. Although the largest protests by Koreans in postwar Japan concerned their right to operate autonomous Korean schools in Japan, Korean activists frequently worked in coalition with the Japanese Left, especially members of the JCP, in calls for Japan's democratic revolution and the overthrow of the emperor system. Following the dissolution of the largest postwar Korean organization, Choryŏn, in 1949 and the establishment of Mindan in 1946 and Chongryun in 1955, Korean engagement with Japanese politics diminished in size and strength as Mindan and Chongryun discouraged Korean involvement in Japan's domestic affairs. Although Korean residents and Japanese leftist activists engaged in mass protests against the 1965 Japan-ROK Normalization Treaty, Korean involvement centered on their opposition to the South Korean government. Nevertheless, the momentum of the Hitachi Employment Discrimination case propelled widespread local movements and two key national movements: the antifingerprinting movement and the local voting rights movement.

Antifingerprinting Campaign
From 1952 to 1982, all foreigners over the age of fourteen residing in Japan for more than a year were required to submit their fingerprints in the process of registering with local authorities under the Alien Registration Act of 1952, a process that had to be repeated every three years.

Those who refused to be fingerprinted were subject to imprisonment for up to one year or a fine. In 1982, the minimum age was raised from fourteen to sixteen and the renewal period was extended from three to five years. This revision also increased the fine for those who refused to be fingerprinted and made them ineligible for reentry permits. The law was revised again in 1987 so that foreign residents were required to submit their fingerprints only once in their lifetimes. At the same time, this revision added another significant penalty: those who refused to be fingerprinted were required to renew their alien registration cards every two years, instead of every five years. After a decadelong struggle led by Korean residents, the Diet abolished the fingerprinting requirement for permanent residents in 1993 and, eventually, for all foreign residents in 1999. The fingerprinting requirement was reinstated in 2007; however, those with special permanent-residency visas, the vast majority of whom are prewar Korean immigrants and their descendants, are exempt.

For many Korean residents, the fingerprinting process was a degrading experience that only foreign residents and criminals were required to undergo. Until 1971, foreign residents had to have all of their fingers printed using a "rotating" method that was identical to the fingerprinting process for criminals. A revision of the law in 1971 eased the process to a single fingerprint (of the left index finger) and another revision in 1985 replaced the "rotating" method with a flat fingerprint and introduced a colorless ink to replace the thick black ink used previously (Tanaka 1995: 93–4).

In 1980, Han Jŏng Sŏk, a first-generation Korean resident whose family immigrated to Japan during the colonial period, started the antifingerprinting movement when he refused to submit his fingerprint as he was renewing his alien registration card at the Shinjuku ward office in Tokyo. His widely publicized case had a domino effect on the rest of the entire foreign-resident community, resulting in a struggle that lasted more than a decade and involved thousands of Korean and other foreign residents who refused to submit their fingerprints and the aforementioned revisions to the policy in 1982, 1985, and 1987 before the fingerprinting requirement was abolished for permanent residents in 1993. In 1985 alone, more than 10,000 of the 360,000 foreign residents who renewed their alien registration cards refused to submit their fingerprints (Iwasawa 1986: 156).

The tactics used by activists in the antifingerprinting movement replicated previous movements by Korean residents: protests, lobbying, and litigation. At the same time, Patricia Steinhoff (1989: 186) points out that the movement differed in one fundamental way: participation required individual civil disobedience with "serious personal consequences" ranging from arrest to deportation to disqualification from naturalization. Rather than fan the flames of the movement, however, government officials frequently declined to enforce the law even as they reserved the right to do so. Such selective enforcement diluted the strength of the movement as Steinhoff (1989: 187) describes: "The protestors are denied the satisfaction of a victory, the publicity of heavy arrests, and even the strategy of clogging the judicial system."

Because the movement began on the heels of local and national victories for the Korean-resident community and coincided with Japan's ratification of international covenants on human rights and refugees, however, it gained immediate national and international attention and support. Many of the same actors who supported Pak Chŏng-sŏk in the Hitachi case – such as the KCCJ, the NCCJ, and the Japanese Bar Association Committee on Human Rights Protection – took leading roles in the protests and publicity campaigns. By 1986, the National Mayor's Association and approximately one thousand local assemblies submitted resolutions requesting abrogation or amelioration of the fingerprinting requirement as well as the requirement that foreign residents carry their alien registration cards with them at all times (Iwasawa 1986: 156). Although appeals to international human rights norms by foreign-resident defendants who refused to be fingerprinted were largely unsuccessful in the courts, they resonated strongly with international bodies, including the UN Human Rights Commission.

Mindan and Chongryun had initially opposed the antifingerprinting movement on the grounds that it encouraged Korean residents to violate Japanese law, which directly contradicted both organizations' policy of adhering to the Japanese legal system. Some members of Chongryun further maintained that the fingerprinting requirement was a necessary consciousness-raising experience for Korean youth who, upon turning sixteen, were confronted with their Korean identities often for the first time. It was said that without this sort of "rite of passage," Koreans in Japan would assimilate themselves completely into Japanese society without ever having to acknowledge their true identities (interview with Tanaka Hiroshi, 31 May 1995, Tokyo). As Han Jŏng Sŏk recounts, "Neither the South Korean state nor the *zainichi* organizations offered me any help [when I was prosecuted for refusing to submit my fingerprint in 1980]. It was the Japanese that came to my aid – my lawyers worked pro-bono, the Japanese press publicized my case, and several Japanese individuals offered support" (interview with Han Jŏng Sŏk, 30 March 1999, Tokyo). As the movement gained significant exposure in 1985, however, Mindan began to encourage Korean residents to "reserve" their fingerprints without necessarily violating Japanese law (Strausz 2006: 651). Soon thereafter, South Korea began to put considerable pressure on Japan to abolish the fingerprinting requirement and, after Japan and South Korea signed the 1991 Memorandum of Understanding that clarified the legal status of Korean residents in Japan, the Diet abolished the fingerprinting requirement for permanent residents in 1993.

Local Voting Rights Movement

The antifingerprinting movement proved to be the most successful mass mobilization of Korean residents for a single cause in Japan's postwar history. Although diplomatic pressure from South Korea was critical in abolishing the fingerprinting requirement in 1993, few would deny the central role played by Korean grassroots movements. There have been no mass movements on the scale of the antifinger-printing movement since that time; nevertheless, subsequent social movements in the Korean community have followed its blueprint, developed alongside local movements of the 1970s and 1980s, of grassroots mobilization linked to regional networks of Korean and Japanese activists that appeal to local community citizenship, democracy, and international human rights norms. One of the central Korean movements that emerged in the late 1980s was the local voting rights movement.

Korean claims to voting rights dates back to the early postwar period when the Korean organization, Choryŏn, rallied for the reinstatement of voting rights for Korean residents together with calls for Korean representation in the Japanese government. Choryŏn's position, however, was based on the premise that Koreans, as "liberated nationals," should take part in Japan's democratic reconstruction alongside other Allied nationals. The contemporary movement for local voting rights, in contrast, centers on the idea that Korean and other foreign residents are permanent, contributing members of Japanese society who deserve equal citizenship rights, which was the basis for other Korean movements in the 1970s and 1980s. A citizens' organization in the city of Kita-Kyūshū was the first to make a formal petition for the enfranchisement of foreign residents in the city's local elections in 1975. They declared that Korean and other tax-paying foreign residents who had lived in Japan for three or more years should be given voting rights in local elections, citing examples of Western democracies that had granted voting rights to foreign residents or were in the process of doing so by the mid-1970s, including Canada, Denmark, and New Zealand.

Following the aforementioned local victories in gaining social welfare rights for Korean residents in the 1970s and 1980s, Mintōren made suffrage for foreign residents one of its central priorities in 1987. Again, Korean and other foreign residents made their claims through protests, direct lobbying of local officials, and litigation. Between 1993 and 1996 alone, more than 1,200 local governments submitted resolutions to grant local voting rights to foreign residents. By 2005, this number rose to more than 1,500 and an additional 170 municipalities had passed ordinances to allow foreign residents to vote in local referenda. As I mention in Chapter 1, a number of local governments also began to establish assemblies and advisory councils to represent the interests and opinions of foreign residents in their communities around this time, such as the Kawasaki City Representative Assembly for Foreign Residents that was established in 1996 and the Tokyo Metropolitan Government's Foreign Citizens' Advisory Council that was established in 1997.

Litigation became a highly useful tool to draw attention to the movement at the national level. A lawsuit filed by eleven Korean residents in 1990 claimed that the exclusion of tax-paying permanent residents, who were previously Japanese nationals until the 1952 San Francisco Peace Treaty, was illegal. A group of Korean residents formed the political party *Zainichitō* (Zainichi Party) in 1992 and ran an election campaign for several Korean-resident candidates during the upper-house elections that year. During the following year, the party brought a lawsuit against the Japanese government claiming the right of foreign residents not only to run for elections but also, with sufficient votes, to win seats in an election. In a landmark decision, the Supreme Court ruled in 1995 that granting local voting rights to foreign residents was not unconstitutional, which directly contradicted the stance of opponents to local voting rights and added considerable momentum to the movement.

Unlike previous movements involving citizenship rights, Mindan supported the local voting rights movement relatively early on and offered its official support in 1994, when it organized a petition campaign. By 2002, Mindan had declared the suffrage issue its top priority in the 1 January edition of its official newspaper, *Mindan Shimbun*. Chongryun remains opposed to the movement, arguing that suffrage would accelerate Korean assimilation into Japanese society. Mindan's early support of the movement at the closing stages of the antifingerprinting movement helped move the issue to the purview of the South Korean government. During Kim Dae Jung's presidency (1998–2002) in particular, the issue became a central source of negotiation between South Korea and Japan concerning the Korean-resident population. During his first visit to Japan as president in 1998, Kim brought up the local voting rights issue in his meeting with Prime Minister Obuchi Keizō. Kim subsequently vowed to address the issue in South Korea, and, after a series of meetings among government officials, South Korean and Japanese nongovernmental organizations (NGOs), and Korean-resident activists, South Korea became the first Asian country to grant local voting rights to foreign residents in 2005 (implemented in 2006).

Finally, in July 2000, the New Komeito Party introduced a bill to the Diet that would grant local voting rights to foreign residents. As I discuss in the following chapter, the bill had the support of members in the ruling coalition, including the Liberal Democratic Party's (LDP) Secretary-General Nonaka Hiromu, as well as the opposition Democratic Party and Communist Party. It also generated heated opposition from conservative members of the LDP, who voted against it. Between 2000 and 2006, the New Komeito Party submitted the local voting rights bill to the Diet six times, but the bill remains under debate as of this publication. Although the bill gained renewed support when Ozawa Ichiro, the president of the Democratic Party of Japan, pledged to work toward its passage following his January 2008 meeting with Lee Sang-deuk, South Korea's National Assembly Deputy Speaker and

special envoy of President Lee Myung Bak, conservative members of
the LDP remain adamantly opposed to the bill.

THE "KOREAN PROBLEM" IN POSTWAR JAPAN

Postwar Japan's citizenship policies that linked nationality with ethnocultural identity established the boundaries for negotiation between
state and nonstate actors. Although Japanese state policies excluded
Koreans from the community of Japanese nationals, they did not
expel them from the boundaries of the Japanese nation-state. As a
developing democracy, Japan could not resort to such measures as
genocide, mass imprisonment, or forced repatriation to manage the
"Korean problem."[16] Instead, immigration and citizenship policies
served as important control mechanisms for shaping Japanese racial
politics and justifying the political, social, and economic exclusion of
former colonial subjects. Using the American model, Japan's immigration policies protected Japan's borders from unwanted immigration, which included new migrants as well as returnees among the
Korean population. Meanwhile, Japan's citizenship policies sought
to ensure the political and cultural assimilation of former colonial
subjects who chose to remain in Japan and become Japanese nationals, assuming that the remainder of the noncitizen population would
repatriate.

Nevertheless, postwar immigration and citizenship policies that
excluded former colonial subjects from the body politic did not result in
the latter's retreat from Japanese politics and society. Instead, Korean
political engagement varied according to the historical context and,
specifically, the political opportunities that were available to the community. As American Occupation officials embarked upon the task of
transforming a defeated former imperial power to a modern democracy, Koreans viewed themselves as participants in leading Japan's
postwar reconstruction. Rather than interpret their foreign citizenship
as the source of the community's powerlessness, Koreans objected
to their treatment as Japanese nationals by Occupation authorities,

---

[16] However, a number of Japanese officials made unsuccessful attempts to initiate the
process of forced repatriation and some Korean political prisoners were freed only
under specific conditions (usually repatriation).

arguing that they belonged to the victorious Allied armies with rights and privileges that *surpassed* the defeated Japanese.

Cold War politics shifted the goals of American policy in Japan, which led to the dissolution of the major postwar Korean organization in Japan and the establishment of the pro–North Korea Chongryun and pro–South Korea Mindan. Although foreign citizenship status continued to be the basis for political organization within the community, Chongryun and Mindan reproduced the asymmetries of Japanese citizenship to equate Korean nationality with Korean ethnic identity in order to garner support for their competing homeland regimes. Despite their extreme political rhetoric, both organizations remained relatively stable and autonomous throughout the Cold War largely due to their declarations of noninvolvement in Japanese domestic politics. In return for organizational survival, Mindan and Chongryun facilitated the creation of a politically docile community vis-à-vis the Japanese state. Hence, repressive state policies *alone* did not create a disempowered community. Under Mindan and Chongryun's leadership, the Occupation's solution to the "Korean problem" remained intact: one could either abandon any Korean cultural affiliation and become a "proper" Japanese citizen or accept the limitations of noncitizen status to preserve one's Korean identity.

As native-born generations of Korean residents came of age, Mindan and Chongryun's legitimacy in the Korean community began to fade and the contradictions of Japanese citizenship and immigration policies vis-à-vis Koreans began to unravel. The Occupation's solution to the "Korean problem" in the realm of Japanese national security was no longer sufficient in the realm of Japanese democracy. Although many Koreans have maintained their Korean nationalities, most do not intend to repatriate to Korea, as was the assumption in the early postwar years. Accordingly, new movements by younger generations of Korean activists pose a direct challenge to the institution of Japanese citizenship and its many layers of practice in Japanese society.

In effect, the "Korean problem" has come full circle from the Occupation: Korean groups are asserting their rights as foreign residents and forcing the Japanese government to reconsider its citizenship and immigration policies. The following chapter explores the ways that Korean activists have responded to the challenges and opportunities of the post–Cold War era, focusing on three approaches to diversifying

democracy in Japan. New generations of Korean activists have reinterpreted the meaning of citizenship as identity *and* practice as they
engage in "citizens movements" to democratize Japanese society. As
these groups search for a new foundation for defining Korean identity
beyond nationality alone, they have begun to adopt political strategies
that require radical change in a society that has heretofore purported
cultural and ethnic homogeneity.

4

Citizenship as Political Strategy

In July 2000, the New Komeito Party, a member of the ruling coalition, drafted a bill to grant foreign residents the right to vote in local elections. Although the local voting rights bill gained support from the ruling coalition and opposition parties, conservative members of the Liberal Democratic Party (LDP) argued that the bill was unconstitutional and that granting voting rights to foreign residents would reduce the already low naturalization rates among Korean residents. Such a move, they claimed, would provide further incentive for Koreans to maintain their "privileged status" without declaring allegiance to Japan. As a countermeasure, the LDP drafted legislation in 2001 aimed at easing naturalization requirements for special permanent residents. The proposed legislation would allow special permanent residents to acquire Japanese citizenship by declaration alone and would involve a simple registration process. Proponents of the bill argue that Koreans in Japan have already assimilated into Japanese society and that easing naturalization procedures would give them greater freedom to choose their nationalities.

Both bills, which as of this publication have remained under debate in the Diet since their introduction, appear to benefit the Korean-resident community in Japan; nevertheless, Korean reactions have been mixed. Most Korean activists support the voting rights bill, for which a wide section of the Korean community has lobbied since the mid-1980s. In contrast, Korean activists have been among the most vocal opponents of the naturalization bill. Rather than embrace the bill for reducing the barriers to full citizenship for the Korean community, many Korean activists contend that the bill is an attempt to reverse the rights gained by years of activism and that it is a continuation of Japanese state efforts to forcibly assimilate Koreans into the Japanese mainstream (Kashiwazaki 2006).[1]

Based on their legal status, we would expect social movements in Japan's Korean community to center around the quest for political inclusion, in the form of citizenship acquisition, similar to the movements of historically disenfranchised communities elsewhere. However, even as Japanese leaders have encouraged Koreans to become Japanese nationals from the 1980s, Korean activists have not mobilized the community to do so. Why have Korean organizations focused their efforts on gaining partial citizenship rights for foreign residents and rejected opportunities to gain full membership for the Korean community?

This chapter examines the ways that Korean organizations have mobilized the community around their foreign citizenship status in the post–Cold War era to gain political visibility and strength in Japan. Rather than naturalize and become an overlooked, statistically insignificant section of the voting population, Korean activists use their non-citizen status as the basis for political empowerment. Especially in recent years, native-born Korean activists have found strength in the community's position as the oldest, most established foreign-resident group in Japan. They have thus emerged as leaders of the country's burgeoning immigrant population. The following section analyzes the logic of using foreign citizenship as a strategy for political empowerment by focusing on the costs and benefits of political incorporation for the Korean community. I then discuss the context in which this strategy emerged and flourished following significant shifts in Japan's political and social landscape. Finally, I examine three approaches to citizenship that have shaped contemporary Korean movements to bring about social change and political empowerment for the foreign-resident community.

---

[1] A minority of Korean proponents, such as Chŏng Dae-kyun (2001), a second-generation Korean resident and professor at Tokyo Metropolitan University, maintains that Korean acquisition of Japanese nationality will widen the definition of Japanese identity, leading to a "multiethnic, multicultural and global community" (quoted in Asahi Shimbun, 11 January 2002).

THE COSTS AND BENEFITS OF POLITICAL INCORPORATION

Given the rising number of naturalizations within the Korean community, why do Korean community activists continue to seek rights and recognition as foreign citizens, and reject opportunities to gain full citizenship for their community? At first glance, the explanation to this puzzle may appear to lie in organizational survival. We might surmise that Korean organizations are attempting to retain their membership base by discouraging their members from naturalizing. However, such a strategy is largely self-defeating and short-lived.

First, the rising number of naturalizations within the Korean community indicates that the incentives of naturalization outweigh the disincentives for a growing segment of the community. Although the naturalization rate had been increasing steadily since the mid-1950s, the number of Koreans who naturalized in the late 1990s nearly doubled the figures of the 1980s. Since 1995, approximately ten thousand Korean residents have naturalized every year (see Table 1.3). Aside from the two most prominent advantages of full citizenship – voting rights and the right to run for public office – acquiring Japanese citizenship yields immediate material gains, such as freedom from employment restrictions, eligibility for fellowships and scholarships limited to Japanese nationals, as well as the advantages of carrying a Japanese passport in international travel.[2] In addition, as many of my interviewees pointed out, Japanese nationals often receive preferential treatment for bank loans over foreign nationals. Although special permanent residency provides a secure legal status, acquiring Japanese nationality affords individuals protection from deportation and the rollback of legal rights and/or social benefits for permanent foreign residents. Permanent foreign residents must also apply for reentry permits every few years. Finally, we cannot discount the symbolic and practical benefits of full citizenship status.

Conversely, the material costs of naturalization for individual native-born Korean residents are relatively low. The stated requirements for naturalization applicants are easily met by most adult Korean

---

[2] A Japanese passport provides greater convenience in international travel than does a South Korean passport. E.g., Japanese passport holders often do not have to apply for visas to countries where there is a requirement that South Korean passport holders do so.

TABLE 4.1. *Marriage Trends of Korean Residents in Japan*

Year	Total Registered Marriages	Married to (North and South) Korean Nationals		Married to Japanese Nationals[a]	
		No. of Cases	%	No. of Cases	%
1960	3,524	2,315	65.7	1,172	33.3
1965	5,693	3,681	64.7	1,971	34.6
1970	6,892	3,879	56.3	2,922	42.4
1975	7,249	3,618	49.9	3,548	48.9
1980	7,255	3,061	42.2	4,109	56.6
1985	8,627	2,404	27.9	6,147	71.3
1990	13,934	2,195	15.8	11,661	83.7
1995	8,953	1,485	16.6	7,363	82.2
1996	8,804	1,438	16.3	7,261	82.5
1997	8,540	1,269	14.9	7,178	84.1

[a] The category of "Japanese Nationals" may include those of Korean ancestry.
Source: Japan Ministry of Health and Welfare 1961–97.

residents (see Table 1.1). In addition, because Article 9 of the postwar constitution prohibits Japan from having a standing army, naturalized citizens are not subject to military duty. Furthermore, given their high levels of cultural assimilation, most native-born Korean residents would not have to make significant changes to their lifestyles to become Japanese citizens. In terms of language, culture, and education, the majority of Korean residents have more in common with the Japanese than they do with South or North Koreans in the peninsula. Likewise, the symbolic costs of naturalization are not terribly high for native-born Korean residents who are generations removed from the experience of Japan's colonial era. Although many Korean residents consider themselves to be ethnically Korean, few feel any national affiliation to the North or South Korean states. Moreover, for many in the Korean community, Japanese nationality is no longer considered a betrayal of one's Korean identity; on the contrary, younger generations in the Korean community are increasingly emphasizing the level of one's Korean "consciousness" (*ishiki*). To be sure, these factors have likely contributed to the growth of naturalizations within the Korean-resident community since 1995.

Second, intermarriages between Koreans and Japanese now constitute more than 80 percent of all marriages among Korean residents, and the children of such marriages have been eligible for Japanese nationality through either their father's or mother's nationality since 1985 (see Table 4.1). Thus, we can speculate that the majority of Koreans in Japan will be Japanese nationals in the decades to come. Consequently, discouraging members from naturalizing is not only an ineffective strategy, but it also excludes a significant and growing portion of the Korean community.

A more effective strategy for organizational survival would involve changing membership rules to include Japanese nationality holders in order to retain their membership and changing the focus of their activities to attain greater political representation within Japanese electoral politics by building strong voting blocs and supporting Korean candidates for political office. Korean activists could work within the system as citizens with full rights rather than outside of the system as foreigners. Although numerous organizations have implemented the first change regarding membership rules, none has implemented the second change (although several individuals have naturalized in order to run for political office).

In order to implement the second change, Korean activists could lobby for the insertion of *jus soli* (birthright citizenship) into Japan's citizenship laws, so that native-born residents from the third generation would automatically gain Japanese nationality, and pressure lawmakers to pass the LDP-sponsored bill that would ease naturalization procedures for native-born residents. Given that both of these measures have been implemented in other advanced industrial democracies and the second measure in particular has the support of the dominant party, one or both of these proposals could gain traction in the Diet. As I mentioned earlier in this chapter, however, the most vocal opposition to the LDP bill has come from Korean and other proimmigrant activists.

If the LDP bill were to pass, native-born permanent residents, most of whom are Korean, could gain Japanese nationality through a simple process of registration or declaration, similar to second-generation foreign residents in a number of European countries that have descent-based citizenship policies. To be sure, the most commonly cited disincentive of naturalization among native-born Korean residents in Japan today is the paperwork involved in the application process. Although there is no fee associated with naturalization applications – which

reached $675 in the United States as of this publication – natural-
ization applicants often pay significant amounts in attorney fees to
prepare documents verifying their family histories. For those who elect
to prepare the documents themselves, the process of document preparation alone can take months or even years. Because most naturalization applicants in the Korean community have not lived in Japan for
longer than three generations, this process necessarily entails requesting family registration documents from the local hometown offices
of an applicant's parent, grandparent, or great-grandparent in South
Korea. Interviews with local officials during the naturalization process have also been known to be stressful, and sometimes humiliating,
for naturalization applicants. Soo Im Lee, a professor at Ryukoku
University who naturalized in 2001, recounts that there was an aston-
ishing lack of privacy during the interview process. As she sat in the
waiting room awaiting her interview, she recalls that she could hear
every detail of the interview in progress, which was highly disturbing
given the personal nature of the interview. During her own interview,
the local presiding official claimed that her desire to be a Japanese
national was too weak and that she did not exhibit enough humility
(interview with Soo Im Lee, 8 September 2008, Tokyo; also see Lee
2002).

    Given these circumstances, it may appear that Korean activists pro-
vide a profound disservice to the Korean community by thwarting state
efforts to ease naturalization procedures for native-born residents and,
instead, focusing their efforts on gaining additional rights for foreign
residents, rather than specifically addressing how Koreans can gain
political power as Japanese nationals. To be sure, the movement for
local voting rights for foreign residents that gained headway in Japan
from the 1990s (to the present) is consistent with patterns of claims
making by foreign residents in other industrial democracies. Since the
1970s, the case for expanding the franchise to noncitizen residents has
gained momentum in Europe and, more recently, in the United States.
In Japan's case, however, the primary beneficiaries of this movement's
success – which has been spearheaded by Korean activists from as early
as 1975 – would be the growing immigrant population of Chinese,
Nikkei Brazilians, Filipinos, and South Koreans, rather than prewar
Korean immigrants and their descendants. If not organizational survival, what is the logic behind mobilizing for foreign-resident rights

when Japanese nationals will soon outnumber foreign nationals in the community of prewar Korean immigrants and their descendants?

As I demonstrate in the remaining sections, Korean activists in contemporary Japan have focused less on the struggle for policy reforms and more on a battle of ideas since the 1990s. Rather than organizational survival, I argue that Korean organizations have mobilized the Korean community around their foreign citizenship status as a tool to gain political visibility in Japanese civil society. Decades of harsh discrimination, legal insecurity, and individual "passing" as Japanese have contributed to the Korean community's social and political invisibility, which contemporary Korean activists view as the community's central problem. Direct forms of discrimination against Korean residents – ranging from ethnic slurs to employment discrimination – are less visible in present-day Japanese society than they were two decades ago; nonetheless, most Korean residents use their Japanese aliases in their daily lives and continue to "pass" as Japanese. Although the high rates of intermarriages between Korean and Japanese nationals may signal harmonious relations between the two communities, the numerous cases in which such marriages are contingent upon the naturalization of the Korean bride or groom suggest otherwise. As one Korean activist describes,

Direct discrimination against Koreans has lessened such that some Koreans say that they have never experienced discrimination. But these are Koreans who continue to use their Japanese names. Most Korean parents give their children Japanese names so that they will not experience discrimination.... Discrimination in Japan is indirect, difficult to discern, and hard to identify.... This type of discriminatory practice is often more severe than institutional discrimination because it's so hard to recognize and prove.... (Bae Jung Do, lecture, Yokohama Asia Festival, 27 October 1998)

Naturalization tends to exacerbate the problem of "passing" among some Koreans. For example, some naturalized Koreans have kept their Korean backgrounds secret even from their children (Field 1993: 644; Asakawa 2003: 140–50). Most Koreans who naturalize are either apolitical or uninterested in associating with other Koreans. Politically active individuals are a small minority within this group. Moreover, Korean activists have found that it is exceedingly difficult to mobilize Japanese nationals of Korean descent. Not only are they hard to locate (most have Japanese names and do not identify themselves as being of Korean descent), but also they are not interested in either publicizing their Korean identities or fighting against discrimination that they feel they no longer experience. As another activist explains, there are more Japanese nationals in the Korean community than ever before, yet the same problems linger (interview with Suh Jung Woo, 17 August 1999, Osaka).

Despite their social invisibility and their small numbers in relation to the dominant Japanese population, Korean residents, who make up less than 1 percent of the total Japanese population, have exercised considerable political clout specifically as foreign residents. As Ehashi Takashi (1998), a leading activist from the 1965 and 1970 protests against the U.S.-Japan Mutual Security Treaty (*Anpo*) protests, remarked about Korean movements in the 1970s to remove the nationality requirement in civil service employment, "there are probably only 1,000 people or so working on the issue of the Nationality Clause, with perhaps 100 at the center. It is amazing to me that a couple of hundred people have been able to budge a society of 120 million people" (cited in Wender 2005: 229).

Unlike Mindan and Chongryun, however, new generations of Korean activists are not engaged in a futile effort to prevent Koreans from becoming Japanese nationals, because few would deny that Japanese nationals will outnumber foreign nationals in the Korean community in decades to come. To be sure, the emphasis is less on *Korean* nationality – especially its relationship to the North and South Korean states – and more on *foreign* citizenship status. By expanding the practice of citizenship at the grassroots level to include all residents of Japan regardless of nationality, this strategy aims to transform the meaning of citizenship in Japan so that 1) it is no longer associated with ethnocultural identity; 2) citizenship rights are not held exclusively by Japanese nationals; and 3) citizenship acquisition becomes an empowering choice rather than a disempowering process in which the naturalization applicant must ask for the "privilege of naturalization" (interview with Soo Im Lee, 8 September 2008, Tokyo). By changing the symbolic significance and institutionalized privileges associated with Japanese nationality – the basis for social and legal discrimination in postwar Japan – new generations of Korean activists aim to diversify Japanese society, such that "passing" as Japanese becomes not only unnecessary but also meaningless because "Japanese" would no longer be associated with a single ethnocultural identity. This approach, therefore, is distinctly geared toward bottom-up change. For many Korean activists, top-down efforts to ease the political incorporation of Korean residents would result not in social change but the co-optation of Korean social movements. They view the LDP's proposed bill to ease naturalization requirements for permanent foreign residents as a classic attempt to quell dissent through strategic concessions. Although the concessions – eliminating the requirement to adopt a Japanese name for naturalization applicants and the proposed measure to eliminate the formal naturalization process entirely for native-born permanent residents – are significant, they, nevertheless, do not contradict earlier state efforts to resolve the "Korean problem," which has been to make the Korean-resident population invisible through assimilation and naturalization. Given the Korean community's high rates of cultural assimilation as well as their phenotypical similarity to the dominant Japanese population, facilitating the process by which Koreans acquire Japanese nationality would likely exacerbate the Korean community's social and political invisibility. Korean identity in Japan would then become associated with postwar South Korean immigrants, thus eradicating the category of Koreans as a historical minority in Japan and burying an episode in Japan's history that most would rather forget. Furthermore, by making Japanese citizens of an already indistinguishable Korean-resident population, the state can reappropriate the dominant discourse on Japanese cultural homogeneity and reinvent Japan as a "closed" country that cannot manage the chaos of opening its doors to foreigners.

The long-term goal, therefore, is to win the battle of ideas over immigration, citizenship, and, more broadly, democratic inclusion in contemporary Japan so that policy reforms reflect on-the-ground practices. Under present conditions – in which Japanese nationality continues to be associated with ethnocultural identity among Japanese and non-Japanese residents alike and in which antiimmigrant hostility and nationality-based discrimination compel foreign residents to pass as Japanese – policies that would facilitate naturalization for Korean residents would likely serve the state's interest in assimilating the population. These same policies would take on an entirely different meaning if they were products of grassroots movements and pressure. As one activist puts it, "According to Japan's official mono-ethnic [*tanitsu minzoku*] principle, nationality [*kokuseki*], citizenship [*shimin*], and nation [*minzoku*] are the exclusive terrain of the Japanese. A grass-roots approach to the citizen [*shimin*] concept by contrast includes Japanese nationals [*kokumin*] as well as foreign residents" (interview with Yi In-Ha, 2 September 1999, Kawasaki).

THREE APPROACHES TO DIVERSIFYING
JAPANESE DEMOCRACY

Since the 1990s, there has been a distinct shift in Korean political activism from the entrenchment of the Korean community to the diversification of Japanese democracy. Unlike the homeland-focused, insular Mindan and Chongryun whose engagement with the Japanese state was largely reactive to direct violations of Korean human rights in Japan, new generations of Korean activists have taken a proactive approach in order to bring about social change in Japan. In partic-ular, they have reinterpreted the meaning of citizenship as identity *and* practice as they engage in movements to democratize Japanese society.

Korean social movements of the 1970s and 1980s aimed to secure institutionalized rights for foreign residents and, ultimately, recogni-tion of their humanity. In order to establish the minimum conditions under which prewar Korean immigrants and their descendants could carry out their lives in Japan as permanent residents, Korean activists sought access to health insurance, social welfare benefits, public-sector jobs, and pensions for the Korean-resident community. This movement for partial citizenship rights was nothing short of a civil rights move-ment seeking recognition of a subordinate group's humanity, equality, and full citizenship.

Following a series of events and legal victories (discussed in Chap-ter 3) that conferred upon Korean residents a secure legal status, access to numerous social welfare benefits, and greater opportunities in pri-vate and public-sector employment, Korean social movements became less confrontational and more localized. Although Korean activists continue to engage in lobbying, litigation, and protests, these tools tend to be reserved for specific issues and cases, with the exception of the national movement for foreign-resident enfranchisement. In this way, Korean movements have paralleled other social movements of 1960s and 1970s Japan where mass mobilization, protests, and landmark legal cases were eventually met with concessions – mostly minimal – from Japanese officials, which then had a demobilizing effect on the movements. As Susan Pharr (1990) argues, this minimalist concession strategy was a form of conflict aversion that made the movements less contentious and more issue-based. Patricia MacLaughlan (2003) notes further that, in the case of the consumer movement, there was a distinct shift from lobbying state officials to increasing public awareness of the new rights and privileges gained by the reforms and monitoring their enforcement by local governments. A key difference between Korean and other Japanese social movements is that limited government concessions have not necessarily depoliticized the former.

On the contrary, the limited victories of the 1970s and 1980s have only pushed activists to turn their attention to their broader communities – whether in the form of their local communities, the wider foreign-resident population, or Japanese society as a whole – in espousing social change. Korean activists, especially since the 1990s, have aimed to remove the roots of discrimination against Koreans in Japan, which they locate in postwar Japan's framework of nationality. Most Korean activists argue that social and structural discrimination in Japanese society is based on nationality; therefore, they aim to gain social and structural equality in Japan specifically for those who are the targets of discrimination: foreign residents. In order to eliminate nationality-based discrimination, foreign residents must be recognized as equal members of Japanese society regardless of their nationalities.

National- and local-level reforms implemented directly or indirectly in response to Korean claims strengthened the position from which Korean activists could make further demands for social change – with a secure legal status that would allow them to engage in open protests without fear of deportation and social welfare benefits and broad employment opportunities that underscored the incongruity between Korean residents' daily lives as full members of their communities and their disenfranchisement as foreign nationals. They were also followed by the onset of heightened immigration to Japan.

Changes in Japan's political and social landscape since the late 1980s gave Korean activists an unparalleled opportunity to shape public debate on the problems of immigration and citizenship in Japan. As I discuss in the following chapter, the demand for unskilled labor resulted in the rapid influx of foreign workers from developing countries in the 1980s and ultimately led to the phenomenal growth of immigrant communities in Japan. In the absence of national immigrant incorporation policies, local governments and civil-society organizations have stepped in to provide services aimed at integrating new immigrant groups into Japanese society. As a consequence, the issues and causes long championed by Korean activists – such as multicultural education, voting rights for foreign residents, proposals for antidiscrimination legislation, and programs to raise awareness of discrimination in Japanese society – are at the center of public debate. These developments have presented Korean activists with a new set of challenges and opportunities to empower not just Koreans but the entire foreign community in Japan.

Korean activists have responded to their new opportunities in different ways. Although some have transformed themselves into umbrella organizations for all foreign residents and their advocates, others continue to focus on the Korean-resident community. This chapter divides contemporary movements in the Korean community, especially since the 1990s, roughly into three categories: 1) grassroots organizations that concentrate on local communities; 2) local and national organizations that focus on issues specific to the Korean-resident community; and 3) research organizations that engage less in grassroots politics and more in the "battle of ideas." Each of these groups is rooted in distinct approaches to citizenship and Korean political empowerment in Japan. Local grassroots organizations in the first category base their activism on the "resident as citizen" concept that views foreign residents as citizens of their local communities with attendant rights and duties. Korean organizations in the second category base their movements on what I call the "group-rights approach," which puts emphasis on the specificities of the Korean community's history in Japan. The last category of Korean organizations refers primarily to those that serve as a forum for debate and intellectual exchange, centered on the concept of "cosmopolitan citizenship." In a number of cases, the various Korean organizations under discussion overlap in their approaches, claims, and, in the case of the last group, members.

Local Citizenship: Resident as Citizen

The local citizenship approach comes directly out of Mintōren, the organization that emerged from the Hitachi Employment Discrimination Trial in the early 1970s based on a loose coalition of Korean and Japanese activists. As I discuss in Chapter 3, Mintōren was established as a decentralized grassroots organization that had chapters in areas with relatively large Korean populations, such as Osaka, Kanagawa, and Kawasaki. These local chapters were loosely tied together based on two central concepts: 1) "living together in harmony" (*tomoni ikiru*), modeled after the cooperative practices and joint leadership between Korean and Japanese activists; and 2) the resident as citizen concept, which maintained that Korean residents were full members of their local communities worthy of equal rights and treatment. The local organizations that emerged out of Mintōren have become relatively independent entities with closer ties to their local governments than with other former Mintōren chapters. Most of these organizations work in close cooperation with their local governments and many have become nonprofit organizations (NPOs) that receive funding from their local governments. The activities in which these organizations engage vary according to the needs of foreign residents in each local community but tend to revolve around educational programs for foreign-resident adults and children and welfare services for the elderly.

One of the most widely acknowledged organizations of this type in the Kantō region is the Kawasaki Fureaikan (Fureai Hall), a public organization for cultural exchange primarily between Japanese and Korean residents, which is located in the heart of the Sakuramoto district of Kawasaki city.[3] This area contains a large concentration of Korean laborers and their descendants who were enlisted by the Japanese government to build military factories in the city during World War II. According to the *Kawasaki Fureaikan Tenth Year Anniversary Magazine* (13 June 1998), the stated purpose of the center is to "eradicate discrimination and create a tolerant local society"

---

3 The name *fureai* comes from the Japanese verb *fureau*, which means "to open one's heart" to others.

and to "let everyone live up to his or her potential." As a nonprofit organization, the Fureaikan receives its funding from the local Kawasaki government. The staff is comprised of a more or less equal number of Korean and Japanese residents of Kawasaki, while the clientele is about 80 percent Japanese and 20 percent non-Japanese, reflecting the makeup of the local population (interview with Bae Jung Do, 23 February 1999, Kawasaki).

Before the hall opened in 1988, the project stirred considerable controversy in the city. In 1987, the Kawasaki city government planned to build the hall and assign administrative responsibility to the Seikyusha (Blue Hill Association), an ethnic Korean social welfare foundation set up in 1973 to provide after-school activities for children of Korean and Japanese residents in the area. Local Japanese residents opposed the construction of the hall because they believed Koreans would dominate (*Japan Times*, 22 August 1987). To overcome these objections, the city assigned three Japanese municipal officials to work at the center, including one who served as the first director. In 1990, Bae Jung Do, a second-generation Korean resident and Mintōren activist, replaced the Japanese director.

Despite the controversy surrounding its opening, the Fureaikan eventually established itself as a central community resource for Kawasaki city residents. Although most Korean activists in Japan concentrated their activities on Korean human rights, the Fureaikan focused on the local responsibilities of Korean and Japanese residents alike. Hence, the goal of the Fureaikan is the horizontal integration of the local community rather than the entrenchment of the ethnic Korean community. Central to this approach is the appeal to citizenship in its broadest sense at the local level: citizenship is correlated with residence rather than nationality.

As Bae Jung Do explains, Kawasaki, like most other Japanese cities, lacks public facilities (or citizen spaces, *shiminkan*) in which the entire community can come together, with the exception of public libraries. Other community organizations such as senior citizen centers or support groups for foreigners tend to foster sectionalism, separating community members by age, sex, nationality, and so forth. The Fureaikan proposes to bring together not only Japanese and foreign-resident members of the community but also the young and the old, men and women, and various social, economic, and political groups. In recent years, the Fureaikan has addressed the needs of new foreign residents in Kawasaki, such as Filipinos, *Nikkei* Brazilians, Chinese, and newly arrived South Koreans.[4] Because the new foreign residents' concerns differ from those of Korean residents who have lived in Japan for generations, the Fureaikan has expanded its scope of activity. In addition to such activities as classes in Korean language and arts, social clubs for Korean and Japanese residents of all ages, and public lectures on Korean history and the Korean community in Japan, the community center now conducts Japanese-language classes for new immigrants – which had previously been offered in the form of literacy education for the elderly first generation of Korean residents – and training seminars for volunteers working with recent immigrants. The Fureaikan also hired a Filipina resident on its staff in 1998 who directs an after-school program for Filipino children called the *Dagat* Club.

Nevertheless, the Fureaikan's philosophy and activities have garnered criticism from segments of the local Japanese citizenry as well as some Korean community activists. Japanese critics claim that the Fureaikan privileges its Korean members and thereby engages in reverse discrimination. For example, the Fureaikan sponsors after-school activities specifically for Korean children through the *Kenari* Club, with the stated purpose of fostering Korean pride and solidarity.[5] Bae Jung Do notes that Korean-resident children, who spend most of their time with Japanese children, need a space where they can gain confidence in themselves in order to persevere in their local communities. In contrast, Japanese residents complained that the club unfairly excludes Japanese children who may want to learn about Korean culture. Korean critics, in turn, contend that Fureaikan activists invest too much energy and resources in the Japanese community. Former activists from Mintōren in Osaka as well as the Kawasaki Seikyusha question how much independence the Fureaikan can maintain when it receives funds from Kawasaki city. Some claim that the Fureaikan has been co-opted by Kawasaki city officials and have gone so far as to accuse the Fureaikan of being part of the "establishment" (interview, 7 September 2008, Osaka).

---

[4] Whereas Koreans made up 83% of all foreign residents in Kawasaki in 1985, they made up only 47% in 1996 (Ishizawa 1998).
[5] *Kenari* is the Korean name for *forsythia*, which is a traditional Korean plant.

Despite criticism from the Japanese and Korean communities, Fureaikan activists believe that participation in the local community is a crucial step in gaining social recognition for the broader foreign community in Japan. For example, Reverend Yi In-Ha, the founder of Seikyusha, observed in 1999 that the Korean community had reached a crossroads. The Japanese government has addressed most of the demands made during the civil rights movements of the 1970s and 1980s, such as the elimination of the fingerprinting requirement and the right to national health care and welfare benefits. In addition, overt discrimination toward Koreans is less visible today than it was twenty years ago. Consequently, younger generations of Koreans lack interest in joining civil rights movements and are increasingly choosing the route of assimilation and naturalization. But Yi explains that participation in the local community is qualitatively different from assimilation. Because Japanese society is changing rapidly, Yi feels that the next step in the civil rights movement is to create coalitions with other marginalized groups such as other foreign and minority groups, the disabled, women, and so forth. Winning basic rights for Koreans alone is not sufficient. He argues that a movement that does not work with other marginalized segments of the society loses its *raison d'être* as a citizens' movement. Hence, he calls himself a "transformist" as opposed to a "conformist" (interview with Yi In-Ha, 2 September 1999, Kawasaki).

The Fureaikan is part of a network of grassroots Korean and Japanese citizens' movements that seek to raise awareness of and tolerance for cultural diversity within Japanese society. Their activities range from movements for the readoption of Korean ethnic names (led by the group, *Minzokumei o torimodosu kai*) to movements for local voting rights for foreign residents. The logic of this approach is that when differences are shared – not polarized – Korean ethnicity will no longer be a private burden to hide but a public identity to celebrate. By conceptualizing an ethnic Korean culture within the larger Japanese society as commonsensical, these groups are attempting to transform the basis of Japanese social attitudes and state policies toward the Korean community from denial to toleration for differences in a multiethnic society (interview with Bae Jung Do, 23 February 1999, Kawasaki). In this sense, the culture concept in these movements is closely linked with power. The term *fureai* can be deeply subversive according to Bae Jung Do: "Not only does it suggest 'to meet,' 'to talk,' 'to learn,' and 'to make contact,' but also may denote 'to fight,' 'to struggle,' and 'to challenge'" (lecture, 27 October 1998).

Differences and Group Rights

During a recent interview, a second-generation Korean resident explained to me why he continues to focus his work specifically on the "oldcomer" or *zainichi* Korean community despite the growing numbers of recent South Korean immigrants, or "newcomers," in Japan:

Newcomers have no history in Japan. For example, one newcomer asked me why do you [oldcomer Koreans] feel the need to send your children to a Korean school instead of a regular Japanese school? Newcomers are voluntary immigrants who don't relate to our history as immigrants who were forced to come to Japan. They don't understand how important Korean schools are to us because they never had to struggle to recover their cultural heritage and language [in the aftermath of forced cultural assimilation during the Japanese colonial era in which Korean colonial subjects were forced to adopt Japanese names as well learn the Japanese language and punished when they spoke in Korean]. This stems from the difference between involuntary immigrants who are politicized because of their history versus voluntary immigrants who focus on economic success. (interview with Pak Yŏng Ho, 6 September 2008, Kawasaki)

This position lies at the core of the "group-rights" approach among Korean organizations that make claims to rights based on their history in Japan as former colonial subjects. Unlike claims made by indigenous populations in Japan and elsewhere, this approach closely parallels those made in the U.S. African American community that seek monetary and substantive reparations for historical injustices that they view as the root of present-day marginalization. Korean organizations in this category seek to secure cultural, social, and political rights that were taken away from former colonial subjects either during the colonial period or in the postwar era when Koreans were denationalized. They also seek reparations for past atrocities. Accordingly, most of the movements that take a group-rights approach make claims to educational rights in the forms of accredited Korean schools and ethnic education in Japanese schools, antidiscrimination legislation specifically for foreign residents, and historical redress and reparations for the first generation of former colonial subjects. Although the first two goals have the potential to benefit other foreign residents in Japan, the last one pertains exclusively to Korean and Chinese residents. One of the organizations in this category, *Zainichi Korian Jinken Kyōkai* (Human Rights Association for Koreans in Japan; hereafter referred to as HRKJ), was established in 1995 by former members of Mintōren's Osaka chapter to address what they viewed was a premature shift in focus from the Korean community to a Japan-centered multiculturalism. Mintōren's informal networking style of organization also became a source of friction for some of its members. After a series of victories achieved by Mintōren at the local level in the 1970s and 1980s, membership in the organization gradually dwindled, especially among Koreans. Eventually, Japanese members assumed leadership positions in a number of regional offices, such as the Kanagawa Mintōren. Suh Jung Woo, the president of HRKJ, describes why he decided to create a new organization separate from Japanese Mintōren members:

> We [Koreans] became a minority in our own movement.... I'm not saying that Japanese involvement is bad. But if the subjects of the movement – Koreans – do not stand up and raise their voices, how can the movement go forward?... The Japanese members had an idealistic vision of a colorblind society. Whereas Chongryun and Mindan are based on extreme ethnonationalism [*minzokushugi*], Mintōren was based on the principle that everyone is the same, that there are no differences between Koreans and Japanese. In other words, their [Mintōren's] philosophy is in complete and extreme opposition to ethnonationalism. Some younger members even claimed that the practice of Koreans marrying other Koreans was in itself reactionary, that it didn't embody the concept of coexistence [*kyōsei*]. If Japanese and Koreans are to live in harmony with one another [*tomo ni ikiru*], they argued, Koreans must marry Japanese [*nihonjin to kekkon suru beki da*]. (interview with Suh Jung Woo, 17 August 1999, Osaka)

With one central office in Osaka, HRKJ represents a larger network of Korean organizations that seeks the empowerment of the Korean community at the local and national levels. These organizations, based largely in Osaka, Fukuoka, and Hiroshima, include the *Osaka Kokusai Rikai Kyoiku Kenkyū Senta* (Osaka International Understanding Educational Research Center, also known as Korean Minority Japan or KMJ), the *Zenkoku Zainichi Korian Hogosha Kai*

(National Association of Korean Guardians), and the *Yao-shi Zainichi Korian Kōreisha Fukushi o Susumeru Kai* (Yao City Association for the Advancement of Korean Senior Citizens' Welfare). Although these organizations tackle national-level issues, their primary work centers on the concerns of Korean residents in their local communities. For example, the Osaka organizations focus their efforts on providing services to elderly first-generation Korean residents in the community and offer support to Koreans seeking to file lawsuits related to discrimination and reparations. Although the Hiroshima organizations engage in similar activities, they put emphasis on literacy education in their services for the elderly first generation, many of whom cannot read or write in either Japanese or Korean. The Fukuoka organizations, in contrast, concentrate their efforts on helping first-generation Koreans gain access to their pensions.

The stated purpose of HRKJ is to protect the rights of Koreans in Japan as well as to level the structural gap between Koreans and Japanese.[6] Their approach is two-pronged: centralized activities aimed at increasing Korean political power at the national level, and local, grassroots activities aimed at changing Japanese society. The target of the former approach is the Japanese legal system. Suh points out that Koreans lack legal and institutional protection in the Japanese legal system despite the democratic reforms enacted during the American Occupation of Japan. Although Japanese laws specifically address the rights of women, children, *burakumin*, and the disabled, among others, there is no mention of Korean residents in any Japanese law.

Further, Suh notes that discrimination against Koreans cannot be attributed solely to the ideology of Japan as a homogeneous nation: "Whites are of a different ethnicity, but they are not necessarily discriminated against. Why [do Japanese] discriminate against Asians, but not so much against Whites? They are both of different ethnicities" (interview with Suh Jung Woo, 17 August 1999, Osaka). Instead, he describes discrimination against Koreans and other Asians in general as an historical problem directly linked to Japanese imperialism: "Japan exploited Asian resources in order to catch up with the West.

---

[6] The following description of HRKJ and Suh's philosophy comes from three interviews that I conducted with Suh in Osaka on 17 August 1999, 8 September 1999, and 7 September 2008.

That is the pattern of Japan's modernization. Koreans in particular were the source of Japan's cheap labor" (interview with Suh Jung Woo, 17 August 1999, Osaka). For Suh, discrimination against Koreans stems from historically rooted, structural inequalities that must be addressed at the national level. Thus, Suh argues that the task at hand is to implement laws that specifically address Korean residents vis-à-vis the Japanese state. To that end, Suh maintains that Koreans need to acquire political power through political activities, lobbying, and, most importantly, establishing voting rights.

The basis for the latter approach – local activities aimed at changing Japanese society – lies in grassroots citizen movements. Suh maintains that the most important goal of these movements is to generate public discussion and debate about discrimination against Korean residents in Japanese society. With the rapid increase in the "newcomer" foreign population, government officials and the public alike often ignore the less visible problem of discrimination against the "oldcomer" population. Although the new era of "coexistence" (*kyōsei*) has reduced cases of direct discrimination against Koreans, it has also generated a false sense of security among Japanese and Koreans that discrimination no longer exists, according to Suh. Moreover, the burden of "coexisting" with the Japanese rests primarily on Koreans. But in some ways, Suh assumes that burden. Many of HRKJ's activities are aimed at educating the Japanese about the history of Koreans in Japan in order to change policies that are rooted in that history. Japanese officials have shown a greater willingness to grant political concessions to Koreans, such as social welfare benefits and proposals for local voting rights, than to acknowledge any wrongdoing in the past.

In order to reform state policies, Japanese society must first concede that the problem of discrimination against Koreans exists, according to Suh. Policies regarding prewar Korean immigrants and their descendants will, in turn, set precedents for those regarding new immigrants. Accordingly, HRKJ vigilantly documents and publicizes specific cases of discrimination against Korean residents and strives to identify causal factors. For example, in their study of employment discrimination cases, HRKJ found that most companies lacked basic diversity training within their employment systems. In response, HRKJ launched a monthly diversity-training seminar specifically for Japanese executives in 1998 called *Zainichi Korian no Jinken o Kangaeru Kai* (Research Organization on the Rights of Korean Residents in Japan).

Suh argues that Korean residents in Japan essentially have dual nationalities. Although they are legally North or South Korean nationals, they are de facto Japanese citizens. Nationality, for Suh, is simply a label. His South Korean nationality is nothing more than a frame (*waku*) or a receptacle (*iremono*) because the content (*nakami*) of his citizenship is Japanese. Although he has a South Korean passport, he points out that, "If someone were to ask me which country I am a national [*kokumin*] of, I wouldn't know how to answer" (interview with Suh Jung Woo, 8 September 1999, Osaka). Thus, for him, his informal Japanese "citizenship" is more important than his formal Korean nationality.

Nevertheless, he acknowledges that the reality of his citizenship status is unnatural, unresolved, and anomalous because Japanese citizenship policies remain rooted in the ideology of a homogeneous nation. He asserts that Japanese citizenship policies as they exist are not voluntary. As long as the Japanese citizen is defined as belonging to an ethnically homogeneous nation, Koreans cannot make the decision to naturalize of their own free will. Naturalization requires cultural assimilation. Furthermore, he is not convinced that formal Japanese citizenship status will necessarily eradicate discrimination against Koreans.

Suh notes that many fellow Koreans have accused him of being "assimilationist"; however, Suh considers Korean ethnonationalism in Japan to be the ultimate form of assimilation. He contends that the Korean community's adherence to the doctrine of ethnic homogeneity is a product of Japan's ethnonationalism. He questions the usage of the term *minzoku* (ethnicity, nation, race) within the Korean community. In the post–World War II era, the definition of the Korean *minzoku* has been associated with North or South Korea, not necessarily with the Korean diasporic groups that preceded the establishment of the ROK and the DPRK. But Korean society in Japan is distinctly different from that in North and South Korea. Nevertheless, he doubts that a single Korean resident would call him or herself a member of the Yamato (Japanese) *minzoku*. He believes it is unhealthy for Koreans to aspire to be part of either the Korean or Japanese *minzoku*, which he views as an oppressive construction. Korean residents, according to Suh, make up a Japanese minority group of Korean (*Chōsen*) ancestry and, accordingly, may legitimately claim the same rights as Japanese nationals.

Cosmopolitan Citizenship

Although the bulk of Korean movements have taken place at the grass-roots level, Korean activists have waged another subtle movement that has centered on the battle of ideas between Korean activists and Japanese officials regarding immigration and citizenship. As I discuss in the following chapter, postwar Japanese policies regarding foreign residents have centered on control and assimilation. Reforms that have widened rights for the Korean-resident community, for example in the early 1980s, reflect not only international human rights norms but also the policy positions of Ministry of Justice officials, such as Sakanaka Hidenori, who maintained that such reforms would compel Korean residents to further assimilate into Japanese society, naturalize, and, eventually, disappear. In this sense, these reforms were closer to "preemptive concessions," to use Susan Pharr's (1990) term, than socially transformative pieces of legislation.

In contrast, postwar Korean activism has centered on antiassimilation, confrontation, and social change. A wide spectrum of activists have aimed to dismantle the postwar framework of Japanese nationality, which equates nationality with ethnocultural identity, by disassociating nationality and citizenship through various means – some have pushed for local voting rights for foreign residents, others have called for the abolishment of the current naturalization (*kika*) system, and still others have focused on ethnic and multicultural education. Up until the 1980s, such differences between movements – despite their common goals – were the basis for divisive politics within the Korean community, especially because they were tainted by strong ideological disputes between the pro–North Korea Chongryun and the pro–South Korea Mindan.

Kim Kyu Il, a first-generation Korean resident, founded in 1982 the *Zainichi dōhō no seikatsu o kangaeru kai* (Korean Research Organization; hereinafter referred to as Kangaeru kai), which is an independent, nonprofit ethnic Korean organization, to provide a forum for Korean residents of all ideological stripes to engage in debate that would create a unified vision for the Korean-resident community. Although many of the group's members were active in other Korean organizations that engaged in such ideological battles, including Mindan, Chongryun, and Mintōren, they came together for forums and conferences based on a single source of commonality: they were all Waseda University graduates. Although the organization rarely engaged in grassroots movements – especially because most of its members refused to associate with one another outside of the Kangaeru kai meetings – it developed into a type of umbrella organization in which members could identify common problems facing the Korean-resident community across ideological lines and seek collective solutions.

Since its founding, the group has been supported entirely by contributions from the Korean-resident community and centered its activities around annual symposia and the publication of *Uri Seikatsu* [Our Lives], an annual journal of essays and articles related to the Korean community. Its members, most of whom have graduated from Waseda and other elite universities in Japan, consist primarily of professionals and intellectuals as well as activists from other Korean and Japanese voluntary associations. The vast array of political viewpoints held by its members, who range from first- to fourth-generation Korean residents – including Chongryun school graduates, bicultural activists, and some virulently anticommunist Mindan members – has often resulted in heated debates at the symposia.

For example, the 1998 symposium focused on four controversial themes: 1) the accelerating rate of naturalization in the Korean community; 2) patterns of marriage (concentrating especially on intermarriages); 3) the changing definition of Korean identity; and 4) assimilation. Although these topics have been raised at numerous conferences about Koreans in Japan, the coordinator of the 1998 symposium noted that this was the first symposium to cross ideological lines (especially between Mindan and Chongryun) in order to engage in a public debate about defining and discussing the Korean experience in Japan. According to Kim, it is precisely this form of open discussion that holds the group together and promotes the development of active citizens.

Kim believes that Japan is on the road to the creation of what he calls an "advanced citizen society" (*senshin shimin shakai*).[7] Although

[7] The following description of Kim Kyu Il's philosophy is taken from three interviews that I conducted with him on 3 February 1999, 30 March 1999, and 4 September 2008 in Tokyo as well as several published interviews conducted by Oh Son Sam in 1997 (Kim 1997). Although he is an established intellectual, Kim has not penned his own work largely because he is legally blind.

citizens of the nineteenth and twentieth centuries were members of class societies, Kim envisions that the twenty-first century will usher in a classless society of self-referential citizens whose rights are based on their common humanity rather than on the particularistic projects of individual states. This concept of citizenship is based on universal human rights and Kantian world citizenship, rather than on state-sponsored rights and national citizenship.

Kim is convinced that Japan, as an advanced industrial democracy with a "middle-class society," is close to reaching such an advanced citizen society, and that Koreans in Japan are crucial to its realization. In contemporary Japan, state and nonstate actors define the concept of the citizen narrowly as either a formal member of the state (*kokumin*) or a local resident (*jūmin*) according to Kim. In both cases, an arbitrary leader defines the subject and sets the parameters for his or her participation. Koreans in Japan have also engaged in this narrow form of citizenship either as national members of North or South Korea through Chongryun and Mindan or as local residents seeking integration into Japanese society. But for Kim, citizenship in its fullest sense entails transcending the narrow confines of authority and engaging in an interactive process of social criticism. As former colonial subjects and ongoing participants in Japan's postwar democratic project, Koreans in Japan are uniquely qualified and capable of critiquing Japanese societal constructs, and posing the questions important to the current historical moment.

Thus, according to Kim, efforts by the Japanese state and some segments of its population to completely assimilate Koreans into Japanese society are harmful for Japan's democratic development. Moreover, official statements denying the existence of a Korean minority within Japan contradict the level of progress already achieved in Japanese society. In a panel discussion on the idea of a "borderless society," Kim remarked, "In a city as cosmopolitan as Tokyo, is it so difficult to conceive of the existence of Korean residents within the city?" (Kim Kyu Il, Yokohama Asia Festival, 3 November 1998). The active Korean citizen opens up opportunities for debate, dialogue, and criticism. As Kim explains, "In a society that demands conformity and espouses homogeneity, the active presence of the Korean citizen pushes the boundaries of the state's universalizing discourse and opens up opportunities for reshaping social relations . . . the [exercise of citizenship by] the Korean citizen furthers the democratic development of the Japanese citizen" (interview with Kim Kyu Il, 30 March 1999, Tokyo).

Kim compares the role of the Korean citizen in Japanese society to that of other foreigners who opened Japan's borders and society. The "first" opening of Japan refers to Commodore Matthew Perry's arrival on Japan's shores in 1853 and the subsequent imposition of unequal treaties by American and European powers. This event led to the Meiji Restoration (1868–1912), a period characterized by rapid modernization and dramatic political, economic, and social change in Japan. The "second" opening denotes the implementation of democratic political and social institutions during the American Occupation of Japan (1945–52). Finally, Japan's scholarly and popular press has identified recent attempts at internationalization (*kokusaika*) as Japan's "third" opening. In Kim's words, "While the third 'opening' of Japan is supposed to be conducted by the Japanese people, I believe that Korean residents will be at the center of the pivotal change from nation-state to citizen-state" (Kim Kyu Il, Yokohama Asia Festival, 3 November 1998).

Since the late 1990s, the ideological divisions within the Korean-resident community have diminished significantly, and, Kim notes, younger generations of Korean residents have grown weary of "confrontational politics" within the Korean-resident community and vis-à-vis the Japanese state. He also points out that many Korean residents have gained influential positions in Japanese society as college professors, journalists in major newspapers, and executives in major corporations. As he puts it, "There is not a single area where Koreans have not penetrated [Japanese society]" (interview with Kim Kyu Il, 4 September 2008, Tokyo). Accordingly, Korean residents have an unprecedented opportunity to influence Japanese society from positions of leadership. Especially with the so-called Korea-boom (*hanryu* in Korean; *kanryu* in Japanese) in Japan, in which South Korean popular culture has gained widespread attention and recognition, Kim argues that Koreans – as members of Japanese society – must take up the responsibility to reshape the public sphere through active citizenship. Kim's engagement in the "battle of ideas," therefore, is a type of citizenship practice employed by a growing segment of the Korean-resident population that does not fit conventional understandings of political participation but, at the same time, is not apolitical.

Kim's vision of citizenship coincides with that of Bae Jung Do and Suh Jung Woo in its emphasis on participation and responsibility over rights and demands. All three make strong distinctions between the instrumentalist view of nationality at the state level, and the interactive interpretation of citizenship at the local and international levels. Although the three approaches differ in their particular projects, they are nonetheless based on the premise that Koreans are permanent and vital participants in Japanese society.

EXPANDING THE BOUNDARIES OF CITIZENSHIP

Although the goals and strategies of Korean citizens' movements vary – ranging from efforts to gain specific rights for former colonial subjects of Korean descent to local grassroots movements to provide support and multicultural education for foreign communities to activities aimed at challenging popular conceptions of Japanese national identity and raising public awareness of social discrimination in Japan – they converge in their mobilization around foreign citizenship: as a legal status worthy of civil, social, and political rights akin to Japanese nationals; as a social category that challenges assumptions about Japanese ethnocultural homogeneity; and as the basis for developing a multicultural society and encouraging democratic revitalization. This approach to citizenship encompasses four interrelated dimensions: 1) formal membership in a state, or legal status; 2) symbolic significance, including the collective identities of those defined as citizens and noncitizens; 3) an assortment of rights and responsibilities, which may overlap between citizens and noncitizens; and 4) practice, or civic engagement according to the republican definition of citizenship. As indicated in Figure 4.1, the individual categories become more expansive as they move away from the domain of the state toward those of citizens and noncitizens. The placement of the last category – the practice of citizenship – at the bottom of the pyramid signifies the predominant role played by citizens and noncitizens in shaping the practice of citizenship as well as the relatively wide arena that this category encompasses. The construction, implementation, interpretation, and contestation of each of these categories involve

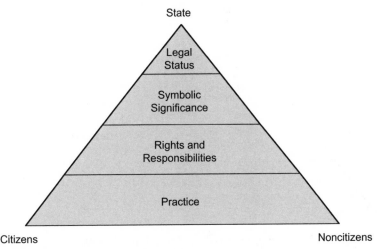

State

Legal
Status

Symbolic
Significance

Rights and
Responsibilities

Practice

Citizens   Noncitizens

FIGURE 4.1. An interactive approach to citizenship.

the triangular interaction of the state, citizens, and noncitizens to vary-
ing degrees.[8]

Applying this multidimensional framework of citizenship to the case
of Japan, we can see that citizenship is a tool for Korean-resident
activists to negotiate the terms of the foreign community's political
incorporation in Japan (see Figure 4.2). As legal status, foreign citizenship status gives activists a political voice disproportionate to their
small numbers, especially in comparison to their naturalized counterparts who constitute a miniscule section of the voting population. The
symbolic significance of nationality as ethnocultural identity differenti-
ates an otherwise highly assimilated, phenotypically indistinguishable
minority from the dominant Japanese society and, consequently, provides compelling evidence of cultural and ethnic diversity in Japan as
well as the problem of discrimination in Japanese society. The rights

---

[8] I acknowledge that the term *noncitizen* encompasses a broad category of distinct
groups such as recent immigrants (including legal and illegal immigrants, migrant
workers, etc.), permanent foreign residents, refugees, stateless persons, and varieties
of "second-class" citizens (nationals who do not have full citizenship and immigration
rights). Although this book focuses on legal foreign residents, I have chosen to refer to
them periodically as "noncitizens" in order to delineate their structural position vis-à-
vis citizens and the state and their fluid self-representations as sojourners, immigrants,
foreign residents, and so forth.

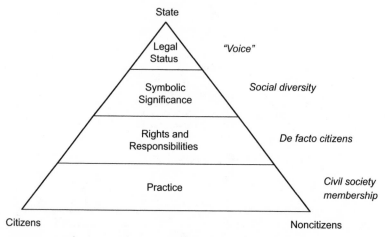

FIGURE 4.2. An interactive approach to citizenship (applied).

and responsibilities that foreign residents have acquired throughout the past few decades have made them, in effect, de facto citizens of Japan. Finally, as a practice in Japanese civil society, citizenship has increasingly become associated with local politics, nongovernmental organization (NGO) and NPO activities, and grassroots movements, including those led by foreign-resident activists. Moreover, because this concept of citizenship is based on community and residence, foreign residents are recognized as "citizens" of Japanese civil society.

Rather than the preservation of a distinct Korean culture, therefore, native-born generations of Korean activists seek to reshape Japanese society. The issue at hand is no longer Korean identity but the quality of Japanese democracy. Representing a foreign community that has resided in Japan for four generations, Korean community activists are particularly well suited to democratize Japanese society by expanding the boundaries of citizenship, in terms of membership rules and its larger significance in Japanese society. Their engagement in movements for local voting rights, antidiscrimination laws, and recognition for foreign residents sheds light on the incongruity between the daily lives of Korean residents as integral members of Japanese society and their legal positions as foreigners.

Hence, the movements associated with these models are not quests *for* citizenship but are ongoing citizenship practices. Although they may ultimately strive for full citizenship for the Korean community, it is not the same citizenship that the state seeks to grant to Korean and other foreign residents. Japanese nationality, for Korean activists, represents social conformity, political passivity, and silence. To naturalize the Korean community en masse is akin to putting a muffle on the community's voice. Thus, they are thwarting state efforts to grant Koreans the "privilege" of Japanese nationality, which is not the same as full citizenship in practice. Mobilizing around their foreign citizenship is part of a strategy to transform a passive process of political inclusion – naturalization (*kika*) – into an active and empowering choice for the community – citizenship acquisition (*shiminken o shutoku suru*), complete with all its attendant rights and responsibilities. The goal, therefore, is to develop a society in which "coexistence" means acknowledging group differences and equality rather than the current practice that avoids confrontation and pressures non-Japanese groups to "pass" as Japanese.

5

Destination Japan

Global Shifts, Local Transformations

Kim Kyu Il, who heads the Korean organization *Kangaeru kai*, recounted an ironic experience he had while riding the subway in Tokyo. A small group of *Nikkei* (ethnic Japanese) Brazilians were gathered together in front of the sliding doors of a crowded train heading toward the bustling Ikebukuro district. This group caught the attention of many of the passengers because, as Kim put it, they were speaking loudly in Portuguese. After observing the group for some time, Kim un-self-consciously commented in Japanese to his riding companion, also a Korean resident, "There certainly are a lot of foreigners in Japan today" (interview with Kim Kyu Il, 30 March 1999, Tokyo).

In many respects, Japan typifies so-called recent countries of immigration. Conservative lawmakers and bureaucrats resist efforts to liberalize immigration policies, despite Japan's labor shortages, aging population, and low fertility rates, and focus their efforts on curbing illegal immigration. Pressures from businesses to import labor have been addressed through short-term solutions that amount to a type of guest-worker program. Immigrants with temporary visas often struggle to meet their basic needs, as they have limited access to health care and social services, are vulnerable to exploitation by their employers, and, if they overstay their visas, are in danger of immediate deportation. Although antiimmigrant violence is considerably lower in Japan than in Europe, antiimmigrant hostility manifests itself in statements by politicians, public notices about foreign criminality, and media reports that link foreigners with crime and disorder.

At the same time, there are distinct aspects that belie the claim that Japan is a recent country of immigration. Compared to its European counterparts that have experienced heightened immigration since the mid-1960s and 1970s, Japan's recent encounter came much later, with the lion's share arriving since the late 1980s. During the decade after their arrival, however, local governments invited foreign residents to voice their interests in local referenda and advisory councils, numerous schools instituted multicultural education into their curricula, hundreds of nongovernmental organizations (NGOs) provided services and advocacy for immigrants, the national Diet debated a bill that would grant foreign residents local voting rights, and mainstream organizations and media declared Japan a multicultural society. Not only have these developments taken place much more rapidly than in southern European countries that have seen a dramatic increase in the immigrant population since the 1980s, but also they contrast strikingly with the slow pace of reforms within Japan pertaining to problems in the electoral system, the economy, and the health care system.

This chapter analyzes how the political choices made by Korean actors have institutionalized paths available to recent immigrants on three levels: policies, local institutions, and ideas. Recent immigrants arrived in Japan just as the smoke from various critical struggles regarding foreign residents' legal status and citizenship rights began to settle. These struggles had led to a major change in the government's approach to managing the foreign-resident population. Whereas immigration policies that were established in the early postwar period treated foreigners as sojourners, policy reforms from the late 1970s reflected the state's recognition of the foreign population as permanently settled residents. These reforms – which were directly or indirectly shaped by Korean legal victories, lobbying efforts, and social movements – have afforded foreign residents in Japan generous social welfare rights, widening the gap between temporary and permanent residents. Meanwhile, local governmental institutions and civil-society organizations have filled the lacuna left by official closed-door policies at a remarkable speed in part because they are extensions of existing organizations and programs aimed at the Korean-resident community. In many cases, the same activists who had participated in Korean social movements and organizations have shifted their attention to recent immigrants, using similar tools to mobilize communities, raise public awareness, and lobby officials. Finally, ideas about citizenship, multiculturalism, and democracy that have been associated with recent immigrants originate, in many cases, in past and current Korean social movements.

IMMIGRATION CONTROL, PART I: FROM EXCLUSION TO ASSIMILATION

Since it was formulated in 1951, Japan's Immigration Control Law has been based primarily on control, as the name of the law implies. In the years leading to the passage of the law, government officials aimed to resolve three central immigration issues facing Japan at the time: 1) the legal status of former colonial subjects whom they hoped to repatriate en masse; 2) illegal immigration primarily from the Korean peninsula, including many former colonial subjects who repatriated to Korea but returned to Japan for reasons relating to security and livelihood; and 3) the activities and movements of former colonial subjects within Japan who were increasingly viewed as a security threat due to their involvement in what were perceived to be procommunist activities. These issues were addressed by 1) unilaterally declaring all former colonial subjects aliens and making alienage the basis for exclusion in public-sector employment, welfare benefits, and electoral politics, among other things; 2) tightening border controls; and 3) instituting a strict system of alien registration that would require foreigners to submit their fingerprints and carry their alien registration cards with them at all times and, thereby, allow government authorities to closely monitor their whereabouts. The Immigration Control Law was an imperfect solution to the so-called Korean problem.

This approach based on control and exclusion, which some have called the "1952 system" (Yamawaki 2001), began to unravel as the second generation of Korean residents came of age in the 1960s and 1970s. As I discuss in Chapter 3, the second generation of Korean activists identified themselves as permanent, contributing members of Japanese society, rather than as sojourners who would eventually repatriate to their homeland, which was how the first generation of Korean leaders defined themselves. Consequently, Korean movements of the 1970s and 1980s challenged the exclusionary nature of Japanese society and laws by making claims to civil and social rights as foreign residents permanently settled in Japan on the basis of their equality to their fellow Japanese citizens.

In the midst of the Korean civil rights movement, a young immigration official named Sakanaka Hidenori wrote an essay proposing a new approach to immigration control based on assimilation and naturalization rather than exclusion, which won first prize in the Immigration Bureau's essay contest in 1975. Although justifying strict closed-door policies on the claim that immigration would have a destabilizing effect on Japan's homogeneous society, Sakanaka warned that Korean residents in Japan threatened to pose a "minority problem" (*shōsū minzoku mondai*) because of their positions as cultural and legal foreigners in Japan (Sakanaka 1989: 191–228). He recommended, instead, a policy approach that would encourage Koreans to assimilate into Japanese society and naturalize, which later came to be known as the "Sakanaka thesis" (*Sakanaka ronbun*). The Immigration Bureau published Sakanaka's essay that year in its monthly report *Nyūkoku kanri geppō* (Monthly Report on Immigration Control). In the following year, the Ministry of Justice released a white paper on immigration control stating the need to clarify the legal status of Koreans in Japan and that referred explicitly to Koreans as "settled" residents for the first time (Yamawaki 2001: 291–5).

Sakanaka further elaborated on his proposal regarding Korean residents in 1977, noting three possible routes that Korean residents could take: repatriation, continued residence in Japan as foreigners, or continued residence in Japan as Japanese nationals (Sakanaka 1989: 160). Most Koreans in Japan at the time were following the second route of residing in Japan as foreigners, which Sakanaka regarded as detrimental to Japanese society. Given that the majority of this population were native-born residents with little cultural or emotional attachment to the homeland, or "quasi-Japanese" (*jun nihonjin*), Sakanaka proposed that they should be treated as permanent members of Japanese society, rather than as foreigners. This shift would entail addressing problems of discrimination, education, employment, and social welfare. By respecting their human dignity and rights, Sakanaka argued, Koreans would *naturally* choose to go the route of assimilation and naturalization, thereby ensuring that Japan would successfully avoid the "minority problem" that plagued other industrial democracies. He also predicted that, as the rate of intermarriages between Korean residents and Japanese nationals grew, the majority of the Korean population in Japan would be Japanese nationals by the early twenty-first century, thereby leading to their "natural extinction" (*shizen shōmetsu*).

As detailed in Chapter 3, the Hitachi Employment Discrimination Trial of the early 1970s and numerous local movements by Korean residents had forced the issues of employment discrimination, social welfare rights, and education on the table and a number of local governments and private companies had already made significant reforms and concessions when Sakanaka's essays were published. Japan ratified the International Covenant on Economic, Social and Cultural Rights (ICESCR) and the International Covenant on Civil and Political Rights (ICCPR) in 1979 and the Convention Relating to the Status of Refugees in 1982 that gave rise to major reforms to confer foreign residents equal rights to social welfare benefits such as public housing, child care allowances, and health insurance and extended "exceptional" permanent residency (*tokurei eijyū*) to former colonial subjects and their descendants who were not already permanent residents by virtue of the 1965 Japan-ROK Normalization Treaty. In contrast to the heavy-handed efforts by officials to pressure Koreans to assimilate to the point of "indistinguishability" in the 1970s and 1980s, the Ministry of Justice gradually eased naturalization procedures for Korean residents and, in a 1985 amendment to the Nationality Act, eliminated its "recommendation" for naturalization applicants to adopt a Japanese name (Kim 1990; Sakanaka 1999; Takenaka 1997: 303). This amendment accompanied another major revision that would allow individuals to gain Japanese nationality through either their father's or mother's nationality, which followed Japan's ratification of the Convention on the Elimination of All Forms of Discrimination against Women in the same year. These reforms, which Sakanaka helped formulate, marked the beginning of what Yamawaki Keizō (2001) calls the "1982 system" of immigration control based on assimilation instead of exclusion and that treated Korean residents as permanent residents instead of sojourners. The new system, however, did not shield Japan from confronting a "minority problem," as the largest mass mobilization of Korean residents – the decadelong antifingerprinting movement – coincided with its installation. When the fingerprinting requirement was abolished for permanent residents in 1993, there was little doubt that Korean residents would not settle for second-class citizenship.

The arrival of new immigrants during this period starkly contrasted the state's exclusionary approach to immigration into Japan with the 1982 system's assimilationist approach to foreign residents already settled within its borders. Having responded to Korean-resident claims through piecemeal reforms that avoided confrontation but, at the same time, anticipated their gradual and "natural" assimilation through cultural assimilation, naturalization, and intermarriage – as opposed to immigrant incorporation programs or reforms to citizenship policies that would proactively speed the process of turning foreign residents into Japanese nationals – the state was wholly unprepared to deal with a new wave of immigrants who would also go the route of settlers instead of sojourners. Although closed-door immigration policies focused heavily on controlling population movements and curbing illegal immigration, policies toward foreign residents already settled in Japan treated them as de facto citizens with social welfare rights almost on par with Japanese nationals. Consequently, Japan unintentionally embodied the liberal model of the "hard on the outside, soft on the inside" immigration state (Bosniak 2006).

IMMIGRATION CONTROL, PART II: EXCLUSION
AND ASSIMILATION

Japan, like other advanced industrial societies, experienced labor shortages at the height of the country's rapid economic growth in the 1960s. Rather than import foreign labor, however, Japanese officials and corporations met labor demands by automating production, shifting production abroad, and tapping into alternative sources of domestic labor, including women, students, and the elderly, as well as the rapidly growing population of rural migrants and seasonal workers.[1] As Takeyuki Tsuda and Wayne Cornelius (2004) point out, Japan was the only advanced industrial democracy in the world that did not import foreign unskilled male workers between the end of World War II and the late 1980s. Immigrant women constituted the first wave of foreign workers in the late 1970s to the mid-1980s; they were imported

---

[1] Japan's rapid economic growth period in the 1960s coincided with the country's greatest rural-urban exodus. In the late 1960s, approximately 4 million farmers migrated to urban areas on an annual basis (Lie 2001: 9; Mori 1997: 55–7).

primarily from the Philippines, Thailand, South Korea, and Taiwan to fill the demand in the so-called entertainment industry.

By the time Japan faced another labor shortage in the 1980s, alter-native sources of domestic labor were depleted. Internal migration shrunk by more than a million in the decade following the 1971 peak, and a reverse migration of urban populations to surrounding regions, due to rising land prices, contributed to a structural change in Japan's labor market (Mori 1997: 56). Women, who were a crucial source of part-time, underpaid labor in the 1960s, increasingly entered the labor force as full-time, white-collar professionals after graduating from four-year colleges. As Leonard Schoppa (2006: 76) points out, labor shortages in the 1980s opened up unprecedented career options and employment opportunities for women. Japan's economic growth also expanded advancement opportunities for young Japanese men, who grew disdainful of blue-collar work. The only domestic source of alternative labor, then, was the elderly, who would increasingly work alongside young foreign workers (Lie 2001: 10). Small and medium-sized firms were the hardest hit by this labor shortage as they were unable to fill labor demands in what are commonly referred to as the "3K" (*kitanai, kitsui,* and *kiken*) industries in Japanese and the "3D" (dirty, difficult, and dangerous) industries in English.

As Japan's "bubble economy" (1986–91) flourished and the Japanese yen grew in strength – reaching an all-time high of about 80 yen per U.S. dollar in April 1995 – Japan became an attractive des-tination for migrant labor.[2] Additionally, many Asian laborers who had previously worked in the Middle East began to migrate to Japan after they lost their jobs due to declining oil prices (Kashiwazaki 2000: 452). The growth in demand and supply spurred the expansion of pri-vate brokers and intermediaries in Japan and various sending countries that organized and promoted labor migration to Japan. These agents exploited many of the structural changes brought about by economic globalization, such as transnational corporations, advances in telecom-munications, technological innovations, and cheap airplane tickets, in

---

[2] After the United States, Britain, France, West Germany, and Japan (Group of Five) signed the Plaza Agreement in September 1985, the Japanese yen jumped from ¥243 per U.S. dollar in September 1985 to a value of ¥153 in September 1986 (Hamada and Patrick 1988: 122). In August 2009, the Japanese yen was valued at ¥94 per U.S. dollar.

order to forge passports and visas and otherwise facilitate illegal foreign migration to Japan (Sellek 2001: 37). From the late 1980s, large numbers of foreign workers entered Japan with tourist visas and overstayed their three-month limit, thus establishing a formidable illegal immigrant population that reached a high of three hundred thousand in 1993 (SOPEMI 2007).

Japanese government officials responded to the internal demand for foreign labor through the creation of legal loopholes that undermine but do not necessarily violate official policies that prohibit the admission of unskilled workers and discourage immigrant permanent settlement. The 1990 revision to the Immigration Control and Refugee Recognition Act reorganized and expanded visa categories from eighteen to twenty-seven. Only four visa categories – permanent resident, spouse or child of a Japanese national, spouse or child of a permanent resident, and long-term resident – allow for unrestricted economic activities. Visa categories that allow for work permits are limited to professional and technical fields, such as professors, artists, engineers, journalists, and researchers, and the law continues to forbid, *in principle*, work permits for unskilled labor. Other foreigners, however, may be granted special permission to work for a designated period of time. As a result of this revision, employers have at their disposal three central legal options for recruiting unskilled foreign labor: hiring foreign laborers with visas that allow for unrestricted economic activities, offering "on-the-job training" to "trainees," and hiring college and precollege students who have special permission to work temporarily (Mori 1997: 95–133).

The most effective way that Japan has been able to import unskilled foreign labor while maintaining a policy that explicitly prohibits the admission of unskilled foreign labor has been through the recruitment of *Nikkei* foreign workers. Like the other "special" category of foreigners, the *Nikkei* are the exception to the rules. Extending *jus sanguinis* to immigration policies, foreign workers of Japanese descent (up until the third generation) and their families automatically qualify for one of three visa categories that allow for unrestricted economic activities: long-term resident, spouse or child of a Japanese national, and spouse or child of a permanent resident. Their visa status also allows them to reside in Japan for up to three years and can be renewed an indefinite number of times. Consequently, their legal status parallels that of permanent residents, which makes them the exception to the policy that discourages the permanent settlement of immigrants. However, unlike ethnic Germans (*Aussiedler*) from Eastern Europe and the former Soviet Union who migrated to Germany in the 1990s, the *Nikkei* do not automatically qualify for Japanese citizenship. Like all other foreigners, they must undergo the process of naturalization in order to become Japanese nationals.

The official explanation for the "*Nikkei* exception" to Japan's immigration policies is that the government is providing ethnic Japanese with the opportunity to visit their relatives in Japan, learn the Japanese language, and otherwise explore their cultural heritage.[3] However, the makeup of the *Nikkei* immigrant population leaves no doubt that the primary objective of this policy is labor recruitment. Although the largest population of *Nikkeijin* resides in the United States, almost all *Nikkei* immigrants who entered Japan with long-term residency visas following the 1990 revision were Brazilian and Peruvian nationals, most of whom were recruited to work for small and medium-sized firms in the construction and manufacturing sectors.[4] In 2004, South American nationals accounted for more than half of all foreigners working in the manufacturing sector (SOPEMI 2006). The Brazilian population alone experienced almost a fivefold increase in the decade following 1990, from 56,000 to 254,000 in 2000. In 2007, their numbers reached almost 317,000, making them the third-largest foreign-resident group in Japan after Chinese and Koreans. Takeyuki Tsuda (2003) estimated that approximately one-fifth of the entire *Nikkei* Brazilian population were residing in Japan in 2003.

The second major loophole for importing unskilled labor involves manipulation of the "trainee" and "technical intern" visa categories, which in combination form the basis of a de facto guest-worker program. Trainees are granted a one-year visa with the stated purpose of acquiring technical skills through classroom instruction and practicum.

3 This justification contrasts strikingly with Germany's "law of return" for *Aussiedler*, which is based on the idea that "ethnic brothers and sisters" are returning home to Germany (Brody 2002: 94).
4 An anthropologist who conducted fieldwork in Japan during a two-year period noted that very few *Nikkei* South Americans visited their Japanese relatives while residing in Japan. The handful that did visit their relatives commented that their reception was cold or that their relatives seemed embarrassed to see them (Roth 2004: 3-4).

Since 1990, Chinese nationals have made up the largest proportion of foreigners with trainee visas. Because they are not supposed to work for wages under this program, they receive only a "trainee allowance." Trainees are especially vulnerable to exploitation by employers because they are not recognized as "workers" by law and thus, not protected by labor laws and health insurance systems (Kashiwazaki 2000: 453).[5] As one might predict, this highly unregulated trainee system contributed to the growing illegal immigration problem because many trainees over-stayed their visas and/or abandoned their positions for higher-paying jobs elsewhere.

In April 1993, the Ministry of Justice unveiled the Technical Intern Training Program (TITP) to combat growing illegal immigration. This program, which officially aims to enable foreign nationals who have undergone a certain level of training in Japan to further improve their skills through on-the-job training, allows foreigners to stay in Japan for up to three years under an employment contract (Ministry of Justice 2008a). Nonetheless, because small and medium-sized firms that do not have the resources to provide classroom instruction or jobs that require significant training primarily utilize these programs, they remain tools for employers to hire cheap, unskilled foreign labor. Among the most common types of work that "interns" have engaged in through this program are women and children's apparel production, welding, and plastic molding. In 2007, the Ministry of Justice revised its guidelines for companies using technical internship programs; the guidelines now prohibit participating companies from engaging in "inappropriate management," such as confiscating employees' passports and alien registration cards and barring them from leaving the company dormitories, as well as "unfair conduct" (Ministry of Justice 2008a).

The third central source of legal migrant labor comes from foreign students. The vast majority of foreign students enrolled in Japanese schools (precollege students) and colleges work either part-time or full-time and, since 2004, are permitted to stay in Japan for 180 days after graduation with a "temporary visitor" residence status so that they may find employment. In 2007, the number of foreign students

---

5 Furthermore, trainees frequently sign contracts that tie them to their employers and subject them to deportation if they abandon their training.

in Japan reached a peak of more than 132,000, of whom 65 percent were Chinese nationals. Generally, college students can receive special permission to change their visa status to one of three categories: engineer, specialist in humanities/international services, or intracompany transferee. More than ten thousand foreign students changed their residence status in 2007 so that they could work in Japan after graduation (Ministry of Justice 2008a). Nevertheless, precollege and college students made up more than 7 percent of all illegal immigrants in Japan in January 2008 because significant numbers overstayed their visas or engaged in economic activities that were not permitted by their residence status.

Through these loopholes, the state has managed to meet labor market demands and give employers alternatives to recruiting illegal immigrants while maintaining an official closed-door policy. Because these loopholes allow immigrants to reside continuously in Japan for up to three years at a time, however, they have inadvertently contributed to the growth of the long-term and, increasingly, permanent foreign-resident population. The number of general permanent residents (*ippan eijyusha*) more than doubled between 1995 and 2000 alone, from a little more than 63,000 to more than 145,000 (Ministry of Justice 1998, 2001). The 2000 figure tripled to almost 440,000 in 2007 (Ministry of Justice 2008b).

The growth of temporary and "settled" foreign populations in Japan created new dilemmas and opportunities for the local communities in which they resided. Without official immigrant incorporation policies or programs to assist new immigrants, local governments and civil-society organizations were left to deal with the growing population of foreign residents, most of whom were not fluent in Japanese language or customs, on their own. At the same time, the lack of a central directive gave them considerable flexibility to come up with creative solutions to integrate them, often using existing resources. Although some of the local communities in which significant numbers of immigrants settled had almost no foreign residents in their midst, such as Hamamatsu, others such as Osaka, Kobe, Kawasaki, and Yokohama had extensive experience in working with foreign residents and had already implemented numerous initiatives that aimed not only at their integration but their political empowerment as well.

LOCAL GOVERNMENTS AND THE CREATION OF LOCAL
IMMIGRANT INCORPORATION PROGRAMS

The contradictions between immigration policies that officially closed
the door to immigration and local realities where foreign populations,
many ,of them residing illegally in Japan, were growing in size and
importance led to a bureaucratic nightmare for local governments.
Although Ministry of Justice officials could turn a blind eye to the
swelling ranks of immigrants in Japan, local government officials were
forced to create some sort of immigrant integration program to maintain social and political stability in their communities. Even foreign
residents deemed temporary or unwanted by the national government
need assistance as they settle, adapt, and reside in their local communities. In some cities such as Tokyo and Hamamatsu, where foreign
residents made up more than 3 percent of the total population in
2009, local governments simply could not ignore the foreign-resident
population because of their relative size vis-à-vis the local population.
Rather than police immigrant populations or concentrate their efforts
on identifying illegal immigrants, many local governments turned to
another national state-sponsored program, *kokusaika* (internationalization), to guide immigrant incorporation.

The *kokusaika* campaign began in the 1980s as a state-sponsored
effort to boost Japan's competitiveness and influence in a rapidly globalizing world. This goal was to be achieved through full participation in
international institutions, technological innovation, increased tourism,
exchange student programs, and English-language instruction, among
other things. However, this campaign inadvertently heightened international and national pressure to open Japan's markets to foreign services and goods and implement internationalization within (*uchinaru
kokusaika*).

With the rapid growth of the foreign population since the 1980s, a
number of local governments with relatively large immigrant populations took it upon themselves to put immigrant integration at the center
of the local internationalization campaigns. Most of the local officials
actively involved in developing immigrant incorporation programs
have operated out of their local government's "international office"
(Pak 2000: 249). Included in the directive issued by the Ministry of

Home Affairs in 1995 for implementing local internationalization was a call to create an environment in which Japanese and foreign residents could live together comfortably, which includes providing administrative services and education assistance to Japanese and foreign residents alike. Municipal authorities used this directive as a tool to manage some of the problems encountered by recently arrived foreigners in their communities, including housing discrimination, language barriers, and access to education and medical care. Implementing immigrant incorporation programs under the banner of internationalization has also been an important source of revenue from the central government. Thus, various local governments have created services specifically for recently arrived immigrants that range from Japanese-language classes, multilingual information brochures, and legal consultation services to financial support for emergency medical care and limited political representation (Kashiwazaki 2002).

These services and programs, however, were not created anew. Many of the policies directed toward recent immigrants are extensions of policies or proposals that emerged prior to their arrival and well before the Ministry of Home Affairs issued its 1995 directive on local internationalization. As I discuss in Chapter 3, a number of local governments with substantial Korean populations implemented reforms to widen foreign-resident rights to include social welfare benefits and employment opportunities years before national-level reforms in the late 1970s and early 1980s. From the 1980s, cities with large populations of Korean residents, such as Osaka and Kawasaki, established ethnic education programs for Korean-resident schoolchildren in order to offer instruction in Korean language and introduce them to Korean music, dance, and other cultural activities. Many of the multicultural education programs created for new immigrants, moreover, are modeled after Korean ethnic education curricula in that they offer cultural activities aimed at preserving the target group's ethnic identity and offer language instruction in the children's mother tongue as well as in Japanese.

One of the most noteworthy programs that many local governments implemented for foreign residents was the system of assemblies and advisory councils through which foreign residents could represent their interests. Given that many immigrants struggled to meet their basic needs due to language and cultural barriers, legal obstacles, and social discrimination, participation in local politics may not have been a high priority for them. To be sure, it would make little sense for local governments to create such political bodies for recently arrived immigrants given the urgency of their other needs. The development of local institutions for foreign residents' political participation, however, was very much in tune with what had become a nationwide movement for local voting rights led by Korean activists by the late 1980s. As I discuss in Chapter 3, Korean activists had petitioned their local governments for voting rights since 1975, and most of the major Korean organizations (with the notable exception of Chongryun) had made suffrage for foreign residents a central priority by the late 1990s. Local governments responded to this movement by submitting resolutions in support of local voting rights, on the one hand, and establishing assemblies and advisory councils that would give foreign residents a form of local representation, on the other.

Given that these local councils and assemblies provide foreign residents with the most direct method for representing their interests, they have become influential in shaping and prioritizing local policies and programs for foreign residents. They also demonstrate the disparities between the interests of native-born generations of Korean residents and recently settled immigrants. Although local voting rights is often the central issue for native-born Koreans residents, recent immigrants frequently steer the discussion to Japanese-language instruction for new immigrants and ethnic education for their children. Because native-born Korean residents tend to occupy leadership positions in such representative assemblies and councils – due to their cultural and linguistic fluency and, sometimes, their entrenchment in the local community – their interests have the potential to be overrepresented.

For example, the Kawasaki City Representative Assembly for Foreign Residents (*Kawasaki-shi gaikokujin shimin daihyōsha kaigi*), established in 1996, reserves five of its twenty-six seats for "oldcomer" Korean residents. The city then allocates the remaining twenty-one seats based on gender, age, and nationality as well as individual qualifications and experience. The only qualifications that potential assembly members must meet are a legal visa status, Japanese-language fluency, local residency, and an age requirement (18 or older). In recent years, the assembly was successful in pushing for local reforms related to housing and the translation of government publications into foreign languages. Pak Hae-sook, a South Korean national who immigrated to Japan in 1997, served on the assembly for three years. During her tenure, she noted that Mindan and Chongryun representatives almost always brought up the local voting rights issue during assembly meetings and spent considerable time arguing over the issue. As I mentioned in Chapter 3, Mindan supports the voting rights bill while Chongryun opposes it. She had joined the assembly in order to push for the implementation of ethnic education programs for immigrant children but found that "oldcomers" invariably had a stronger voice than "newcomers" during the meetings (interview with Pak Hae-sook, 6 September 2008, Kawasaki). A Japanese activist who works with recent immigrants put it this way:

My clients deal with routine police harassment. They come to our office because their families are about to be torn apart [because one of the parents' visas has expired]. Honestly, all these pretty words about multiculturalism [*tabunka shakai*], coexistence [*kyōsei*], and the foreign citizen [*gaikokujin shimin*] are just . . . pretty words that don't reflect reality for most new immigrants. Why would an immigrant who is trying to get special permission to live in Japan after having overstayed his visa for 10 years and established a family in Japan lobby for voting rights? They need basic rights for survival, not special rights. (interview, 5 September 2008, Tokyo)

The depth and breadth of local governmental programs and policies to assist new immigrants in their communities, therefore, reflect prior engagement with the Korean-resident community. The Korean civil rights movement of the 1970s and 1980s made clear that Korean residents were permanent members of Japanese society who expected to be treated as equals to Japanese nationals. Subsequent reforms at the national and local levels gave force to Korean claims by equalizing their rights to social welfare benefits, expanding their employment opportunities even in the public sector, and creating local bodies through which they could voice their interests. Although these reforms applied broadly to all foreign residents, they were designed with Korean residents in mind, who made up more than 80 percent of the foreign-resident population until the mid-1980s.

Consequently, new immigration from the late 1980s did not liberalize local governments. On the contrary, local governments were able to address the needs of new immigrants relatively quickly precisely because they already had at their disposal extensive policies and programs designed specifically for foreign residents in their communities. In contrast to claims by antiimmigrant pundits that Japanese society could not possibly deal with the "cultural chaos" of non-Japanese immigrants living in their midst, many local governments displayed considerable creativity and resourcefulness in integrating new immigrants even without national immigrant incorporation policies or state support. Although new immigrants have largely benefitted from these initiatives, some of their more urgent needs have gone unaddressed because the noncitizen rights movement has been based on the struggles of former colonial subjects and their multigenerational descendants whose interests often diverge from those of recent immigrants. Moreover, immigrants with temporary visas and overstayers have been largely overlooked by local governmental initiatives. These gaps have given civil-society organizations opportunities not only to address overlooked areas but also to shift public debate on multiculturalism, citizenship, and democracy.

IMMIGRANTS AND JAPANESE CIVIL SOCIETY

Despite the image of Japan as an immigrant-hostile society, foreign residents have access to hundreds of civil-society organizations that provide services, support, and advocacy specifically for foreign residents. Although some NGOs were formed as issue-oriented groups to meet the immediate needs of new immigrants, other organizations have their origins in the struggles of the Korean-resident community, from the early postwar period to the 1990s. Unlike Japanese activists that worked with Korean and *buraku* groups at the margins of Japanese society in the 1960s and 1970s, many immigrant support groups in contemporary Japan operate at the mainstream of Japanese society, having emerged from the so-called nonprofit organization (NPO) boom that followed the 1995 Hanshin earthquake and the passage of the NPO Law in 1998. Despite differences in the goals and strategies of these organizations, they are not necessarily disparate groups. As I discuss in the following text, many of the groups are linked by a broad network of Japanese and Korean activists, lawyers, academics, and religious organizations that have, in one way or another, participated in the Korean civil rights movement since the 1970s.

Among the group of organizations created specifically for new immigrants, the largest numbers are geared toward supporting the most vulnerable members of the immigrant population: workers with temporary visas, visa overstayers, and immigrant children. As most of the recent immigrants to Japan are migrant laborers, the problems and challenges that they face frequently involve working conditions as well as their living situation. Thus, while struggling to find affordable housing and adequate medical care, many have also had to deal with employment contract violations, unpaid wages, industrial accidents, physical abuse, and sexual harassment. Moreover, undocumented immigrants rarely benefit from social services provided by local governments and are often shunned by other foreign residents who do not want to be associated with them. Consequently, their principal allies and sources of support come from civil-society organizations formed by Japanese nationals.

These organizations fill a critical gap between a central government that provides no immigrant integration programs and local governments that limit their services to foreign residents legally residing in their communities. They are also invaluable in communities that did not have large populations of foreign residents prior to the arrival of new immigrants. In Hamamatsu, for example, where large populations of *Nikkei* immigrants are concentrated, civil-society organizations have played central roles in providing basic services to new immigrants, including offering free medical checkups, translating pamphlets that detail the public services that are available to foreign residents, and appointing teachers who specialize in teaching Japanese as a second language (Asahi Shimbun, 17 October 2001).

Although civil-society organizations often bring immigrant concerns to the attention of local authorities and work with local governments to provide services and support to immigrants in the community, they can, at the same time, become a crutch for local governments that are reluctant to take on particular responsibilities. For example, in her study of local NGO efforts to meet immigrants' educational needs in Hamamatsu City, Keiko Yamanaka (2006) argues that the local government delegated the complex task of socializing immigrant children into Japanese society entirely to women's community organizations, thereby reinforcing traditional gender roles and further marginalizing an issue requiring national attention.

Additionally, Apichai Shipper's (2006; 2008) study of Japanese NGOs offering support, services, and advocacy to illegal immigrants finds that most of these groups have limited resources and, consequently, tend to cater to specific clientele based on occupation, gender, nationality, and locale. For example, he observes that support groups for women focus primarily on Filipina and Thai women who work as "entertainers," while Christian NGOs supply services and consultation mostly to immigrants from countries with large Christian populations, including Filipinas, South Koreans, and *Nikkei* Latin Americans.[6] Because proimmigrant NGOs work primarily to address the immediate needs of recent immigrants, they have provided immigrants with few political socialization skills. What's more, these organizations lack immigrant leadership and have not been able to organize the immigrant community for sustained political action or generate immigrant-staffed organizations.[7] Consequently, immigrant involvement in their political empowerment remains indirect and episodic.

At present, the largest numbers of foreign-resident organizations led by foreign residents come from the Korean community. As I discuss in the previous chapters, Korean organizations in Japan can be divided principally into those that cater exclusively to the Korean-resident population and those that take a broader approach to the foreign-resident community. Those in the former category have, until recently, excluded not only recent immigrants, including "newcomer" South Korean immigrants, but also Koreans with Japanese nationality as well as Korean residents affiliated with opposing organizations. In particular, given that Mindan and Chongryun emerged as official overseas organizations representing South and North Korea respectively, they are qualitatively different from proimmigrant NGOs and independent Korean organizations that are voluntary in nature and have no official ties to the state (although some have close ties to their local governments). Nevertheless, as they are faced with dwindling memberships, they have increasingly broadened their appeal to larger segments of the Korean-resident population.

---

[6] Rather than perform on stage, most "entertainers" work as hostesses in the industry known in Japan as *mizu shōbai* (water trade, in reference to bars, cabarets, restaurants, and so forth) and as prostitutes (Sellek 2001: 37–8, 160–1).

[7] There is a clear distinction between proimmigrant organizations led by Japanese activists and immigrant or foreign-resident organizations led by immigrants and foreign residents.

Among the Korean organizations in the latter category, some, such as Mintōren, began as pan-ethnic organizations that focused primarily on the Korean community in their early years but incorporated the challenges facing new immigrants shortly after their arrival. Others, such as *Zenchōkyō* (*Zenkoku zainichi chōsenjin kyōiku kenkyū kyōgikai*, or the National Association for the Study of Education for Korean Residents), emerged as specifically Korean organizations but shifted their focus to new immigrants in what they perceived to be a common struggle. After *Zenchōkyō* resolved to tackle issues relating to the education of all foreign residents in Japan, instead of just Korean residents, the group, which was established in 1979, changed its name to *Zenkoku zainichi gaikokujin kyōiku kenkyū kyōgikai* (National Association for the Study of Education for Foreign Residents), or *Zengaikyō*, replacing the word *Korean* (*chōsenjin*) with *foreigner* (*gaikokujin*) (Asahi Shimbun, 17 December 2002).

Most of the Korean organizations that have incorporated the concerns of new immigrants came out of the Korean civil rights movement, which has shaped current advocacy efforts pertaining to foreign residents in three central ways. First, the strategies employed by previous Korean social movements have established a blueprint for current activism and advocacy efforts directed toward the Korean and non-Korean foreign-resident communities. As I discuss in Chapter 3, Korean social movements in the 1970s and 1980s were largely grassroots movements that centered on local communities. Although several movements gained national attention and helped bring about national-level reforms, they aimed primarily to change the conditions of their local communities and, in most cases, gained the support of many local officials. This decentralized, grassroots approach was certainly not unique to Korean movements at that time; on the contrary, it reflected a broader shift toward grassroots citizens' movements in Japan, beginning with the environmental movements of the late 1960s and early 1970s (Broadbent 1998; McKean 1981). At the same time, these citizens' movements by foreign nationals linked the position of foreign residents with that of Japanese nationals under the banner of citizens demanding change, on the one hand, and demonstrated the possibilities of noncitizen political engagement through litigation, lobbying, and protest, on the other. Korean social movements in the 1970s and

1980s, therefore, established the "resident as citizen" concept well before the aftermath of the 1995 Kobe earthquake popularized it.

Second, the central actors from Korean social movements of the 1970s and 1980s continue to influence Korean activism and proimmigrant civil-society organizations today. The same network of supporters who played leading roles in the Hitachi Employment Discrimination Trial, the antifingerprinting movement, and local movements for social welfare and employment rights in the 1970s and 1980s remain at the forefront of current movements for local voting rights, antidiscrimination legislation, and appeals for special residence permissions by visa overstayers, among other issues. This network includes groups such as the Korean Christian Church in Japan (KCCJ), the National Christian Council in Japan (NCCJ), and the Japanese Bar Association Committee on Human Rights Protection as well as individual activists and academics such as Suh Yong-dal of Momoyama Gakuin University, who is at the forefront of the local voting rights movement; Komai Hiroshi of the University of Tsukuba, who has lobbied on behalf of visa overstayers; and Satō Nobuyuki of the Research Action Institute for the Koreans in Japan (*Zainichi kankokujin mondai kenkyukai*, or RAIK), who leads current efforts to pass the Basic Law for Foreign Residents in Japan. Accordingly, new immigration to Japan did not create a break in the movement for foreign residents' rights; rather, it provided the ongoing movement with added momentum.

Third, the ideas that emerged out of earlier Korean social movements continue to shape how activists, and even some local governments, approach political empowerment for the foreign-resident community. Political mobilization in the Korean and non-Korean foreign-resident communities continues to concentrate on empowering foreign residents *as foreign residents*. Instead of guiding new immigrants on the path to naturalization, local institutions and civil-society organizations have promoted their rights as foreign residents and encouraged their participation in the public sphere as "foreign-resident citizens" (*gaikokujin shimin*). Aside from cases involving the legal status of children born out of wedlock or stateless persons, advocacy groups have not demanded revisions to Japan's citizenship policies on behalf of new immigrants and have focused their efforts on easing permanent-residency requirements instead. Naturalization rates remain low even as permanent-residency applications have soared, despite the fact that the residency requirement for the latter is twice that of the former. Rather than a destabilizing force in Japanese society, foreign residents have been heralded as a potential source of democratic revitalization in Japan, as I discuss in the following section. This approach, which separates nationality from citizenship, contrasts strikingly with the national government's aim to assimilate and naturalize the "settled" foreign-resident population, as argued in the Sakanaka thesis. As one South Korean immigrant explains,

I feel very comfortable being a foreigner [in Japan]. There's a lot that I can do because I am a foreigner. I decided to keep my maiden name even after I married my [Japanese] husband because I want people to know that I am a foreigner and not a Japanese person. I also felt it was important to show solidarity with *zainichi* Koreans who put such importance on *honmyo sengen* ["declaring one's Korean name"]. Without our *zainichi sŏnbae* ["elders," *senpai* in Japanese], we [foreigners] would not be able to engage in citizens' movements. They are the leaders of the foreign community. (interview with Pak Hae-sook, 6 September 2008, Kawasaki)

THE LANGUAGE OF CITIZENSHIP

Recent efforts by Korean activists, civil-society organizations, and local governments have been pivotal in reshaping the local landscape and providing new opportunities for traditionally underrepresented social actors to shape debate on citizenship, diversity, and democracy. In particular, their attempts to incorporate foreign residents into the public sphere have led to subtle yet significant changes to the language of citizenship in Japan, so that foreign residents are increasingly recognized as citizens of their local communities. Hence, although shifts in the global economy have had little impact on Japanese citizenship and immigration *policies*, they have brought about significant changes to local citizenship *practices*.

The language of citizenship in Japanese signifies the growing dichotomy between citizenship at the state and local levels as well as that between citizenship as policy and practice. Although the term *citizenship* translates directly into Japanese as *shiminken*, this term is not used in Japanese government documents or legal texts to refer to citizenship as a policy. Rather, the Japanese government employs *kokuseki* (nationality) to refer to legal-juridical membership in the state and *kokumin* (literally, people of the country) to refer to citizens. *Shiminken* is usually reserved to discuss citizenship in North America and Europe as well as the rights and duties associated with being a full member of the polity.[8]

At the same time, Japanese voluntary associations have increasingly used the term *shimin* (literally, people of the city, or townspeople) in reference to their locally based movements (*shimin undō*, or citizens' movements) and community organizations (*shimin dantai*, or citizens' groups).[9] *Shimin* transcends the implied passivity and formality of *kokumin* in order to connote an active member of civil society. Furthermore, in this case the usage of the term *shimin* is based on community rather than on state membership, which opens up the possibility of recognizing foreign residents as citizens in the sense of their being members of a civil society.

A handful of local governments, such as those in the cities of Kawasaki and Toyonaka, and civil-society actors explicitly identify foreign residents as "citizens" using the term *shimin*. Still, the most common term used is *jūmin* (resident), the connotations of which alternate between *resident* and *citizen*. The concept of *jūmin* is rooted firmly in territory rather than state membership or legal status and, thus, includes all residents of a particular community. Based on the principle of *jus domicili*, foreign residents are local citizens who pay taxes, participate in the community, and contribute to the common good. Local governments that have taken a proactive stance toward foreigners in their communities have applied this definition of resident-as-local-citizen as the basis for providing foreign residents with social

---

[8] These terms in their Korean pronunciations, *kukjŏk* and *kukmin* respectively, are used in the same way in South Korea. Although the root, *kuk* (or *koku* in Japanese), literally means country, it is also closely associated with the modern terms *nation* and *nation-state*. The North Korean state refers to its citizens as (*Chosun*) *kongmin*, which can be translated as "citizen" or "the public." The root, *kong* (or *kō* in Japanese), translates into "public" and is closely associated with the "civic" or "civil" spheres.

[9] The German terminology for citizenship and nationality displays striking similarities. Although the term *burge* refers to "bourgeois" and "citizen," the term *Staatsburgerschaft* literally translates into "citizen of the state" and is closely associated with the term for nationality, *Staatsangehorigkeit*. In like manner, the concept of citizenship used in reference to the "citizenship initiatives" of the 1970s that led to the Green Movement in Germany implies "active involvement in the affairs of the city at the local level" (Smith and Blanc 1996: 75).

services, consultative voice, and/or voting rights in local referenda. They have also extended this concept to national-level debates on granting local voting rights to foreign residents.

However, this locally rooted concept of the citizen goes beyond services and rights. Local state and nonstate actors have actively encouraged foreign residents to participate in the community as citizens. The Kawasaki City Representative Assembly for Foreign Residents serves as a forum for foreign residents to "contribute to the formation of the local community, promote mutual understanding, and promote foreign resident participation in the city administration" (City of Kawasaki 2006). Likewise, many local government pamphlets that have been produced specifically for foreign residents encourage them to participate in public life or work with other community citizens for the common good. Civil-society organizations and think tanks have also encouraged foreign residents to participate in the public sphere, linking their active engagement with democratic revitalization. For instance, Keidanren, Japan's most powerful business organization, called for the cultivation of a "vibrant diversity" in which foreign residents participate actively in revitalizing Japanese society in its "Japan 2025" report (Nippon Keidanren 2003). Similarly, one of the recent "challenge books" (*charenji bukks*) issued by the government think tank, the National Institute for Research Advancement (NIRA 2001), explicitly links the reinvigoration of citizenship practices in Japan with equal social, economic, and political rights for foreign residents.

The concept of active citizenship contrasts strikingly with that of citizenship acquisition in Japan, especially among Korean residents. Han Jŏng Sŏk, a pioneer of the antifingerprinting movement in the 1980s, contends that the meaning of naturalization (*kika*) in present-day Japan is not equivalent to that of acquiring nationality (*kokuseki o shutoku suru*). Whereas the latter concept implies the rights and responsibilities of citizenship (*shiminken*), the former presupposes cultural assimilation (*nihon minzoku ni naru koto*, or becoming part of the Japanese nation/race/ethnicity) (interview with Han Jŏng Sŏk, 17 October 1998, Tokyo). Moreover, a number of Korean activists that I interviewed stated that the only condition under which they would be willing to naturalize would be within a system of birthright citizenship (*jus soli*) similar to that in the United States.

At the same time, most of the native-born activists that I interviewed with South or North Korean nationality interpreted their rights within the boundaries of their legal status as "special permanent residents" in Japan and their obligations as tax-paying residents of their local communities (*jūmin*) and members of their organizations. Discussions of their civic identities ranged from residents of their local communities, members of their organizations, and Korean residents in Japan. The vast majority of the activists I interviewed interpreted their Korean nationalities narrowly as legal status. Although they often identified themselves as being "Korean" (e.g., *Hanguk saram* or *Chosun saram* in Korean and *Kankokujin* or *Chōsenjin* in Japanese; literally, a Korean person) or "Zainichi Korean," they rarely referred to themselves as North or South Korean "citizens." Moreover, all of my interviewees reserved the term *shimin* to refer to their *participation* in their local communities or in their voluntary associations.

NONNATIONAL CITIZENSHIP, MULTICULTURALISM, AND DEMOCRACY

Japanese official responses to the growth of the immigrant population have been remarkably shortsighted. Recent immigration policy reforms have aimed primarily to curb illegal immigration and accommodate labor shortages through unofficial mechanisms that do not violate the official closed-door policy. Because current immigration policies are based on the notion that immigration to Japan is temporary and controllable, they have entirely overlooked the problems of immigrant integration, social change, and democratic accountability. Current population projections, however, make clear that labor shortages will only become more severe in the years to come.[10]

With declining fertility rates and increased longevity, Japan's already high ratio of elderly citizens to working-age population is expected to surpass 25 percent by 2017 and reach more than 35 percent

---

[10] Beginning in 2005, Japan's total population has been decreasing at an annual rate of −0.02%. The UN Population Division (2007) predicts that the annual rate will reach −0.78% from 2045 to 2050. These numbers are based on medium variant projections.

of the total population by 2050.[11] Meanwhile, the estimated working-age population is expected to decrease to about 60 percent of the total population by 2020 and approximately 54 percent by 2050 (National Institute of Population and Social Security Research 2002). In order to alleviate labor shortages and the fiscal burdens of a large elderly population, Japan will need to admit an unprecedented number of immigrants. The UN Population Division (2000) estimates that Japan will have to admit approximately 647,000 immigrants every year simply to maintain the size of the current working-age population. With immigration on this scale, the foreign population could constitute more than 30 percent of the total Japanese population by 2050.

In recent years, the Liberal Democratic Party (LDP) and the Ministry of Justice have pushed forward proposals that reflect a move toward a type of assimilatory multiculturalism. In 2001, the LDP introduced a bill to ease naturalization procedures for Korean residents by eliminating the lengthy screening process and allowing Koreans to use Korean names that are currently not recognized by the Ministry of Justice. Sakanaka gave a speech to Mintōren activists in 1998 encouraging Korean residents to naturalize with their Korean names. Taking a stance remarkably similar to Korean-resident activists, he located the root of discrimination against Koreans to their alienage. But, in direct contrast to Korean activists, he proposed that Koreans can overcome discrimination by becoming Japanese nationals, thereby eliminating the basis of their discrimination. Instead of using nationality as the basis for Korean identity, he suggested that Koreans focus their efforts on making Korean names the basis for maintaining an ethnic Korean identity so that they could live as Japanese nationals with full rights while "expressing their ethnic roots" (Sakanaka 1999: 15–22). For Sakanaka, the structural effect has become the descriptor: Koreans are discriminated against because they are foreigners but, as Japanese nationals, they can maintain their ethnic Korean identity

---

[11] Japan's fertility rate has fallen by more than 25% since 1970 and, at the present rate of 1.27 (average number of children per woman), is among the lowest in the world (Papademetriou and Hamilton 2000: 15–16; UN Population Division 2007). According to UN (2007) estimates, Japan had the oldest population in the world in 2005 (with a median age of 42.9) and is estimated to have the second-oldest population in the world in 2050 along with South Korea (median age 54.9; Macau is expected to have the oldest population with a median age of 55.5).

without discrimination. Korean activists, in contrast, argue that Koreans were denationalized because of their ethnocultural identity; as a result, renationalization through naturalization requires Koreans to give up their ethnocultural identity first, which would then eliminate the basis of their discrimination. Whereas Sakanaka argues that Koreans can escape discrimination through naturalization, Korean activists maintain that only complete cultural assimilation akin to the colonial policy of *kōminka* (forced cultural assimilation, or "imperialization") would have that effect. Sakanaka's "encouragement" of naturalization by using Korean names has been interpreted by some activists as the Japanese state's attempt to hinder the development of multiethnic, collaborative projects between members of the Korean and other foreign communities that would challenge the fundamental nature of Japanese citizenship and immigration laws rather than the specific ways they violate the rights of the Korean community.

Meanwhile, the Ministry of Justice has adopted the language of "coexistence" (*kyōsei*) to justify stricter rules for alien registration, including the reinstatement of the fingerprinting requirement in 2007, as well as enacted measures to reduce illegal immigration by half, including increased efficiency in deportation proceedings (Ministry of Justice 2008a). This usage of the term *coexistence* stems from the limited multiculturalism embraced by local governments and the popular press since the late 1990s. The idea of "coexistence with foreigners" (*gaikokujin to no kyōsei*) is based on conflict avoidance, maintenance of the status quo, and ethnic privatization.[12] Although it derives from the concept of "living together in harmony" (*tomoni ikiru*) that Korean activists espoused from the early 1970s, it differs in fundamental ways, as a former Mintōren activist describes:

"Coexistence" [*kyōsei*] is based on the internationalization campaign [enacted by the national government] instead of the local community. It replaced the subject of "everybody" [as in "everybody in the community can live together in harmony"] to only Japanese and foreigners so that foreigners are treated as guests [instead of members of their local communities]. . . . Policies regarding foreign residents [that rest on the coexistence principle] then trace problems

---

[12] This privatization of social conflict is consistent with the ways that Japanese authorities have responded to social protests in the past. Susan Pharr (1990: 207) observes that, "Perhaps no major nation in the world places a greater cultural emphasis on conflict avoidance."

that foreign residents encounter to their lack of assimilation. A complex local problem regarding immigrant children's education and delinquency is interpreted simply as their inability to communicate, which then gets "resolved" by policies that require local governments to provide services for Japanese language instruction. . . . It also assumes that progress has already been made because "coexistence" is about maintaining stability, not creating change. (interview with Bae Jung Do, 3 September 2008, Kawasaki)

Rather than redefining what it means to be a Japanese citizen and advancing genuine social change, this approach, therefore, encourages superficial toleration of foreign cultures and avoidance of social conflict. Thus, it is a type of assimilatory multiculturalism in that it acknowledges that despite differences between Japanese and foreign residents, all can live together peacefully by tolerating these differences and making the differences tolerable. It simultaneously calls for cultural recognition and the sanitization of cultural differences, thereby neutralizing their political effects (Hooker 2005). It also places a heavy burden on foreign residents to minimize their differences so that they do not provoke antipathy on the part of their fellow Japanese residents. When Japanese and foreign residents are encouraged to engage in cross-cultural exchanges, they are expected to introduce each other to superficial, homogeneous, and sanitized cultural traditions devoid of historical content and critical thought. Foreign residents in particular are responsible for making the exchange palatable to Japanese tastes (not too spicy!).

Additionally, this limited multiculturalism does not recognize diversity among Japanese citizens.[13] Although all residents may be "citizens," there remains a distinct separation between Japanese citizens and foreign citizens. Hence, the concept of the "citizen" in Japanese civil society has yet to fundamentally change the dominant understanding of what it means to be Japanese. Rather, recent immigrants to Japan have reinforced the "us" versus "them" distinction that native-born foreign residents have long problematized.[14] Even as new immigrants

[13] Seung-Mi Han (2004) notes that local governmental efforts to politically incorporate foreign residents also pressure foreign residents to dilute differences between themselves in order to present a "united front."
[14] Native-born foreign residents do not fit well into the "other" category. They are just like "us" in terms of physical appearance, language, and culture, but they are not one of "us" because of their nationality, which leads to the inevitable question of why and the uncomfortable historical memory of Japan's colonization of Korea.

have become increasingly visible in Japanese society, "oldcomers" and their history continue to remain largely invisible. As Suh Jung Woo describes,

Some say that our insistence in asserting our identities as Koreans or protesting against discrimination is counterproductive to living in harmony with the Japanese.... The issue at hand is not about avoiding Japanese discrimination [but facing it head on]. Minorities need to raise their voices loudly in order to be heard. I think that sidestepping discrimination on the notion that Koreans and Japanese are the "same" is a new type of assimilationist rhetoric [*shin dōka shugi*].... The current era of coexistence [*kyōsei*] is highly individualistic and does not tolerate direct discrimination. At the same time, it does not acknowledge discrimination, either.... We must acknowledge that despite superficial civility, discrimination still exists in Japanese society. (interview with Suh Jung Woo, 17 August 1999, Osaka)

Several Korean-resident activists have commented that internationalization efforts have tended to underscore Japanese ignorance of the history of Koreans in Japan. Japanese audiences at various "international cooperation" events and lectures on Koreans in Japan inevitably ask second- and third-generation Korean-resident activists how long they have lived in Japan or compliment them on their fluent Japanese (Bae 1999: 5).

At the same time, Korean grassroots movements to gain rights and recognition specifically as foreign residents have had a profound influence on the ways in which local actors approach immigrant incorporation and empowerment. The "active foreign citizen" concept that challenges the hidden assimilated minority approach, in particular, opens up opportunities for traditionally underrepresented groups to express their preferences even as the formal, national realm of politics remains closed to the elite (LeBlanc 1999). It is also consistent with calls from various sectors of Japanese civil society to decentralize power and allow for greater local autonomy (Smith 2000). By emphasizing political participation and community engagement – for Japanese and foreign residents alike – this concept stresses the importance of practicing citizenship. Unlike the concept of nationality, this understanding stresses that citizenship is something that must be constructed, not granted. Although local incorporation efforts have not translated into national immigrant incorporation policies, they are consistent with patterns in other advanced industrial democracies. That is, national political institutions such as political parties are no longer playing important roles in immigrant incorporation and political socialization. Rather, a wide range of local organizations – such as religious institutions, labor unions, NPOs and NGOs, and ethnic voluntary associations – have come to fill these roles in the contemporary era (Andersen and Cohen 2005). By acting as conduits through which immigrant groups can express their political interests and demands, these local organizations have become important sources of democratic accountability for those who are formally excluded from the political process in Japan. As local practices end up diverging significantly from national policies, they open up the space for contestation, deliberation, and, possibly, policy reform and social change. Accordingly, the ways that Korean activists and civil-society organizations have reshaped the meaning of citizenship as practice provide a potentially powerful tool for reshaping Japanese democracy.

Conclusion

Today, everyone feels that Japan's economy and politics have hit a wall.... Japan is a society in which those in power dispense benefits to a narrow body of supporters and force others to conform.... To change this conformist trait, it is essential that Japan be reborn as a society that embraces diversity. Japanese people must tolerate people of different cultures and opinions, respect each other's differences, and try to resolve any social problems through discussion. In short, Japan must become a pluralist democracy befitting an advanced country.

– Masaru Kaneko, *Asahi Shimbun*, Annual Report, 2001

CITIZENSHIP, DIVERSITY, AND DEMOCRACY IN JAPAN

In 1986, former Prime Minister Nakasone Yasuhiro commented that the "considerable number of blacks, Puerto Ricans, and Mexicans" lowered American literacy and intelligence. He explained that Japanese intelligence levels were higher because of Japan's racial purity (*New York Times*, 27 September 1986). Two years later, Watanabe Michio, the former foreign minister of the Liberal Democratic Party (LDP), made a derogatory comment about U.S. African Americans' propensity toward financial delinquency. Again, in 1990, Japan's Justice Minister Kajiyama Seiroku compared foreign prostitutes in Tokyo to African Americans who move into white neighborhoods in the United States and "ruin the atmosphere" (*New York Times*, 18 October 1990).

This series of controversial remarks cannot be attributed simply to the ignorance or hubris of high-ranking officials in Japan. The fact that these comments were publicized at the height of Japan's economic prosperity reflects greater international scrutiny of Japanese politicians at the time, not the development of new prejudices and ideologies. What link these remarks are not only discriminatory attitudes toward minorities within and outside of Japan but also the belief that Japanese superiority lies in the society's racial and cultural homogeneity. Both Japanese officials and outside observers have attributed modern Japan's economic, political, and social development to its "uniquely homogenous society."

For these and many other Japanese leaders, diversity is a source of instability. Until the late 1980s, Ministry of Justice officials frequently commented that the existence of ethnic minorities within Japanese society was highly undesirable and that foreign residents should assimilate to the point of indistinguishability (Takenaka 1997: 303). Until the late 1970s, foreigners in Japan had few rights and were nearly invisible in the public sphere. A 1980 government report to the UN Human Rights Commission stated that there were no minorities in Japan despite the existence of about 3 million *burakumin*, 1.2 million Okinawans, 600,000 Korean residents, and 24,000 Ainu at the time. Even as government officials denied their existence, foreign residents who were sixteen and older were required to submit their fingerprints and carry an alien registration card with them at all times until 1993. Moreover, foreigners regularly encountered discrimination in employment, housing, and daily life.

Japan's immigration and citizenship policies have remained largely unchanged since their institutionalization in the early postwar period. Nevertheless, the meaning and practice of citizenship have undergone significant transformations. Whereas foreign citizenship once implied deprivation, it has now become a symbol of Japanese multiculturalism and democratic revitalization. Japanese nationality is still commonly associated with Japanese ethnocultural identity; however, the concept of the "citizen" (*shimin*) is increasingly associated with civic engagement and the local community, rather than state membership.

Although international norms, domestic institutions, and recent immigration have triggered incremental reforms, this book has traced the contradictions between the policies and practices of Japanese citizenship and immigration politics to the strategic interaction between Japanese state policies that seek to control and assimilate foreign residents, on the one hand, and Korean grassroots movements that seek to gain rights and recognition specifically for foreign residents, on the other. Japan's restrictive citizenship policies formulated in the context of postwar reconstruction sought to ensure the political and cultural assimilation of former colonial subjects who chose to remain in Japan, assuming that the remainder would repatriate. However, as the majority of the Korean population residing in Japan at the close of the American Occupation did not repatriate, Japan's citizenship policies resulted instead in disturbingly low rates of naturalization and, eventually, the formation of a permanent foreign-resident community that would span several generations.

Consequently, just as a first generation of immigrants primarily from former colonies arrived in postwar Europe, a second generation of foreign residents had already emerged in Japan. Although former colonial subjects in other countries had the option of choosing their nationalities at the time of liberation, postwar Japanese citizenship policies unilaterally stripped Korean and Taiwanese subjects of their Japanese nationality. Because Japan is the only former colonial power to maintain a pure system of *jus sanguinis* since the postwar period, most of its former colonial subjects and their descendants are not Japanese nationals either by choice or circumstance and, consequently, make up one of the largest segments of the foreign population.

Furthermore, Japan's failure to incorporate native-born foreign residents beyond the second generation is directly linked to the postwar reformulation of Japanese citizenship policies whereby nationality, rather than race or ethnicity, became the primary means by which the Japanese state differentiated former colonial subjects from the remainder of the population. To be sure, this ethnocultural understanding of Japanese nationality has created symbolic barriers for former colonial subjects to naturalize. At the same time, it has also provided foreign residents with specific opportunities to negotiate their political incorporation. For a highly assimilated, phenotypically indistinguishable minority group, the paradigm of citizenship-as-difference is a powerful tool for gaining social and political visibility and challenging the dominant monoethnic ideology upon which Japanese citizenship policies are based.

Conventional understandings of citizenship would lead us to assume that immigrants have more to gain as full citizens of their country of residence rather than as legal foreigners. Permanent foreign residents in Japan, however, have gained relative political power *as* foreign residents, not *despite* their foreign citizenship. Rather than naturalize and become a small section of the voting population, foreign-resident activists have increasingly used their noncitizen status as their "voice" to express their opposition to state policies. They have appropriated the dominant discourse that equates nationality with ethnocultural identity in order to challenge the notion that Japan is culturally homogeneous and, thus, generate public debate on Japanese citizenship policies. Especially as they engage in coalitions with other segments of Japanese civil society, their visibility as integral members of Japanese society is increasingly blurring the dichotomy between those who are legally defined as "citizens" and "noncitizens" by the state.

The contradictions between citizenship policies and practices attracted national attention with the rapid influx of immigrants from the 1980s. As numerous officials justified proposals to close Japan's border to immigration on the basis of the dominant monoethnic ideology, foreign-resident activists engaged in movements to disassociate nationality and citizenship and increase awareness of Japanese cultural diversity. The presence of a vocal, articulate, and politically savvy group of native-born foreign-resident activists posed a formidable challenge to official attempts at reinventing Japan as a closed country that cannot manage the chaos of opening its doors to foreigners.

Meanwhile, changes in Japan's political and social landscape have complemented foreign activists' efforts to diversify Japanese democracy. The increasingly visible presence of recent immigrants has altered Japanese civil society dramatically. Their presence in local communities has generated public debate on Japanese national identity, multiculturalism, and even democratic revitalization. Shortsighted immigration policies have forced local governments and nongovernmental organizations (NGOs) to provide new immigrants with social services and advocacy. Furthermore, shifts in Japanese civil society following the 1995 Hanshin earthquake and the passage of the Nonprofit Organization (NPO) Law in 1998 have created subtle yet significant changes to the language of citizenship in Japan, so that foreign residents are increasingly recognized as citizens.

These shifts have created an opening for social change as Japan recovers from its decadelong recession and faces the challenges of an aging population, severe labor shortages, and low birthrates. Overall, the contradictions of Japan's citizenship and immigration politics reflect the larger contradictions of Japanese democracy. Depending upon where you look, Japanese democracy is either failing or flourishing. Although Japan has all of the institutions of a modern democracy – free and fair elections, universal suffrage, a democratic constitution that guarantees and protects citizen rights, and so forth – a single party, the LDP, has dominated the government since 1955, with only a brief interruption of one-party rule in 1993. Although some have attributed this puzzle to the lack of democratic values among Japanese citizens (Van Wolferen 1990), survey data have revealed a decline in citizen confidence in government and politics – and dissatisfaction with the ruling party in particular – since the late 1980s, similar to the pattern of other trilateral democracies (Pharr 2000). Thus, the LDP has maintained almost continuous one-party rule since 1955 despite its unpopularity. As Ethan Scheiner (2006) argues, the inability of voters to express their dissatisfaction with the government, and the ruling party in particular, through "voter revolts" or party competition suggests a failure of democracy in Japan.

At the same time, Mary Alice Haddad's (2007) examination of voluntary organizations in Japan offers a very different portrait of Japanese democracy, in which citizens have unimpaired opportunities to formulate their preferences and signify their preferences to their fellows citizens and government officials (Dahl 1971). In contrast to claims that Japanese citizens are politically quiescent, Haddad's study unveils high rates of volunteer participation (which surpass those of the United States in organizations such as volunteer firefighters and parent-teacher associations) as well as an increasing pluralization of voluntary associations. Even as voters have not been able to express their dissatisfaction through the electoral process, these civil-society organizations have become important sources of democratic accountability at the day-to-day level: they serve as conduits through which citizens can voice their interests and concerns about specific aspects of their daily lives that are then transmitted back to the government. For Haddad, Japan's vibrant civil-society signals a promising shift in Japanese democracy.

In a system in which voter preferences are not accurately reflected in political outcomes and in which public contestation through the electoral process is effectively blocked, foreign residents who are formally excluded from the political process have been able to voice their concerns and interests through many of the same processes and institutions utilized by average Japanese citizens. The debate on citizenship and diversity in Japan – which has been shaped in part by foreign residents – signifies a distinct shift in the direction of Japanese democracy. On the one hand, it is at the core of post-1998 grassroots efforts to practice democracy from the ground up as an alternative to elite politics. Proimmigrant NGOs emerged at the same time as other NGOs and NPOs that sought to fill a chasm left by an ineffective, unresponsive national government. On the other hand, it represents a cluster of local movements with national significance – similar to the environmental movement of late 1960s and early 1970s Japan – because it challenges the very heart of national state policies and ideologies. Thus, the strategy of using noncitizen status as voice is a potentially powerful one in the Japanese context. Because most citizens in Japan do not view national elections and political parties as the site for social change, it should not come as a surprise that foreign residents do not view naturalization as the path to full citizenship.

Within this new context, noncitizen political mobilization around their foreign citizenship status proves a number of strategic advantages. First, this strategy allows long-term foreign-resident organizations to expand their membership base by including recent immigrants. Second, foreign-resident activists are able to gain political allies by creating coalitions with Japanese activists who are working on behalf of recent immigrants. Finally, mobilizing around their foreign citizenship status helps to increase activists' political visibility. As they work at the edges of the Japanese government to carve out a political voice and rights for the foreign community, they have reframed public debate not only on immigrant incorporation but also on citizenship, diversity, and democracy in Japan.

CITIZENSHIP AS AN INTERACTIVE PROCESS

The contemporary problem of immigrant politics centers on the seeming contradiction between citizenship policy and noncitizen political behavior or, more generally, that between citizenship policy and practice. Ideally, immigrants and foreign residents must acquire full citizenship before they can enjoy the privileges and practices of citizenship. Citizenship policies, however, rarely live up to their ideals. And citizenship practices are usually messy.

The state attempts to control the racial and ethnic makeup of its population through immigration and citizenship policies and may make adjustments to existing policies or create new policies in response to changes in the population. But these policies cannot control the ways that the population – the dominant society and minority communities – interprets, negotiates, and practices citizenship. Although all industrial democracies share the challenges of unprecedented flows of immigration and growing social diversity and many national states have enacted similar policies in response to these challenges, their local governments, institutions, and individuals may adapt to the changing contours of the population in divergent ways. Instead of a highly assimilated community of naturalized citizens, countries with strict immigration and citizenship policies that encourage assimilation may have large communities of highly assimilated, unnaturalized foreign residents, as in Japan. Multicultural policies may create pockets of residentially segregated foreign and minority communities with high rates of unemployment instead of self-sufficient communities engaging in consociational politics, as has been the trend in the Netherlands in recent years. Proimmigrant activists may base their movements on the "right to difference" in one decade and make integrationist appeals to the values of the republic in another decade without changes to official policies, as was the case in France during the 1980s and 1990s.

Although the study of immigrant incorporation tends to focus primarily on state policies, the process by which immigrants become socially and politically recognized members of their countries of residence entails constant interaction among the state, noncitizens, and citizens. In defining citizenship restrictively as formal membership in a state, the concentration is on citizenship attribution and acquisition. An examination of citizenship as formal membership in a state offers insights into state formation and citizenship policy; nevertheless, it tells us little about citizenship as a practice. As a process, citizenship is subject to contestation and redefinition by state and social actors.

Because of the high stakes involved, citizenship can function as a political strategy used by state and nonstate actors to structure relations between citizens and noncitizens as well as between state and nonstate actors. Using citizenship and immigration policies, states can monitor and control, to a certain degree, the internal and external movements of noncitizens (Marx 1998; Solomos 1989) or use citizenship status to racialize or criminalize foreign populations (Ngai 2004; Volpp 2002). State and nonstate actors may reinvent or revise national traditions in order to shape or reshape citizenship policies and practices (Feldblum 1999). Finally, nonstate actors may use citizenship status as a political strategy to negotiate with the state in racial politics and reform citizenship policies and practices (Kastoryano 2002; Klopp 2002).

The findings of this book challenge our conventional understandings of citizenship, which would lead us to assume that noncitizen political activities are aimed at citizenship acquisition alone and that citizenship acquisition is always politically empowering. Given that the perceived benefits of naturalization for many individuals are primarily material, we should not assume that political incorporation automatically leads to political empowerment for immigrant and minority groups. Whereas political incorporation through naturalization reflects immigrant trust in the political system and thereby promotes system-level stability, political empowerment for many immigrants and other disadvantaged groups requires systemic change.

Especially in cases in which citizenship policies are based on ethno-cultural understandings of nationhood, as in Japan, citizenship acquisition may not be the central goal of social movements among noncitizen communities. The relationship between generational status and patterns of noncitizen political engagement in Japan, in particular, problematizes the dichotomous division between "civic" and "ethnic" citizenship policies and their impact on noncitizen political engagement. Putatively homogeneous societies with restrictive citizenship policies will likely have low rates of naturalization among their foreign residents, which will, in turn, result in a relatively large proportion of foreign citizens within the community of immigrants and their descendants.

At the same time, these same citizenship regimes necessarily produce native-born generations of foreign residents, who have at their disposal distinct forms of social and political capital that foreign-born immigrants lack. Although their foreign citizenship may not allow them to vote in national (and possibly local) elections, it does not prohibit their participation in politics. These communities will likely mobilize themselves specifically as foreign residents, rather than as politically incorporated racial and ethnic minorities, and may engage in extraelectoral forms of political participation, which includes but is not limited to homeland politics. Ethnic citizenship regimes may shape the collective identities of immigrants and their descendants as foreign residents, but generational status, historical context, and timing must be weighed when making cross-national, and even intranational, comparisons of the direction and scope of noncitizen political engagement. Rather than political disengagement from the country of residence, low naturalization rates may be accompanied by high rates of extraelectoral political participation. Permanent and native-born foreign residents may have relatively strong bargaining power at the local level as a result of piecemeal extensions of institutionalized rights, which, in practice, may make them de facto citizens. The very stringency of such citizenship policies based on claims of ethnic and cultural homogeneity may provide foreign-resident activists with incentives to challenge existing policies and narrow definitions of membership in the dominant society. Their social movements may be focused on contesting and negotiating the terms of their political incorporation, not simply political incorporation.

Likewise, when invisibility, rather than hypervisibility, is the central challenge that a minority community faces, then the strategies that the community uses for political empowerment will likely differ significantly from conventional approaches used by phenotypically distinct groups. Native-born generations of foreign-resident activists in Japan attribute the persistent social discrimination and political weakness of the Korean-resident community to their social and political invisibility, as opposed to their foreign citizenship status or irreconcilable differences between Koreans and Japanese. Korean residents in contemporary Japan routinely face pressures to pass as Japanese, rather than direct discrimination, and often confront individual Japanese who are ignorant of the community's history in Japan, rather than those who harbor ill will against them. Likewise, present-day Korean residents experience relatively little legal discrimination despite their status as foreign residents; nevertheless, Japanese officials have long been unresponsive to the community's demands for citizenship and immigrant policy reforms – ranging from straightforward requests by naturalized citizens of Korean descent to readopt their Korean names to calls for legislation that explicitly protects the human rights of foreign residents – in part because they denied their very existence.

Consequently, Korean social movements have not centered on the right to acquire citizenship and vote, as has been the case among numerous disenfranchised communities elsewhere at different historical moments; on the contrary, Korean activists have mobilized the foreign community specifically around their foreign citizenship status as part of a strategy to gain political and social visibility in Japan. Even as Japanese officials have publicly promoted the naturalization of permanent foreign residents during the past two decades, Korean activists have thwarted official attempts to politically assimilate the community, arguing that naturalization without social and political change in Japan exacerbates the community's invisibility – among state and non-state actors alike – and thereby contributes to the official claim that Japan is ethnoculturally homogeneous. As they have aligned themselves with recent immigrants in their movements for noncitizen rights and recognition, Korean-resident activists have contested the conditions for naturalization, seeking instead to diversify the meaning of Japanese citizenship. Naturalization, in this case, is not the most effective step toward political empowerment.

Perhaps the most remarkable feature of Japanese immigration and citizenship politics is the state's ability to uphold the façade that Japan is not a country of immigration. But it is precisely the failure to incorporate prewar immigrants and their descendants that has created the current dilemma for Japanese officials as they attempt to control another wave of immigration. The areas in which Japan stands out among advanced industrial democracies directly contradict the official stance that immigration is a new phenomenon in Japan and that Japanese society is homogeneous. That is, the contradictions of Japan's immigration and citizenship politics derive less from Japan's recent immigration challenges, which is the basis for framing Japan as a recent country of immigration, and more from Japan's immigration history as a former colonial power. Ironically, Japanese officials have been resistant to immigration because they do not want the problems that they associate with racial and ethnic diversity in other advanced industrial democracies. Nevertheless, many of the hallmarks of racial and ethnic politics – such as economic and social dislocation, widespread social discrimination, and civil rights movements – have become the defining features of contemporary immigrant politics in Japan.

References

Agrela, Belén, and Gunther Dietz. 2006. "Nongovernmental Versus Governmental Actors? Multilevel Governance and Immigrant Integration Policy in Spain." In *Local Citizenship in Recent Countries of Immigration: Japan in Comparative Perspective*, ed. T. Tsuda. Lanham, MD: Lexington Books: 205–34.

Aldwinckle, David. 1999. "Turning Japanese: Naturalization into Japan Is Not Easy but It Is Possible." In *NKK News*, Tokyo: NKK Corporation; http://www.debito.org/NKKnews599.html (accessed 20 August 2009).

Allen, Ernest, Jr. 1994. "Satokata Takahashi and the Flowering of Black Messianic Nationalism." *The Black Scholar* 24 (1): 23–46.

Andersen, Kristi, and Elizabeth F. Cohen. 2005. "Political Institutions and Incorporation of Immigrants." In *The Politics of Democratic Inclusion*, ed. C. Wolbrecht and R. Hero. Philadelphia: Temple University Press: 186–206.

Asakawa, Akihiro. 2003. *Zainichi gaikokujin to kika seido* [Naturalization and Foreigners in Japan]. Tokyo: Shinkansha.

Bae, Jung Do. 1999. *Zainichi korian: Rekishi, genjyō, mirai* [Korean Residents: History, Present State, Future]. Yokohama, Japan: Yokohama Association for International Communication and Exchange (YOKE).

Baldwin-Edwards, Martin, and Martin A. Schain, eds. 1994. *The Politics of Immigration in Western Europe*. Newbury Park, Ilford, Essex: Frank Cass and Co.

Barnhart, Michael A. 1987. *Japan Prepares for Total War: The Search for Economic Security, 1919–1941*. Ithaca, NY: Cornell University Press.

Beasley, W. G. 1987. *Japanese Imperialism, 1894–1945*. Oxford: Oxford University Press.

Bellah, Robert. 1957. *Tokugawa Religion: The Values of Pre-Industrial Japan*. Glencoe, IL: The Free Press.

Benedict, Ruth. 1946. *The Chrysanthemum and the Sword: Patterns of Japanese Culture*. New York: Meridian Books.

Berger, Thomas U. 1998. "The Perils and Promise of Pluralism: Lessons from the German Case for Japan." In *Temporary Workers or Future Citizens? Japanese and U.S. Migration Policies*, ed. M. Weiner and T. Hanami. London: Macmillan Press: 319–52.

Bleich, Erik. 2001. "The French Model: Color-Blind Integration." In *Color Lines: Affirmative Action, Immigration, and Civil Rights Option for America*, ed. J. D. Skrentny. Chicago: University of Chicago Press: 270–96.

———. 2003. *Race Politics in Britain and France: Ideas and Policymaking since the 1960s*. Cambridge: Cambridge University Press.

Bloemraad, Irene. 2005. "The Limits of De Tocqueville: How Government Facilitates Organisational Capacity in Newcomer Communities." *Journal of Ethnic and Migration Studies* 31 (5): 23.

———. 2006. *Becoming a Citizen: Incorporating Immigrants and Refugees in the United States and Canada*. Berkeley: University of California Press.

Bosniak, Linda. 2006. *The Citizen and the Alien: Dilemmas of Contemporary Membership*. Princeton, NJ: Princeton University Press.

Broadbent, Jeffrey. 1998. *Environmental Politics in Japan: Networks of Power and Protest*. Cambridge and New York: Cambridge University Press.

Brody, Betsy. 2002. *Opening the Door: Immigration, Ethnicity and Globalization in Japan*. New York: Routledge.

Brubaker, Rogers. 1992. *Citizenship and Nationhood in France and Germany*. Cambridge, MA: Harvard University Press.

———, ed. 1989. *Immigration and the Politics of Citizenship in Europe and North America*. Lanham, MD: University Press of America.

Calder, Mari. 2002. "Achieving Power without Power? The Politics of Japanese Immigrant Policy in Comparative Perspective." BA thesis, Department of Government, Harvard University, Cambridge, MA.

Castles, Stephen, and Alastair Davidson, eds. 2000. *Citizenship and Migration: Globalization and the Politics of Belonging*. New York: Routledge.

Castles, Stephen, and Mark J. Miller. 2003. *The Age of Migration: International Population Movements in the Modern World*. 3rd ed. New York and London: Guilford.

Chan, Jennifer, ed. 2008. *Another Japan Is Possible: New Social Movements and Global Citizenship Education*. Palo Alto, CA: Stanford University Press.

Chan-Tiberghien, Jennifer. 2004. *Gender and Human Rights Politics in Japan: Global Norms and Domestic Networks*. Palo Alto, CA: Stanford University Press.

Chapman, William. 1991. *Inventing Japan: The Making of a Postwar Civilization*. New York: Prentice Hall Press.

Chee, Choung-Il. 1983. "Japan's Post-War Mass Denationalization of the Korean Minority in International Law." *Korea and World Affairs* 7 (1): 81–113.

Chen, Edward I-te. 1984. "The Attempt to Integrate the Empire: Legal Perspectives." In *The Japanese Colonial Empire, 1895–1945*, ed. R. H. Myers and M. R. Peattie. Princeton, NJ: Princeton University Press: 240–74.

Chen, Paul Huen. 1988. "From Colony to Neighbor: Relations between Japan and South Korea, 1945–1985." PhD diss., Johns Hopkins University.

Cheong, Sung-hwa. 1992. "A Study of the Origin of the Legal Status of Korean Residents in Japan: 1945–1951." *Korea Journal* 32 (1): 43–60.

Cho, Wendy K. Tam. 1999. "Naturalization, Socialization, Participation: Immigrants and (Non)Voting." *Journal of Politics* 61 (4): 1140–55.

Chong, Dae-kyun. 2001. *Zainichi kankokujin no shūen* [The Demise of Korean Residents]. Tokyo: Bunshun Shinsho.

Chung, Erin Aeran. 1999. "Zaibei korian no mita zainichi dōhō no minzoku ishiki: Esunisiti to nation no hazama de [A Korean American's Perspective on Ethnic Identity in Japan's Korean Community: At the Intersection of Ethnicity and Nation]." *Uri seikatsu* [Our Lives] 14 (August): 146–57.

———. 2009. "The Politics of Contingent Citizenship: A Comparative Study of Korean Political Engagement in Japan and the United States." In *Diaspora without Homeland: Being Korean in Japan*, ed. S. Ryang and J. Lie. Berkeley: University of California Press: 147–67.

City of Kawasaki. *Kawasaki City Representative Assembly for Foreign Residents* 2006; http://www.city.kawasaki.jp/25/25zinken/home/gaikoku/assembly/index.htm (accessed 20 August 2009).

Cohen, Theodore. 1987. *Remaking Japan: The American Occupation as New Deal*. New York: The Free Press.

Communist Party of the United States of America. 1938. "Is Japan the Champion of the Colored Races? The Negro's Stake in Democracy." New York: Negro Commission, National Committee.

Conde, David. 1947. "The Korean Minority in Japan." *Far Eastern Survey* 16 (4): 41–5.

Cumings, Bruce. 1981. *The Origins of the Korean War: Liberation and the Emergence of Separate Regimes, 1945–1947*. 2 vols. Vol. 1. Princeton, NJ: Princeton University Press.

———. 1990. *The Origins of the Korean War: The Roaring of the Cataract, 1947–1950*. 2 vols. Vol. 2. Princeton, NJ: Princeton University Press.

———. 1993. "Archaeology, Descent, Emergence: Japan in British/American Hegemony, 1900–1950." In *Japan in the World*, ed. M. Masao and H. D. Harootunian. Durham, NC: Duke University Press: 79–112.

———. 1997. *Korea's Place in the Sun: A Modern History*. New York: W. W. Norton and Company.

Dahl, Robert. 1971. *Polyarchy: Participation and Opposition*. New Haven, CT: Yale University Press.

DeKay, Charles. 1901. "Who Are the Japanese? Their Ethnic Mixture and Future as a World Power." *New York Times Magazine*, 18 August, 7.

DeSipio, Louis. 1996. "Making Citizens or Good Citizens? Naturalization as a Predictor of Organizational and Electoral Behavior among Latino Immigrants." *Hispanic Journal of Behavioral Sciences* 18 (2): 194–213.

———. 2006. "Transnational Politics and Civic Engagement: Do Home-Country Political Ties Limit Latino Immigrant Pursuit of U.S. Civic Engagement and Citizenship?" In *Transforming Politics, Transforming America: The Political and Civic Incorporation of Immigrants in the United States*, ed. T. Lee, S. K. Ramakrishnan, and R. Ramirez. Charlottesville: University of Virginia Press: 106–26.

deWit, Thom Duyven, and Ruud Koopmans. 2005. "The Integration of Ethnic Minorities into Political Culture: The Netherlands, Germany and Great Britain Compared." *Acta Politica* 40 (1): 50–73.

Dower, John. 1986. *War without Mercy: Race and Power in the Pacific War.* New York: Pantheon Books.

———. 1999. *Embracing Defeat: Japan in the Wake of World War Two.* New York: W. W. Norton and Company and The New Press.

Duus, Peter. 1995. *The Abacus and the Sword: The Japanese Penetration of Korea, 1895–1910.* Berkeley: University of California Press.

Earnest, David C. 2006. "Neither Citizen nor Stranger: Why States Enfranchise Resident Aliens." *World Politics* 58 (January): 242–75.

Eckert, Carter J., Ki-baik Lee, Young Ick Lew, Michael Robinson, and Edward W. Wagner. 1990. *Korea Old and New: A History.* Seoul: Ilchokak Publishers.

Ehashi, Takashi. 1998. "The Battle over the Nationality Clause: Finding Hope in Local Governments – an Interview with Ehashi Takashi." *AMPO: Japan Asia Quarterly Review* 28 (2): 49.

Feldblum, Miriam. 1999. *Reconstructing Citizenship: The Politics of Nationality Reform and Immigration in Contemporary France.* Albany: State University of New York Press.

Field, Norma. 1993. "Beyond Envy, Boredom, and Suffering: Toward an Emancipatory Politics for Resident Koreans and Other Japanese." *Positions* 1 (3): 640–70.

Fiorina, Morris P. 2002. "Parties, Participation, and Representation in America: Old Theories Face New Realities." In *Political Science: The State of the Discipline*, ed. I. Katznelson and H. Milner. New York: W. W. Norton and Company: 511–41.

Freeman, Gary. 1979. *Immigrant Labor and Racial Conflict in Industrial Societies: The French and British Experience, 1945–1975.* Princeton, NJ: Princeton University Press.

Fukuoka, Yasunori. 2000. *Lives of Young Koreans in Japan.* Trans. T. Gill. Melbourne, Australia: Trans Pacific Press.

Fukuoka, Yasunori, and Myung-Soo Kim. 1997. *Zainichi kankokujin seinen no seikatsu to ishiki* [The Life and Consciousness of Young South Koreans in Japan]. Tokyo: University of Tokyo Press.

Gluck, Carol. 1985. *Japan's Modern Myths: Ideology in the Late Meiji Period.* Princeton, NJ: Princeton University Press.

Guiraudon, Virginie. 1998. "Citizenship Rights for Non-Citizens." In *Challenge to the Nation-State: Immigration in Western Europe and the United States,* ed. C. Joppke. Oxford: Oxford University Press: 272–318.

Gurowitz, Amy. 1999. "Mobilizing International Norms: Domestic Actors, Immigrants, and the Japanese State." *World Politics* 51 (3): 413–45.

Haddad, Mary Alice. 2007. *Politics and Volunteering in Japan: A Global Perspective.* New York: Cambridge University Press.

Hailbronner, Kay. 2001. "Citizenship Rights for Aliens in Germany." In *Citizenship in a Global World: Comparing Citizenship Rights for Aliens,* ed. A. Kondo. Houndmills, UK and New York: Palgrave: 100–15.

Hamada, Koichi, and Hugh T. Patrick. 1988. "Japan and the International Monetary Regime." In *The Political Economy of Japan,* ed. T. Inoguchi and D. I. Okimoto. Palo Alto, CA: Stanford University Press: 108–37.

Hammar, Tomas. 1990. *Democracy and the Nation State: Aliens, Denizens, and Citizens in a World of International Migration.* Brookfield, VT: Gower Publishing Company.

Han, Seung-Mi. 2004. "From the Communitarian Ideal to the Public Sphere: The Making of Foreigners' Assemblies in Kawasaki City and Kanagawa Prefecture." *Social Science Japan Journal* 7 (1): 41–60.

Hanami, Tadashi. 1998. "Japanese Policies on the Rights and Benefits Granted to Foreign Workers, Residents, Refugees and Illegals." In *Temporary Workers or Future Citizens? Japanese and U.S. Migration Policies,* ed. M. Weiner and T. Hanami. London: Macmillan Press: 211–37.

Hargreaves, Alec G. 2007. *Multi-Ethnic France: Immigration, Politics, Culture, and Society.* 2nd ed. London and New York: Routledge.

Hayduk, Ron. 2006. *Democracy for All: Restoring Immigrant Voting Rights in the United States.* New York and London: Routledge.

Henderson, Gregory. 1968. *Korea: The Politics of the Vortex.* Cambridge, MA: Harvard University Press.

Hicks, George. 1997. *Japan's Hidden Apartheid: The Korean Minority and the Japanese.* Brookfield, VT: Ashgate Press.

Hideki, Harajiri. 1997. *Nihon teijū korian no nichijō to seikatsu* [The Daily Lives and Affairs of Permanent Resident Koreans in Japan]. Tokyo: Akashi Shoten.

Hill, Robert A., ed. 1989. *The Marcus Garvey and Universal Negro Improvement Association Papers, Volume VI (September 1924–December 1927).* Berkeley: University of California Press.

Hing, Bill Ong. 1993. *Making and Remaking Asian America through Immigration Policy, 1850–1990.* Palo Alto, CA: Stanford University Press.

Hirschman, Albert O. 1970. *Exit, Voice, and Loyalty: Responses to Decline in Firms, Organizations, and States.* Cambridge, MA: Harvard University Press.

Hooker, Juliet. 2005. "Indigenous Inclusion/Black Exclusion: Race, Ethnicity and Multicultural Citizenship in Latin America." *Journal of Latin American Studies* 37 (2): 285–310.

Inui, Kiyo Sue. 1925. *The Unsolved Problem of the Pacific*. Tokyo: Japan Times.

Ireland, Patrick. 1994. *Policy Challenge of Ethnic Diversity: Immigrant Politics in France and Switzerland*. Cambridge, MA: Harvard University Press.

———. 2000. "Reaping What They Sow: Institutions and Immigrant Political Participation in Western Europe." In *Challenging Immigration and Ethnic Relations Politics: Comparative European Perspectives*, ed. R. Koopmans and P. Statham. Oxford: Oxford University Press: 233–82.

———. 2003. *Becoming Europe: Immigration, Integration and the Welfare State*. Pittsburgh, PA: University of Pittsburgh Press.

Iriye, Akira. 1974. "The Failure of Economic Expansionism, 1918–1931." In *Japan in Crisis: Essays in Taisho Democracy*, ed. H. Harootunian and B. Silberman. Princeton, NJ: Princeton University Press: 237–69.

Ishikida, Miki Y. 2005. *Living Together: Minority People and Disadvantaged Groups in Japan*. New York: iUniverse.

Ishizawa, Maki. 1998. "Teijyū gaikokujin no shakaiteki jinken to komuniti [Social Rights for Resident Aliens and Community]." *Shakaigaku nenpō* [Annual Review of Sociology] 27: 69–86.

Iwasawa, Yuji. 1986. "Legal Treatment of Koreans in Japan: The Impact of International Human Rights Law on Japanese Law." *Human Rights Quarterly* 8 (2) (May 1986): 131–79.

———. 1998. *International Law, Human Rights, and Japanese Law*. Oxford: Oxford University Press.

Jacobson, David. 1996. *Rights across Borders: Immigration and the Decline of Citizenship*. Baltimore, MD: Johns Hopkins University Press.

JCS1380/15. 1945. "Basic Initial Post Surrender Directive to Supreme Commander for the Allied Powers for the Occupation and Control of Japan." U.S. National Archives and Records Administration (RG331).

Jones-Correa, Michael. 1998. *Between Two Nations: The Political Predicament of Latinos in New York City*. Ithaca, NY: Cornell University Press.

———. 2001. "Institutional and Contextual Factors in Immigrant Citizenship and Voting." *Citizenship Studies* 5 (1): 41–56.

———. 2002. "Seeking Shelter: Citizenship and the Divergence of Social Rights and Citizenship in the U.S." In *Dual Nationality, Social Rights and Federal Citizenship in the U.S. and Europe*, ed. R. Hansen and P. Weil. New York: Berhahn Books: 233–63.

Joppke, Christian. 1999. *Immigration and the Nation-State: The United States, Germany, and Great Britain*. Oxford: Oxford University Press.

———. 2001. "The Evolution of Alien Rights in the United States, Germany, and the European Union." In *Citizenship Today: Global Perspectives and*

References 191

Practices, ed. T. A. Aleinikoff and D. Klusmeyer. Washington, DC: Carnegie Endowment for International Peace: 36–62.

Junn, Jane. 1999. "Participation in Liberal Democracy: The Political Assimilation of Immigrants and Ethnic Minorities in the United States." *American Behavioral Scientist* 42 (9): 1417–38.

Kang, Chae-on. 1996. *"Zainichi" kara no shiza* ["Zainichi" Perspectives]. Tokyo: Shinkansha.

Kang, Chae-on, and Kim Tong Hoon. 1989. *Zainichi kankoku chosenjin: Rekishi to tembo* [South and North Korean Residents in Japan: History and Prospects]. Tokyo: Rodo Keizaisha.

Kashiwazaki, Chikako. 2000. "Citizenship in Japan: Legal Practice and Contemporary Development." In *From Migrants to Citizens: Membership in a Changing World*, ed. T. A. Aleinikoff and D. Klusmeyer. Washington, DC: Carnegie Endowment for International Peace: 434–72.

———. 2002. "Local Government and Resident Foreigners: A Changing Relationship." In *Japan's Road to Pluralism: Transforming Local Communities in the Global Era*, ed. S. I. Furukawa and T. Menju. Tokyo: Japan Center for International Exchange: 63–88.

Kashiwazaki, Chikako, and Tsuneo Akaha. 2006. "Japanese Immigration Policy: Responding to Conflicting Pressures." In *Migration Information Source*. Washington, DC: Migration Policy Institute; http://www.migrationinformation.org/Feature/display.cfm?id=487 (accessed 20 August 2009).

Kastoryano, Riva. 2002. *Negotiating Identities: States and Immigrants in France and Germany*. Princeton, NJ: Princeton University Press.

Keck, Margaret E., and Kathryn Sikkink. 1998. *Activists Beyond Borders: Advocacy Networks in International Politics*. Ithaca, NY: Cornell University Press.

Kim, Kyeung Duk. 1995. *Zainichi korian no aidentiti to hōteki chii* [The Identity and Legal Position of Korean Residents in Japan]. Tokyo: Akashi Shoten.

Kim, Kyu Il. 1997. "Zainichi to shite, zainichi to tomoni ikiru: Kangaeru kai 15 nen no ayumi to gurando bijon" [Living as a Korean Resident in Japan in Harmony with Korean Residents: The Fifteen Year Journey of the Kangaeru Kai and a Grand Vision]. Interview by Oh Son Sam. *Uri Seikatsu (Saeng'hwal)* [Our Lives] 13: 202–68.

Kim, Yŏng Dal. 1990. *Zainichi chōsenjin no kika* [The Naturalization of Korean Residents]. Tokyo: Akashi Shoten.

Kimpara, Samon, R. Ishida, Y. Ozawa, H. Kajimura, H. Tanaka, and O. Mihashi. 1986. *Nihon no naka no kankoku-chōsenjin chugokujin* [Koreans and Chinese in Japan]. Tokyo: Akashi Shoten.

King, Martin Luther, Jr. 1967. "Beyond Vietnam" speech given at Riverside Church, New York, NY.

Klopp, Brett. 2002. *German Multiculturalism: Immigrant Integration and the Transformation of Citizenship*. Westport, CT: Praeger.

Kondo, Atsushi. 2001. "Citizenship Rights for Aliens in Japan." In *Citizenship in a Global World: Comparing Citizenship Rights for Aliens*, ed. A. Kondo. Houndmills, UK and New York: Palgrave: 8–30.

Koopmans, Ruud, and Paul Statham. 1999. "Challenging the Liberal Nation State? Postnationalism, Multiculturalism, and the Collective Claims Making of Migrants and Ethnic Minorities in Britain and Germany." *American Journal of Sociology* 105 (3): 652–96.

———. 2000. "Challenging the Liberal Nation-State? Postnationalism, Multiculturalism, and the Collective Claims-Making of Migrants and Ethnic Minorities in Britain and Germany." In *Challenging Immigration and Ethnic Relations Politics: Comparative European Perspectives*, ed. R. Koopmans and P. Statham. Oxford: Oxford University Press: 189–232.

Koopmans, Ruud, Paul Statham, Marco Giugni, and Florence Passy. 2005. *Contested Citizenship: Immigration and Cultural Diversity in Europe*. Minneapolis: University of Minnesota Press.

Lahav, Gallya, and Virginie Guiraudon. 2006. "Actors and Venues in Immigration Control: Closing the Gap between Political Demands and Policy Outcomes." *West European Politics* 29 (2): 201.

LeBlanc, Robin M. 1999. *Bicycle Citizens: The Political World of the Japanese Housewife*. Berkeley: University of California Press.

Lee, Changsoo, and George DeVos. 1981. *Koreans in Japan: Ethnic Conflict and Accommodation*. Berkeley: University of California Press.

Lee, Soo Im. 2002. "Kankokukei nihonjin to shiteno aidentiti [Being a Korean Japanese]. *Dōwa mondai kenkyū shiryō* [Research Documents on the Dōwa (Burakumin) Problem]. *Ryukoku daigaku dōwa kenkyukai iinkai* [Ryukoku University Committee on Dōwa Research]: 60–9.

Leheny, David Richard. 2006. *Think Global, Fear Local: Sex, Violence, and Anxiety in Contemporary Japan*. Ithaca, NY: Cornell University Press.

Lie, John. 2000. "Imaginary Homeland and Diasporic Realization: *Kikan Sanzenri, 1975–1987*." *Korean and Korean American Studies Bulletin* 11 (1): J11–J26.

———. 2001. *Multiethnic Japan*. Cambridge, MA: Harvard University Press.

———. 2008. *Zainichi (Koreans in Japan): Diasporic Nationalism and Postcolonial Identity*. Berkeley: University of California Press.

Lien, Pei-te. 1994. "Ethnicity and Political Participation: A Comparison between Asian and Mexican Americans." *Political Behavior* 16: 237–64.

Mackie, Vera C. 2003. *Feminism in Modern Japan: Citizenship, Embodiment, and Sexuality*. Cambridge and New York: Cambridge University Press.

Maclachlan, Patricia. 2003. "The Struggle for an Independent Consumer Society: Consumer Activism and the State's Response in Postwar Japan." In *The State of Civil Society in Japan*, ed. F. Schwartz and S. Pharr. New York: Cambridge University Press: 214–34.

MacMaster, Neil. 2001. *Racism in Europe, 1870–2000*. Hampshire, UK and New York: Palgrave.

Martin, Philip L. 1994. "Germany: Reluctant Land of Immigration." In *Controlling Immigration: A Global Perspective*, ed. W. A. Cornelius, P. L. Martin, and J. F. Hollifield. Palo Alto, CA: Stanford University Press: 189–226.

Maruyama, Masao. 1963. "The Ideology and Dynamics of Japanese Fascism." In *Thought and Behaviour in Modern Japanese Politics*, ed. I. Morris. London: Oxford University Press: 25–83.

McKean, Margaret A. 1981. *Environmental Protest and Citizen Politics in Japan*. Berkeley and London: University of California Press.

Mindan. 1998. *Kankoku Mindan 50 nen no ayumi* [50 Years of South Korean Mindan]. Tokyo: Gogatsu shobō.

Ministry of Justice, Japan. 1998. "Zairyu gaikokujin tokei [Statistics for Foreign Residents in Japan]."

———. 2001. "Zairyu gaikokujin tokei [Statistics for Foreign Residents in Japan]."

———. 2008a. "Shutsu nyukoku kanri tokei nempo [Annual Report of Statistics on Legal Migrants]."

———. 2008b. "Hesei 19 nenmatsu genzaini okeru gaikokujintorokusha toukeini tsuite [Report on Current Foreign Resident Statistics at the End of 2007]."

———. 2009. "Hesei 20 nenmatsu genzaini okeru gaikokujintorokusha toukeini tsuite [Report on Current Foreign Resident Statistics at the End of 2008]."

Mori, Hiromi. 1997. *Immigration Policy and Foreign Workers in Japan*. New York: St. Martin's Press.

National Institute of Population and Social Security Research. 2002. "Population Projections for Japan: 2001–2050." Tokyo: National Institute of Population and Social Security Research.

National Institute for Research Advancement. 2001. *Tabunka shakai no sentaku: Shitizunshippu no shiten kara* [Choosing a Multicultural Society: From the Viewpoint of Citizenship]. Tokyo: Nihonkeizai hyoronsha.

Nippon Keidanren. 2003. "Japan 2025: Envisioning a Vibrant, Attractive Nation in the Twenty-First Century." Tokyo: Keizai Koho Center.

Northup, Robert W. 1974. "The Case of Park Chong Sok and Hitachi Industries." *IDOC* 65: 25–8.

Oezcan, Veysel. 2003a. "Changes to German Law Help Boost Naturalization Numbers." In *Migration Information Source*. Washington, DC: Migration Policy Institute; http://www.migrationinformation.org/Feature/display.cfm?ID=152 (accessed 20 August 2009).

———. 2003b. "Swiss Court Halts Local Plebiscites on Naturalization." In *Migration Information Source*. Washington, DC: Migration Policy Institute; http://www.migrationinformation.org/Feature/display.cfm?ID=162 (accessed 20 August 2009).

Okamoto, Makiko. 1994. "Shokuminchi jidaini okeru aainichi chōsenjinno senkyo undō: 1930 nendai gohan made [The Electoral Movement of Korean Residents in Japan During the Colonial Period: Until the Latter Half of the 1930s]." *Zainichi chōsenjinshi kenkyū* [Historical Research on Korean Residents in Japan] 24: 1–36.

Onuma, Yasuaki. 1986. *Tanitsu minzoku shakai o koete* [Beyond the Myth of the Homogenous Nation]. Tokyo: Toshindo.

Pak, Il. 1992. "'Zainichi ron' ronsō no seika to kadai [The Development and Issues of 'Discourses on Zainichi']." *Horumon bunka [Hormone Culture]* 3: 92–103.

———. 1999. *Zainichi to iu ikikata: Sai to byōdō no jirenma* [Living as a Zainichi: The Dilemma of Difference and Equality]. Tokyo: Kodansha.

Pak, Katherine Tegtmeyer. 2000. "Foreigners Are Local Citizens, Too: Local Governments Respond to International Migration in Japan." In *Japan and Global Migration*, ed. M. Douglass and G. Roberts. New York: Routledge: 244–74.

Pak, Kyŏng-sik. 1989. *Kaihōgo: Zainichi chōsenjin undōshi* [After Liberation: Movements by Korean Residents of Japan]. Tokyo: Sainichi Shobō.

Papademetriou, Demetrios G., and Kimberly A. Hamilton. 2000. *Reinventing Japan: Immigration's Role in Shaping Japan's Future.* Washington, DC: Carnegie Endowment for International Peace.

Peattie, Mark R. 1984a. Introduction to *The Japanese Colonial Empire, 1895–1945*, ed. R. H. Myers and M. R. Peattie. Princeton, NJ: Princeton University Press: 3–58.

———. 1984b. "Japanese Attitudes toward Colonialism, 1895–1945." In *The Japanese Colonial Empire, 1895–1945*, ed. R. H. Myers and M. R. Peattie. Princeton, NJ: Princeton University Press: 80–127.

Pharr, Susan J. 1990. *Losing Face: Status Politics in Japan.* Berkeley: University of California Press.

———. 2000. "Officials' Misconduct and Public Distrust: Japan and the Tri-lateral Democracies." In *Disaffected Democracies: What's Troubling the Trilateral Countries?*, ed. S. J. Pharr and R. D. Putnam. Princeton, NJ: Princeton University Press: 173–201.

Pyle, Kenneth. 1978. *The Making of Modern Japan.* Lexington, MA: D. C. Heath and Company.

Ramakrishnan, S. Karthick. 2005. *Democracy in Immigrant America: Changing Demographics and Political Participation.* Palo Alto, CA: Stanford University Press.

Ramakrishnan, S. Karthick, and Thomas J. Espenshade. 2001. "Immigrant Incorporation and Political Participation in the United States." *International Migration Review* 35 (3): 870–907.

Rath, Jan. 1990. "Voting Rights." In *The Political Rights of Migrant Workers in Western Europe*, ed. Z. Layton-Henry. London: Sage Publications: 127–57.

Reischauer, Edwin O. 1950. *The United States and Japan*. Cambridge, MA: Harvard University Press.

———. 1977. *The Japanese Today: Change and Continuity*. Cambridge, MA: Harvard University Press.

Roberts, Glenda. 2000. "NGO Support for Migrant Labor in Japan." In *Japan and Global Migration*, ed. M. Douglass and G. Roberts. New York: Routledge: 276–301.

Roche, Maurice. 1995. "Citizenship and Modernity." *British Journal of Sociology* 46 (4): 715–34.

Roth, Joshua Hotaka. 2004. *Brokered Homeland: Japanese Brazilian Migrants in Japan*. Ithaca, NY: Cornell University.

Rothstein, Edward. 2006. "Refining the Tests That Confer Citizenship." *New York Times*, 23 January 23, E1.

Rubio-Marín, Ruth. 2000. *Immigration as a Democratic Challenge: Citizenship and Inclusion in Germany and the United States*. Cambridge: Cambridge University Press.

Rudolph, Christopher. 2003. "Security and the Political Economy of International Migration." *American Political Science Review* 97 (4): 603–20.

Ryang, Sonia. 1997. *North Koreans in Japan: Language, Ideology, and Identity*. Boulder, CO: Westview Press.

Sakanaka, Hidenori. 1989. *Kongo no shutsunyūkoku kanri gyōsei no arikata ni tsuite: Sakanaka ronbun no fukusei to shuyō ronpyō* [On the Future of Immigration Control Administration: A Reprint of the Sakanaka Thesis and Its Major Criticisms]. Tokyo: Nihon kajo shuppan.

———. 1999. *Zainichi kankoku chōsenjin seisakuron no tenkai* [The Development of State Policy Discourse on South and North Korean Residents in Japan]. Tokyo: Nihon Kajo Shuppan.

Scheiner, Ethan. 2006. *Democracy without Competition in Japan: Opposition Failure in a One-Party Dominant State*. Cambridge: Cambridge University Press.

Schlozman, Kay Lehman. 2002. "Citizen Participation in America: What Do We Know? Why Do We Care?" In *Political Science: The State of the Discipline*, ed. I. Katznelson and H. Milner. New York: W. W. Norton and Company: 433–61.

Schoppa, Leonard J. 2006. *Race for the Exits: The Unraveling of Japan's System of Social Protection*. Ithaca, NY: Cornell University Press.

Schuck, Peter H. 1998. *Citizens, Strangers and in-Betweens: Essays on Immigration and Citizenship*. Boulder, CO: Westview Press.

Sellek, Yoko. 2001. *Migrant Labour in Japan*. New York: Palgrave.

Shipper, Apichai W. 2006. "Foreigners and Civil Society in Japan." *Pacific Affairs* 79 (2): 22.

———. 2008. *Fighting for Foreigners: Immigration and Its Impact on Japanese Democracy*. Ithaca, NY: Cornell University Press.

Skocpol, Theda. 1992. *Protecting Soldiers and Mothers: The Political Origins of Social Policy in the United States*. Cambridge, MA: Belknap Press of Harvard University Press.

Smith, Anthony. 1986. *The Ethnic Origins of Nations*. Oxford: Blackwell.

Smith, David M., and Maurice Blanc. 1996. "Citizenship, Nationality and Ethnic Minorities in Three European Nations." *International Journal of Urban and Regional Research* 20 (1): 66–82.

Smith, Sheila A., ed. 2000. *Local Voices, National Issues: The Impact of Local Initiative in Japanese Policy-Making*. Ann Arbor: Center for Japanese Studies, University of Michigan.

Soininen, Maritta. 1999. "The 'Swedish Model' as an Institutional Framework for Immigrant Membership Rights." *Journal of Ethnic and Migration Studies* 25 (4): 685–702.

SOPEMI. 2004. "Trends in International Migration: Continuous Reporting System on Migration." Paris: Organization for Economic Cooperation and Development.

———. 2006. "International Migration Outlook: Annual Report." Paris: Organization for Economic Cooperation and Development.

———. 2007. "International Migration Outlook: Annual Report." Paris: Organization for Economic Cooperation and Development.

———. 2008. "International Migration Outlook: Annual Report." Paris: Organization for Economic Cooperation and Development.

Soysal, Yasemin Nuhoglu. 1994. *Limits of Citizenship: Migrants and Postnational Membership in Europe*. Chicago: University of Chicago Press.

Steinhoff, Patricia G. 1989. "Protest and Democracy." In *Democracy in Japan*, ed. T. Ishida and E. S. Krauss. Pittsburgh, PA: University of Pittsburgh Press: 171–200.

———. 1999. "Student Protest in the 1960s." *Social Science Japan* (March): 3–6.

Strausz, Michael. 2006. "Minorities and Protest in Japan: The Politics of the Fingerprinting Refusal Movement." *Pacific Affairs* 79 (4): 641–56.

Suh, Sung. 1994. *Goku chū 19 nen: Kankoku seijihan no tatakai* [Nineteen Years of Imprisonment: The Fight of a South Korean Political Prisoner]. Tokyo: Iwanami Shoten.

Suh, Yong-dal. 2004. "Editorial." *Asahi Shimbun*.

Takenaka, Akira. 1997. "'Nation' and Citizenship in Germany and Japan: A Comparative Study of Citizenship Policies toward Immigrants and Ethnic 'Others'." PhD diss., Columbia University, New York.

Tanaka, Hiroshi. 1995. *Zainichi gaikokujin* [Foreign Residents in Japan]. Tokyo: Iwanami Shoten.

———. 1996. *Q&A gaikokujin no chihō sanseiken* [Q&A Local Voting Rights for Foreign Residents]. Tokyo: Satsuki Shobō.

Toitsu Nippo. 1982. *Zainichi kankoku jinmeiroku* [Records on the Lives of South Korean Residents of Japan]. Tokyo: Toitsu Nipposha.

Tsuda, Takeyuki. 2003. *Strangers in the Ethnic Homeland: Japanese Brazilian Return Migration in Transnational Perspective.* New York: Columbia University Press.

Tsuda, Takeyuki, and Wayne A. Cornelius. 2004. "Japan: Government Policy, Immigrant Reality." In *Controlling Immigration: A Global Perspective,* ed. W. A. Cornelius, T. Tsuda, P. L. Martin, and J. F. Hollifield. Palo Alto, CA: Stanford University Press: 439–76.

UNESCO Japan. *Shiryō III: Zainichi korian no kakaeru mondaiten* [Documents III: Points Related to Zainichi Koreans] 2008; http://www.unesco.jp/teacher/kyozai_f/nikkan/jp/4-8-1.htm (accessed 20 August 2009).

United Nations Population Division. 2000. "Replacement Migration: Is It a Solution to Declining and Ageing Populations?" New York: United Nations.

———. 2007. "World Population Prospects: The 2006 Revision." New York: United Nations.

Valentine, James. 1990. "On the Borderlines: The Significance of Marginality in Japanese Society." In *Unwrapping Japan,* ed. E. Ben-Ari, B. Moeran, and J. Valentine. Honolulu: University of Hawaii Press: 36–57.

Van Wolferen, Karel. 1990. *The Enigma of Japanese Power: People and Politics in a Stateless Nation.* New York: Vintage Books.

Vogel, Ezra F. 1963. *Japan's New Middle Class.* Berkeley: University of California Press.

———. 1979. *Japan as Number One: Lessons for America.* Cambridge, MA: Harvard University Press.

Wagner, Edward W. 1951. *The Korean Minority in Japan: 1904–1950.* New York: Institute of Pacific Relations.

Walters, Ronald W. 1993. *Pan Africanism in the African Diaspora.* Detroit, MI: Wayne State University Press.

Weil, Patrick. 2001. "Access to Citizenship: A Comparison of Twenty-Five Nationality Laws." In *Citizenship Today: Global Perspectives and Practices,* ed. T. A. Aleinikoff and D. Klusmeyer. Washington, DC: Carnegie Endowment for International Peace: 17–35.

Weiner, Michael. 1994a. *Race and Migration in Imperial Japan.* London: Routledge.

———. 1994b. "Race and National Community in Pre-1945 Japan." In *Racial Identities in East Asia,* ed. B. Sautman. Hong Kong: Division of Social Science, Hong Kong University of Science and Technology: 251–66.

Weiner, Myron. 1998. "Opposing Visions: Migration and Citizenship Policies in Japan and the United States." In *Temporary Workers or Future Citizens? Japanese and U.S. Migration Policies,* ed. M. Weiner and T. Hanami. London: Macmillan Press: 3–28.

———, ed. 1993. *International Migration and Security.* Boulder, CO: Westview Press.

Wender, Melissa L. 2005. *Lamentation as History: Narratives by Koreans in Japan, 1965–2000.* Palo Alto, CA: Stanford University Press.

Wihtol de Wenden, Catherine. 1991. "Immigration Policy and the Issue of Nationality." *Ethnic and Racial Studies* 14 (3): 319–32.

Wolbrecht, Christina. 2005. "Mediating Institutions." In *The Politics of Democratic Inclusion*, ed. R. E. Hero and C. Wolbrecht. Philadelphia: Temple University Press: 103–7.

Wong, Janelle S. 2006. *Democracy's Promise: Immigrants and American Civic Institutions*. Ann Arbor: University of Michigan Press.

Woo, Jung-En. 1991. *Race to the Swift: State and Finance in Korean Industrialization*. New York: Columbia University Press.

Yamanaka, Keiko. 2006. "Immigrant Incorporation and Women's Community Activities in Japan: Local NGOs and Public Education for Immigrant Children." In *Local Citizenship in Recent Countries of Immigration: Japan in Comparative Perspective*, ed. T. Tsuda. Lanham, MD: Lexington Books: 97–120.

Yamawaki, Keizō. 2001. "Sengo nihon no gaikokujin seisaku to zainichi korian no shakai undō [Postwar Japan's Policies toward Foreigners and Social Movements by Korean Residents]." In *Kokusaika to aidentiti* [Internationalization and Identity], ed. T. Kajita. Tokyo: Mineruba shobo: 286–318.

———. 2003. "Chihō jichidai no gaikokujin shisaku ni kansuru hihanteki kōsatsu [A Critical Examination of Local Policies for Foreigners]." Meiji University Social Science Research Center Discussion Paper Series, J-2003-10.

Yi, Yu-hwan. 1980. *Nihon no naka no sanjūhachidosen: Mindan, Chōsōren no rekishi to genjitsu* [The Thirty-Eighth Parallel in Japan: The History and Reality of Mindan and Chongryun]. Tokyo: Yoyosha.

Index